The Tropes
of Fantasy Fiction

The Tropes of Fantasy Fiction

GABRIELLE LISSAUER

McFarland & Company, Inc., Publishers
Jefferson, North Carolina

LIBRARY OF CONGRESS CATALOGUING-IN-PUBLICATION DATA

Lissauer, Gabrielle, 1978–
   The tropes of fantasy fiction / Gabrielle Lissauer.
   p.   cm.
   Includes bibliographical references and index.

   ISBN 978-0-7864-7858-3 (softcover : acid free paper) ∞
   ISBN 978-1-4766-1836-4 (ebook)

   1. Fantasy fiction—History and criticism. 2. Science fiction—History and criticism. 3. Speculative fiction—History and criticism. 4. Fiction—Technique. 5. Narration (Rhetoric) 6. Point of view (Literature) I. Title.
   PN3435.L45 2015
   809.3'8766—dc23   2014044407

BRITISH LIBRARY CATALOGUING DATA ARE AVAILABLE

© 2015 Gabrielle Lissauer. All rights reserved

No part of this book may be reproduced or transmitted in any form or by any means, electronic or mechanical, including photocopying or recording, or by any information storage and retrieval system, without permission in writing from the publisher.

On the cover: dragon drawn by the author; castle and background © 2015 Shutterstock

Printed in the United States of America

McFarland & Company, Inc., Publishers
   Box 611, Jefferson, North Carolina 28640
   www.mcfarlandpub.com

To the memory of my Grandma and Grandpa and
my Bubbie and Guv,
who aren't here to see this published
but would have been first in line to buy it.

Also to the memory of Tasha,
who wanted a copy of the book
so she could say she knew me when.
I miss you all.

Acknowledgments

First and foremost, I would like to acknowledge my parents. Without them, I wouldn't be here and I wouldn't be the person I am today. My dad, who has always been there for me, even if it's been silently in the background. He is a quiet rock my family clings to and without him everything would fall apart. Next, my mom, the not-so-quiet rock. Whereas my dad is the shadow in the background who makes everything run, my mom is the person in front who gets all the things done. She's the one who drove me around to libraries when my car died and made sure I kept meeting deadlines. Also, somehow the two of them managed to raise me correctly. Despite what they think or say, it's true. Thirdly, my brother, who put up with me and who loves me and hundreds of other different things that I can't think of to put into words. Fourthly and fifthly, because my brother would never forgive me if I didn't, I'd like to acknowledge my cat Chaucer; he is not the sort of cat who walked across keyboards or sat on them. Instead, he just hacked up a hairball on a library book. And the family parakeet, Avi, who *did* walk across the keyboard and, on that one occasion, managed to close Word. Thus I learned that touchscreens and parakeets do not mix.

Outside of the family, I must mention Professor Hatfield who was the first English literature teacher I had in a subject that wasn't "traditional" English literature. Until then, I didn't realize you could study things like comic books and science fiction/fantasy and be taken seriously. Or, at least, not be completely laughed at. Without that, and his help with my thesis, I doubt this book would be here today.

To Tracey, who helped me with my pre-edit edits. I am a terrible abuser of the comma and rules of grammar and she helped find mistakes. She also helped by pointing out things that I probably should have known.

Chloe didn't actually help me with the writing of this particular

Acknowledgments

work, but she did keep me company throughout the days. She's also here because I promised she would be in the acknowledgments. I'm mentioning Jeremy because I promised him the same thing.

For Ken F, Vegard, Becca, Q, AC, Lee, and Katie Taylor for listening to me rant and rave about *Eragon* and all the other books I read in preparation for this book. It's nice to have someone you can ramble at incoherently and know that they'll feel just as outraged as you. In that same vein, thank you to those who have read the analyses of the books on my LiveJournal and elsewhere. Those were the foundations of this book and helped me realize a lot of what I've written here.

Finally I would like to thank and acknowledge every writer of every book that I've ever read, fiction and non-fiction, good and bad, from *The Muffin Muncher* to *The Norton Anthology of Theory and Criticism* and from *The Fifth Sorceress* to *The Fifth Elephant*.

Table of Contents

Acknowledgments vii
Preface 1
Introduction 5
One. Changing the Story 17
Two. A Matter of Perception 38
Three. The Power of Stories 52
Four. Magic of Fantasy, Fantasy of Magic 64
Five. Not What You Think It Is 75
Six. Heroes and Protagonists, Villains and Antagonists 95
Seven. No Man Is an Island 118
Eight. Fairies and Dragons and Dwarfs, Oh My! 137
Nine. Through the Looking Glass 157
Ten. The Fundamentals 171

Chapter Notes 195
Bibliography 199
Index 203

Preface

Looking back, how I ended up writing this book is a rather long and strange story, at least to me. I've always loved fantasy. Some of the first books I can remember being read to me were fantasy. One was about a muffin-munching dragon and another about a pair of skeletons that lived in a dark, dark basement. My mother also read me *The Hobbit* several times when I was around seven until I started sneaking the book and reading ahead. Then she just let me read it myself. I loved watching *He-Man, She-Ra* and *Dungeons and Dragons* cartoons. I preferred the Dragonlance novels to the Baby-Sitters Club series. If the books had magic or fantasy, I ate them up; good, bad or mediocre, all were read. For my bat mitzvah, my aunt gave me *Dragonsdawn* by Anne McCaffrey, and I never quite recovered from that.

In college, I decided to major in English literature for both my bachelor's and master's degrees. Here I started to really learn about what made a story a good story: all about the traditional ideas of plot, characterization and setting. I started looking at what I read with a critical eye. The real turning point, I think, was my discovering fan fiction around the same time that the *Lord of the Rings* movies came out. Fan fiction is fascinating to explore and read. The quality ranges from "Could be published if it wasn't fan fiction" to "Who let this person near the keyboard?"

As I moved through various kinds of fan fiction, I stumbled upon a different kind of fan fiction: one that criticized bad fan fiction. They went through a fan fiction story and talked about how the characterization of the canon characters was wrong, how the powers new characters didn't fit into the world and, generally, how the stories that were being written weren't *Lord of the Rings* stories but something completely different. All that the characters, locations and items in badly written stories shared with *Lord of the Rings* were the same names. It got me to

Preface

think about the structure of fantasy stories and the sheer amount of effort that was put into them.

Just as I finished my master's degree, a friend recommended Christopher Paolini's *Eragon* to me. Why? Because it was bad. My friend thought I'd enjoy doing a commentary about it. As I explored the fandom and the anti-fandom about the book before deciding to take it on myself, I saw that one of the biggest complaints by the latter was that it ripped off other fantasy novels. Fans returned with the assertion that all fantasy has been done before, so of course *Eragon* appears to rip off other fantasy novels.

It was a fascinating debate and, as I read through *Eragon*, I came to the conclusion that they both might be right. *Eragon*, and the subsequent novels in the series, did use a lot of the traditional fantasy novel tropes and archetypes, which, of course, had been done before and will be done forever after. It's part of the language of fantasy. However, the particular way that Paolini chose to apply these tropes was by borrowing from/stealing from/ripping off others without disguising it very well.

As I started to read more "bad" fantasy novels, such as *The Fifth Sorceress*, the later *Sword of Truth* novels, and some of the *Wheel of Time* series, I noticed that there was often a discrepancy between what the words in the book said and what actually happened. The text would say that a character has X trait but would never actually show that trait in his or her actions. Sometimes the character would show the complete opposite of that trait. And often very different characters shared identical opinions and attitudes.

This bothered me. But I couldn't figure out why the discrepancies existed. It wasn't because the narrators were unreliable. I had read books with unreliable narrators before and they didn't bother me.

Slowly it dawned on me. The books were using a certain lexicon common to fantasy stories, but they were using it as shorthand instead of actual character, plot or world development. They said that a character was a hero or a villain but the actual text—the character's actions—didn't support it!

This idea percolated in my head for a good long time as, in fits and starts, I tried to work out what exactly this meant. All fantasy ideas had been done before—and yet new things were possible; after all, look at all the variations in how writers used the tropes. And one of the ways

Preface

to tell a bad fantasy book was if writers used the tropes … but, in a way, that didn't subvert or invert the tropes straight so much as completely miss the point of the trope they were trying for.

The more I thought about it, the more I realized that these tropes and clichés and archetypes of fantasy made fantasy what it was. Without them, it wouldn't *be* a fantasy novel. This isn't to say that a fantasy novel always requires a wizard or dragons or elves any more than a dessert always requires chocolate. There are hundreds of different ways to make a dessert using chocolate and each one will be different, even if you use the same recipe.

And this is when I decided that fantasy and genre novels were shared experiences with a common lexicon, and it was by using this shared lexicon that the readers and fans of fantasy created and understood what made good and bad fantasy stories.

Introduction

I once belonged to a genre writing group. We would meet on Tuesdays and discuss the stories we'd written. It was open to anyone who wished to come, and we got a lot of interesting people. One time a man came to us because he needed help with a movie script he was writing. He assured us repeatedly that it wasn't a science fiction story, despite the fact that it involved time travel. What he wanted to know was the standard way that time travel worked. After questioning him for about a half hour, we learned that he was under the impression that there was a specific answer and didn't understand that writers made up whatever system they thought worked for their particular story. After all, time travel in *Doctor Who* is different from time travel in *Harry Potter*.

The script writer was surprised that we had no special book to refer to, after all, how else were we supposed to know—for example—what aliens from the planet Preporus Five were called? We made it up, as was everything in fantasy and science fiction. He was, to say the least, very disappointed about the lack of this magic book that apparently all genre writers got upon becoming a genre writer.

However, I can see his point. Genre—or in the case of this book, fantasy—stories tend to have certain elements that repeat themselves no matter what the setting or situation. This gives rise to the idea that all fantasy stories have been done before. And, in a way, this is true. However, in a way, this is *not* true.

The bones of fantasy stories are ancient and have much in common, but the flesh that each author puts over the bones makes each story different. Some authors are better at it than others. When authors fail to create a new version of an old tale, when they let the stitches show, then you get a bad fantasy novel, if not necessarily a bad story, though oftentimes the two do go hand in hand. However, it is possible to learn what makes fantasy work from the bad stories as well as from the good ones.

Introduction

This is what this book is about: how a fantasy story succeeds or fails by how authors apply the tropes and change them to suit the needs of the story. What makes a fantasy story feel successful is how well it employs the known tropes or language of the genre. If employed well, then the story, despite having the same structure as others, feels different. If not, well, then you've read it all before.

What Is Fantasy?

Before we can have any serious discussion of what makes a fantasy story a fantasy story and how one is put together, fantasy[1] itself must be defined so everyone can have a common frame of reference. Fantasy has so many variations and definitions that it's almost like trying to define what happiness is. Everyone has their own concept of it, and some definitions are narrower than others. Generally, they seem to deal with the idea of the fantastic: the supernatural and magic.

But does a fantasy story actually require magic and the supernatural to be a fantasy? It would seem so at first, but then there are books such as the *Temeraire* series by Naomi Novik that don't have any magic in them at all but do have dragons fighting in the Napoleonic War. Then there's Jasper Fforde's *Thursday Next* series, which is not found in the fantasy section of the bookstore despite the fact that the books involve characters in an alternate world that can travel into books and meet the characters that live there. Most people would definitely assume that a series involving people spending time in other books a fantasy novel! Then you have Terry Goodkind and his *Sword of Truth* series; he writes what would be considered traditional fantasy, but, as he says, he isn't writing fantasy at all.[2]

Who is right? It's hard to say.

In the introduction to the *Cambridge Companion to Fantasy Literature*, it is suggested that

> we view fantasy as a group of texts that share, to a greater degree or other, a cluster of common tropes which may be objects, but which may also be narrative techniques. At the centre are those stories which share tropes of the completely impossible and towards the edges, in subsets, are those stories which include only a small number of tropes, or which construct those tropes in such a way to leave doubt in the reader's mind as to whether what they have read is fantastical nor not [James and Mendlesohn, eds., *Cambridge Companion*, p. 1].

Introduction

So what are these tropes mentioned? Unfortunately there are too many to list, but here are a few examples: the hero, the reluctant hero, the anti-hero, the designated hero, the mentor, the death of the mentor, the love interest, the designated love interest, the femme fatale, the innocent girl, the action girl, the damsel in distress, the action girl who spends more time being a damsel in distress, elves, mysterious kingdoms, prophecies, Chosen Ones, mysterious hidden kingdoms/cities/places, evil overlords, a land of evil, a race that is always evil, a secret magical society, villain monologues, specific special objects, mysterious forests, fairy lands, talking animals, magic swords, magic in general, and the quest.

Basically, fantasy seems to be one of those things that people know when they see it, irritating as that is when trying to come up with a definition for it.

But, as suggested in the *Cambridge Companion*, it is this shared lexicon that fantasy readers and writers use that helps us define it. This shared lexicon is admittedly that some aspect of the fantastic—that is, something that is not possible in our own world as opposed to maybe possible given time and progress—must be involved to make it fantasy instead of science fiction, but other than that, it is a rather broad and forgiving genre. It allows us to encompass works from the ancient *Beowulf* to Shakespeare's *A Midsummer's Night Dream* to George R.R. Martin's *A Song of Ice and Fire* series and the *Twilight* series by Stephenie Meyer (even if many would be reluctant to put Shakespeare and Meyer in the same category).

This necessary inclusion of the fantastic makes fantasy the oldest form of storytelling known to man. Perhaps it isn't likely to be admitted in most academic circles, but if fantasy is a story that contains aspects of the fantastic—things that cannot happen in our world—then it most certainly encompasses all of mythology and many classical texts. These texts are the foundations of the modern fantasy story, where the bones are laid and built upon. Without them, there wouldn't *be* any fantasy.

Variations on a Theme

One of the problems that comes with having such an ancient lineage is that people feel that all fantasy has been done before.

In a way this is 100 percent true, but it's like saying that every fruit

Introduction

still life is the same and once you've seen one still life, you've seen them all. But that's not true. Even in a classroom where everyone is drawing the same bowl of fruit, there will be differences—everything from style to position to skill. And just as not every classical symphony will sound the same to a trained musician, not every fantasy novel will read the same to an experienced reader.

Knowing the way fantasy works is essential to writing and reading a fantasy story. In *An Aesthetics of Junk Fiction*, Thomas J. Roberts makes an important point in why people enjoy reading genre fiction: "The writers are like the jazz musicians who give us a familiar melody at the opening of the piece so that we can understand the variations that follow. We do not listen for that melody. We listen for the variations" (Roberts, *Aesthetics*, p. 166).

What does he mean by listening for the variations? Let us look at the Cinderella story as an example. It's a familiar tale that could be considered overdone. The bones of the Cinderella story are as follows:

1. A girl is orphaned and is treated cruelly by her stepmother and stepsisters, being made to act as a servant for them.
2. The girl has a chance meeting with the prince.
3. The prince throws a ball and the girl wishes to go.
4. A supernatural helper appears and gives her a beautiful gown and lets her go to the ball as long as she's back by a certain time.
5. The girl and the prince meet again, the prince enchanted. They fall in love.
6. Midnight strikes/the ball ends/the girl has to get home before anyone discovers she's missing. She flees and leaves a shoe behind.
7. The prince finds the shoe and declares that the only person who can wear the shoe will be his bride.
8. The prince arrives at the girl's house. The stepmother realizes what happened and tries to have one of her own daughters wear the shoe. The shoe does not fit.
9. The real girl arrives and the shoe fits her.
10. The girl and the prince return to the castle to be happily married and something horrid happens to the stepmother and stepsisters.

Two variations on the Cinderella story using the same basic structure are *Ella Enchanted* by Gail Carson Levine and *Phoenix and Ashes* by

Introduction

Mercedes Lackey. Though both are versions of the Cinderella story neither could be mistaken for the other.

Ella Enchanted, to start with, takes place in a world other than ours, where magic is known, if not common. The protagonist, Ella, is gifted or cursed (depending on who you speak to) with obedience. Every time someone gives her a command she has to obey it from jumping up and down to possibly even cutting off her head with an axe. Her father is actually not dead but spends little to no time at home. In fact, at times he is as uncaring as her stepmother through neglect. Ella and the prince spend time getting to know each other. The climax of the book is her breaking the curse as her stepmother urges her—orders her—to marry the prince so that she and her daughters will be provided for instead of trying to get one of her own daughters to marry him. Ella doesn't want to hurt the prince which, given her curse of obedience, she could do if she was married to him, so she has to refuse to marry him—against everyone else's wishes.

Phoenix and Ashes takes place in England during World War I. The stepmother is an Elemental Master, a magic user who can manipulate one of the four traditional elements—in her case, earth. She has Ella's father killed to take over his factories. As for Ella herself, she is a Fire Master and has to learn how to use her powers to free herself. Her prince is actually a shell-shocked Air Master who's the lord of her village. She helps him get over his trauma as much as he helps her free herself from her stepmother and stepsisters. Instead of a shoe, a three-fingered glove is used, which is an inventive way to get around the problem of many people having the same shoe size.

A third interesting case of the Cinderella story is found in *The Fairy Godmother*, also by Mercedes Lackey. The concept is: What is Cinderella supposed to do when she can't have her prince? Become a fairy godmother, of course!

But herein lies the point: "Predictability is an important part of that reading experience, of course. Readers think they know what is coming next, but they are always slightly wrong—which creates the disappointment, surprise, and delight that they associate with the stories" (Roberts, *Aesthetics,* p. 167).

Unfortunately, there is a flip side to this coin. Sometimes a writer will create a story but rely too heavily on the reader's knowledge of the

Introduction

tropes and archetypes without building upon them. It's like creating a movie where the special effects are obvious; you can tell where the green screens are.

Text vs. Meta-Text

The idea of text vs. meta-text deals with what is written on the page (the text) and the reader's expectations from the text (the meta-text). In most cases, the text and meta-text should merge fairly seamlessly; when there is a conflict between the text and meta-text, the conflict should be something that, while possibly jarring, enhances the reader's experience of the story. When the text and meta-text do not enhance the reader's experience, the reader ends up yelling at the book in frustration or disappointment.

A very gross example of this would be if a person were to pick up a book promising to be about Neil Armstrong and his time as an astronaut, but discovered it was about the care of kittens. Obviously, any reader would be upset. The reader was expecting something about astronauts and while kittens are cute, and maybe the reader might even *have* a kitten, this was not the experience he wanted when he picked up this particular book. This disconnection of experience can get all the way down to the nitty-gritty of world-building details and character actions. People will claim that characters are acting out of character for a reason. If the reader didn't have expectations, then he would just accept what is written on the page.

Because of this, the concept of text vs. meta-text zigzags between read-response criticism and formalistic criticism as ways of reading and exploring the text. Like the formalistic style, meta-text requires the story to stand alone without necessarily engaging in authorial intent. The author may say all she wants that she *intended* her work to be a combination of the tragedy of *Romeo and Juliet* with the lyrical styling of *Sir Gawain and the Green Knight,* but it is the text that will confirm or dispute her intention. A work should stand on its own merit without commentary from the author. The author may intend all sorts of things, but none may actually come out in the story. This is where the meta-text comes in.

Introduction

Readers have mental guidelines of what they understand a fantasy story (in our case) to be and how the text should exist. The text should produce a coherent narrative without authorial assistance.

At the same time the audience—more important, the informed audience—is essential to looking at the idea of text vs. meta-text. In Peter Jackson's *Lord of the Rings* and *Hobbit* movies, animals never speak—not the great eagles or the orcs' wargs, even though they do in the actual books. So when Jackson wants the spiders of Mirkwood to speak in *The Desolation of Smaug*, he has a problem. The audience has already been conditioned by the previous movies to not expect talking animals in this version of Middle-Earth. If the spiders were to suddenly start talking, audiences would find it difficult to believe. After all, why should spiders be the only creatures that can speak?

So Jackson pulls a bit of an author's saving throw[3] with Bilbo and the One Ring. The Ring has already been shown to have random magical properties when worn, so why couldn't it translate what the spiders are saying? While it might not be necessary for the spiders to speak, the ambiguous nature of the ring allows Jackson to give them understandable speech without breaking his previous rules of animals not being able to speak in Westron.

Reading in a meta-textual context requires the reader to have an intimate knowledge of, in this case, the fantasy genre. They must know what a "hero" is. They understand that when someone refers to a character as a wizard that the character is a magic user of some sort. They carry a mental dictionary of terms and concepts long agreed upon by previous authors who constantly build upon their predecessors' work. When someone not familiar with the genre is confronted with the concept of a wizard, she may only assume it refers to an old man with a beard wearing robes and a pointy hat.[4] The idea that "wizard" could also encompass characters that use guns, such as Harry Dresden from Jim Butcher's *Dresden Files* series, would challenge their narrow idea of the "wizard" concept. However, genre readers are fluent enough to realize that the idea of a wizard is not so much defined by the way a person looks—his age and clothing—but instead by the fundamental fact that wizards are individuals that can use magic. They understand the essence of the concept of "wizard." They are able to take the archetype and generalize it to cover broader territory. If confronted with a character who

Introduction

is called a wizard but doesn't use magic they are more likely to call foul than if the wizard is a young man who uses a gun. In fact, they might be more interested in the latter, for the oft-cited reason "Well, if they have guns, why don't they just shoot the bastard instead of using magic?"

This is why many fantasy fans have issues with the vampires from the *Twilight* saga. The vampires of this series don't meet their meta-textual knowledge of what makes a vampire a vampire, and the series doesn't follow or build upon the previous lore of vampires. "Everyone" knows that vampires don't sparkle. But if a reader isn't conversant in the meta-textual knowledge of what a vampire is, she accepts what the text—*Twilight* and its sequels—tells her a vampire is. Then, when confronted with a traditional vampire, such a reader would have the same problem that the conversant individual has with *Twilight* vampires, especially if she goes back to books such as *Dracula* or to the movie *Nosferatu*, where the vampire is a monster that needs to be destroyed. A *Twilight* fan may have heard vaguely that vampires are injured by holy objects or garlic but the *Twilight* books prove these notions wrong. As *Twilight* and its sequels are her only frame of reference, the *Twilight* fan accepts this as true. Thus, her meta-textual knowledge of what makes a vampire a vampire is different than that of the more experienced genre reader.

However, she may not necessarily be wrong. In their distilled essence, Western vampires are undead (usually) humans (usually) who drink blood (usually), and the *Twilight* vampires do fulfill those requirements. Now, does this make the *Twilight* books good? No. They just qualify as vampire books. The *Twilight* saga violates other matters of text vs. meta-text, but this will be discussed later in the book.

Text vs. meta-text also deals with the concepts of continuity, which is vital in fantasy stories. Since the writer is coming up with an entirely new way of how the world works by adding the use of magic or by creating an entirely new world altogether, he or she must make sure that it is consistent throughout the story and series to make the world both plausible and believable. The author can't just say, "Oh, it's magic," because that destroys the integrity and believability of the world. The readers must be given a set of rules, which they must be able to trust the author to follow.

If the reader is told from the beginning that magic only works by speaking spells and then later silent magic is shown to work, then the

Introduction

author had better have a good reason for this change (such as "the use of silent magic is limited to a deaf character who only uses sign language") or the reader's trust is broken. Once this happens, it's harder for the reader to be involved in the world, as he cannot believe in it. This idea is more fully discussed in Chapter Ten.

Finally, on the flipside of the writer-reader/text vs. text-meta equation, the writer assumes that the reader is familiar with the language of fantasy so he can use it without having to explain it from the very beginning. He doesn't have to say that a wizard is an individual that uses magic and this is how the magic works. Instead, he can say that wizards can only use magic by learning it from books while a sorcerer is someone who is born with the innate ability to use magic. He takes the essence of a person who uses magic and relies on the reader to adjust his definition of the idea to suit the particular story at hand.

The trick is not to rely too much on the reader's knowledge of concepts as shorthand. The writer still must continue to use his definition, especially with concepts like "hero" and "villain," because those have very particular connotations. If a character's concept or role is X but the character never acts as X, then the text and the meta-text disconnect. In fact, it is this disconnect, this moment of the reader losing connection with the work and having to think about what he just read, that is the heart of the text vs. meta-text moment.

A writer creates a moment of text vs. meta-text when he can give a reader a "Say what?" moment. When skillfully done, this lets the reader know that something different is going to occur in the story and that his expectations of the text have met a turnaround moment. These are not necessarily moments recognized by the characters themselves—such as the serving boy really turning out to be a girl—but instead a change in the narrative certainty and outcome. Having the serving boy be a girl may be a surprise to the characters, but it's a common convention in stories, and one that might be expected. However, killing off the character assumed to be the hero and protagonist three-fourths of the way through the book is not. Heroes are supposed to survive. Good wins over evil. To throw this concept into doubt causes the reader an important moment of uncertainty and then drives him to read further. How does a story develop when the character set up as the noble hero is quite dead? If the writer is clever enough, you get something like George R.R.

Introduction

Martin's *Song of Ice and Fire* series. If not, then the reader will likely feel cheated and not even finish the book.

But it is that "Say what?" moment of dissonance that is the true point of the text vs. meta-text. The reader's assumptions have been challenged and that should drive him forward into interaction with the narrative and text.

And it is this dissonance that this book aims to explore. The conceit is that, yes, all of fantasy has been done before, so much so that it has created a language and set of rules that is followed to create a story. That being said, fantasy's language, rules and tropes give writers a framework to create and explore new ideas which couldn't be done without them. They allow writers to question the importance of story in our everyday lives. And by comparing and contrasting various fantasy works, this book will show what makes a good fantasy good and a bad fantasy something that has been seen before.

The Book

Now that the purpose of the book has been discussed, let's look at the contents. The first part of the book looks at the natures of meta-text and of genre itself; the second part dives more into the building blocks of the fantasy story and what makes some versions successful and others not.

Chapter One: Changing the Story looks at Jasper Fforde's *Thursday Next* series, Terry Pratchett's *Discworld* series and Mercedes Lackey's *Five Hundred Kingdom* series; how they deal with the idea of metafiction within the actual story setting; and how characters use the idea of stories to influence and change their own personal stories within the books themselves without actually breaking the fourth wall. Chapter Two: A Matter of Perception looks at the *Twilight* saga. Only the fact that it is designated a romance series makes people look at it *as* a romance series, even though many of the tropes that are found within it can be and are often used in horror stories … and not merely the vampires and werewolves. Here, the meta-text and the text itself show the disconnects from the romance story genre and why, despite what the text says, they're really something from a horror novel.

In Chapter Three: The Power of Stories, I discuss this. For example,

Introduction

the sheer fact that stories such as the *Dresden Files* and the *Iron Druid Chronicles* take place in the modern-day world requires the characters to be genre-savvy, especially if they reference pop culture. For Chapter Four: Magic of Fantasy, Fantasy of Magic, the question, "Is magic even necessary for fantasy?" will be asked, looking at Naomi Novik's *Temeraire* series, which has no magic but many of the hallmarks of fantasy, and Terry Goodkind's *Sword of Truth* series, which apparently isn't fantasy according to its author, as well as Magical Realism. Finally, there are the ways of telling a fantasy story when the typical archetypes and story structure are subverted, such as in the *Song of Ice and Fire* series and the *Codex Alera* series, which are discussed in Chapter Five: Not What You Think It Is.

Moving into the actual building of a fantasy world, Chapter Six: Heroes and Protagonists, Villains and Antagonists, dissects the natures of the hero and villain vs. the protagonist and antagonist. It looks at how, in fantasy fiction, people often meld the protagonist and hero into a single character and do the same for villains and antagonists, though there is often a great deal of difference. Also, it describes four different kinds of heroes and villains that can be found in fantasy stories. Chapter Seven: No Man Is an Island looks at the side characters and their importance to the plot and to the creation of the world around them, be they secondary characters, minor characters or background characters and gets to the heart of the matter with romance and love interests. Do all fantasy stories require love interests? And when you have a shoehorned-in love interest, what happens to the character dynamics? From there, in Chapter Eight: Fairies and Dragons and Dwarfs, Oh My! we will look at how the various stock fantasy races have been portrayed over the years, from vampires to fairies and dragons to griffins and everything in between. In Chapter Nine: Through the Looking Glass, we look at the secondary world versus the urban fantasy, and the idea of the masquerade that is often employed in urban fantasy (but not secondary worlds) to hide magic from mundane eyes because of fear. Finally, we move onto Chapter Ten: The Fundamentals, which explores the settings of a fantasy story and the importance of world consistency and continuity. How is a story affected when things in the world do not match up from book to book or even from chapter to chapter? Also, there will be a brief discussion on the nature of "in-jokes" and references to other stories and how, if done poorly, they can feel out of place in the story's setting.

CHAPTER ONE

Changing the Story

> "I think it means 'change the story,'" said Ponder, without looking up. "At a saving of five pence."
> —*The Science of the Discworld II: The Globe*
> by Terry Pratchett, Ian Stewart and Jack Cohen

One of the things that most readers don't often remember is that they are acting as voyeurs of other people's lives. They read stories about strangers' lives. From the most intimate sexual moments to the most banal making of a sandwich to someone's greatest triumphs overthrowing the worst evils known to man, the reader is privy to it all.

This voyeuristic aspect is rarely acknowledged. Even in stories told in the first-person, it is generally assumed that the narrator does not know that he or she is a character in a book. Instead, much like in the beginning of *Heart of Darkness,* they are merely recounting their adventure to a friend or at least (in theory) an eager listener. Sometimes the character records their life as if writing an autobiography, again without giving any indication that the speaker realizes that he or she is a fictional character. Thus, the reader is allowed to peer into and engage in worlds not their own.

When characters break the fourth wall—that is, when they appear to acknowledge the existence of the reader or viewer (and I say "appear to" because it is the author who writes the character acknowledging the fourth wall)—the façade of voyeurism is brought to light and makes the viewer think more about the form and function of what it is they're experiencing. The fourth wall is that imaginary barrier that protects the reader from the world and allows the characters within the stories to act without having to worry about the fact that they are, for example, sneaking into the secret lair of the bad guy with someone bumbling along behind them. Unless that someone is their sidekick. They continue about their lives, oblivious to the invisible eye following them around.

The fourth wall can be broken in many ways. Sometimes it's done for humor's sake; other times, as a commentary on how fiction media works; and sometimes as a commentary on the real world itself and how people themselves may just be characters in their own stories.

In the typical manner of breaking the fourth wall, the characters will "turn" to acknowledge either the existence of the audience or the fact that they are fictional. In cartoons such as Warner Brothers' *Animaniacs,* when the Warners are asked by a pilgrim to hand over a turkey, the pilgrim saying, "Give me the bird," Yakko replies, "We'd love to, but the Fox censors won't let us." Or at the end of the famous Bugs Bunny cartoon *What's Opera, Doc,* where a "dead" Bugs Bunny asks the audience why they expected a happy ending; it was opera, after all.

On rare occasions it's even used as a way to drive the plot forward. One such occasion can be found in *Monty Python and the Holy Grail* which cheerfully breaks the fourth wall all over the place. At one point, Arthur and his knights are being chased by the Legendary Black Beast of Aaaaarrrrrrggghhh. In keeping with the style of both the Monty Python television show as well as the rest of the movie, the monster is animated and the chase is subsequently shown as an animated segment. The knights appear to have no way to save themselves when the narrator of the movie tells the audience that the animator suffered "a sudden and fatal heart attack. And thus, the cartoon menace was no more."

While nobody expects the animator to suddenly drop dead, there is no reason why this should have any bearing on either the movie or the characters' peril. While it is a tragedy that the animator died, he could have easily been replaced and the animation continued without interruption to the flow of the movie.[1] This breaking of the fourth wall—making the audience acknowledge that the characters are animated and being chased by an animated creature—and putting into the plot that they are rescued only because of the death of the animator creates a meta-textual moment for the viewers. They are reminded that they are watching a film and that the knights were likely only animated to save money on special effects. It conflicts with how things are normally done within movies or stories. The "real" world shouldn't affect the fictional world. The intrusion in this case brings a humorous moment for the

One. Changing the Story

viewer as they try and process the death of the animator as the savior of the knights, and it allows the knights—in story—to get away from the beast.

Whether the knights acknowledge that this is happening isn't known. However, they do know they are in a film during other points of the movie. Here, the breaking of the fourth wall is used to move the plot forward in a typical Monty Python manner.

This secondary manner of breaking the fourth wall is almost diegetic in its manner. This acknowledgment of the medium forces the viewers to accept the fact that this is how the story progresses. They have to believe that in narrative the characters realize they've been saved by the animator dying.

Moving into diegetic forms of writing that acknowledge that they are a fictional medium brings us to the *Thursday Next* series by Jasper Fforde. This series takes place on an alternate Earth where cloned dodos and time travel are possible and where literature is really serious business. Instead of the *Rocky Horror Picture Show* interactive viewings, they have *Richard III* interactive viewings. People fight with almost religious fervor over who wrote Shakespeare's plays, missionaries going door to door much like Jehovah's Witnesses, trying to convince the validity of someone else having written the Bard's plays. They are considered to be just as annoying.

The protagonist is Thursday Next, a government worker who is assigned to SpecOps 27 literary detectives in Swindon. In the first book, *The Eyre Affair,* Thursday travels into the book *Jane Eyre,* which gets the attention of Jurisfiction, an agency in "Book World" that polices affairs of fictional characters by using real people and fictional people.

Jumping into the fictional world of books is hardly a device found only in the *Thursday Next* series; Cornelia Funke's *Inkheart* Trilogy does it as well. What makes Fforde's books unique is that once in the Book-World, characters acknowledge that they are characters. They acknowledge that there are things like plot devices, such as in *The Well of Lost Plots,* when Thursday is shown "Suddenly, a Shot Rang Out!," a "stolen freeze-dried plot device" (Fforde, *Well,* p. 59). The people in the Book-World even know when their stories are being read and can control it. This happens in *The Well of Lost Plots* when the BookWorld shut down

The Scarlet Letter by closing a story engine and thus rendering casual readers bored with the book. For the class actually studying *The Scarlet Letter*, Thursday and the others have to set off a fire alarm at the students' school (Fforde, *Well*, p. 370). Once that was done, no one could pick up the book because they wouldn't think about it. The BookWorld rulers even controlled what books were printed and where spare characters went, which was why there were so many Gandalf-like characters around.

In the *Inkheart* trilogy, this isn't as necessary because jumping into the book *Inkheart* doesn't affect anything that happens to the "real" physical copy of the book. Instead, it's as if the characters have jumped into another world, much like the Pevensies did when they walked through the wardrobe in C.S. Lewis's *The Lion, The Witch and the Wardrobe*. The characters inside the book *Inkheart* (the version written by one of the characters) act as if they're still in their novel and their lives don't affect what happens when the book is read. If a character were to leave or be added to the book, it isn't reflected in the book for people reading it. They can't tell if someone is all right because it says so in the text. And once things have passed on in the narrative, they can't go back to earlier points in the story. For example, when Dustfinger returns home in *Inkspell,* ten years have passed and his wife has moved on without him. The Ink world can still be affected by writing, but it's done much like a wizard casting a spell rather than actually physically changing the form of the book by the characters themselves. There are no "suddenly, a shot rang out" plot devices that can be bought in the Ink world. Instead, it's just like any other world except that for some people it's fictional because they came from a world where it was a book. But when told this the people within the book world just give them a funny look and think they're crazy.

Fforde also plays with how the reader vs. how the characters perceive things. Since Thursday is an Outlander, while in BookWorld she can see things like character descriptions as written words. In one scene during the beginning of *Something Rotten,* Thursday and Commander Trafford Bradshaw, a character similar to Allan Quatermain from H. Rider Haggard's series of books—one of those African hunter adventure sorts of characters—are in a Western searching for a runaway character. They encounter a group of cowboys that Thursday feels are out of place of the pulpy Western they're in.

One. Changing the Story

For a start, none of them wore black, nor did they have tooled leather double gun belts with nickel-plated revolvers. Their spurs didn't clink as they walked, their holsters were plain and worn high on the hip—the weapon these men had chosen was a Winchester rifle. I noticed with a shudder that one of the men had a button missing on his frayed vest and the sole on the toe of his boot had come adrift. Flies buzzed around the men's unwashed and grimy faces, and sweat had stained their hats half way to the crown [Fforde, *Something*, p. 10].

While this may seem like just an ordinary narrative description done by the author—Fforde—Thursday can tell that they are important and well-described characters. When one of them dies, she says to Bradshaw, "Did you see how much text he was composed of?" I replied angrily. "He was almost a paragraph long..." (Fforde, *Something*, p. 12). So while within the text of the book it seemed as if the characters were being described through the narrative and Thursday's eyes, for Thursday, she was "reading" the text that the cowboys were composed of, much like the readers of the book.

This is something that BookWorld natives can't do. If something doesn't happen in their books, they don't have it in their lives. If breakfast isn't served in the text, then they don't eat it. They don't miss it because it doesn't exist for them. They know of it and ask Thursday about it, but it's not part of their daily routine.

If there aren't dialogue tags when someone speaks, the BookWorld characters can't follow the conversation and they don't know who is speaking. This is contrary to how most people think when they read a book. Readers assume that even though there are no character dialogue tags, the characters themselves still know who is speaking because they are actual people. And yet this scene happens in *The Well of Lost Plots*:

> "Very well," I replied, covering my eyes, "I'll prove it to you. Speak to me in turn but leave off your speech designators."
> "Okay," said Unnamed Police Officer No. 1. "Who is this talking?"
> "And who is this?" added Dr. Singh.
> "I said leave off your speech designators. Try again."
> "It's harder than you think," sighed Unnamed Police Officer No. 1. "Okay, here goes."
> There was a pause.
> "Which one of us is talking now?"
> "And who am I?"
> "Mrs. Singh first, Unnamed Police Officer No. 1 second. Was I correct?"

"Amazing!" murmured Mrs. Singh. "How do you do that?"
"I can recognize your voices. I have a sense of smell, too" [Fforde, *Well*, p. 18].

Since the reader is reading the book, he can't hear the difference between the two voices like Thursday can, much like Mrs. Singh and Unnamed Police Officer No. 1. This puts the reader in a similar situation to the two BookWorld characters. At the same time, they're in the same position as Thursday, because if they were in the BookWorld, they, as Outlanders, would be able to tell the difference.

This succeeds because the book is written in first-person. As a result, we know Thursday's thoughts and can, through her, know what a character made out of a paragraph of text is like. We can see which things are intentional grammatical oversights, such as a character who is described as "an untidy man wearing a hat named Wyatt" (Fforde, *Well*, p. 15). He is supposed to have such poor grammatical construction—for which he apologizes.

Only at one point does Thursday herself feel like she's a book character. In *Something Rotten*, she and her husband are about to have sex when she stops because she can't focus with everyone reading her. Which—to her—is, of course, ridiculous. As she says, "Sorry. I've been living inside fiction for too long; sometimes I get this weird feeling that you, me and everything else are just ... well, characters in a book or something" (Fforde, *Something*, p. 279). But the readers know that this isn't ridiculous at all because they are the ones reading about her and thus are those people that she feels looking upon her.

This is the only time that Thursday breaks the fourth wall. However, it doesn't actually constitute breaking the fourth wall because it makes perfect sense for her to feel that way after having spent so much time in the BookWorld.

Beyond that, the novels themselves—their format and non-story information—are affected by events within the story. Things like chapter titles. In *Something Rotten*, Thursday is told by Emperor Zhark that because of his new contract

> "I have to be given a minimum of eighty words' description at least once in any featured book, and at least twice in a book a chapter has to end with my appearance."
> "Do you get book-title billing?" [Thursday asked.]

One. Changing the Story

"We gave that one away in exchange for chapter-heading status. If this were a novel, you'd have to start a new chapter as soon as I appeared" [Fforde, *Something*, p. 156].

And, if you look at the chapter listings of the book, there are two chapters containing his name: Chapter Seventeen is titled "Emperor Zhark," Chapter Eighteen "Emperor Zhark Again." He also gets his eighty words of description when he first appears at the end of Chapter Sixteen. Thus, the BookWorld is affecting our real world as much as it is the books in their world. Other examples include the missing book *The Great Samuel Pepys Fiasco,* which is listed as being published between *Something Rotten* and *First Among Sequels.* It is crossed off in the listing of books published by Jasper Fforde with the note that it is no longer available. Within the book *First Among Sequels,* we learn the fate of the book and why it's no longer available. In *The Well of Lost Plots,* a subplot involves Thursday helping a detective fiction book try not to get dismantled. The solution is to turn it from hardboiled detective fiction into a detective series involving nursery rhyme characters. These become the Nursery Crime Series—which are also written by Fforde. So apparently the second series wouldn't exist if Thursday hadn't created it in while in the BookWorld.

There is also the mobilefootnoterphone, which is like a cell phone except that it uses footnotes to communicate. The story carries on in the main body of the text and, at the same time, there are conversations between the character in the body of the text and the person they're speaking to on the mobilefootnoterphone.[2]

In this way, Fforde plays with the medium of a book and uses it to move the plot forward, making contact with the world the stories take place in.

Fforde's books are one step removed from the traditional breaking of the fourth wall. They are using the tropes of stories but only within the BookWorld itself. Outside of the BookWorld, the characters from the books are told they are in the real world and that the real world doesn't work like it does in stories. Yet the "real world" of Thursday Next sort of does, because *Thursday Next is* a novel series. So, the fourth wall is only broken within the book itself but the characters never acknowledge the existence of outside readers—that is, us. The fact that the books take place in such an obvious alternate world helps readers suspend their disbelief to the point that they can accept the playing around with the form. Readers know that such things can't exactly happen in our world, but in a world where cheese is a highly regulated substance and you can make your own dodo in a kitchen sink, it seems a bit more plausible.

Flatworlds and Traditions

However, there is an interesting mix between the ways that the *Thursday Next* series and the *Inkheart* trilogy play with the fourth wall. The tropes of stories are acknowledged within the books themselves; however, the characters within the books don't acknowledge that they themselves are characters within books. This pattern can also be found in Terry Pratchett's *Discworld* series and Mercedes Lackey's *Five Hundred Kingdoms* series. Both of these series consciously use familiar tropes found in stories to affect the characters' world, and they acknowledge that this is what they are doing. However, both series do so in different ways. Even so, the fourth wall here isn't broken.

Everybody Knows...

In the *Discworld* series, the physical form of the novel is used to create effects that help tell the story in similar ways to the *Thursday Next* series. This is especially true in regards to the use of font faces for various characters. Death tends to talk IN SMALL CAPS. In *Men at Arms,* one character is able to think in *italics,* which is, as the text comments, dangerous. One character in *The Truth,* Mr. Tulip, manages to curse by saying "---ing" all the time. The dash isn't a substitution for a curse word; he manages to say the "---" as well as the "ing" attached to it. It is a "speech impediment" (Pratchett, *Truth,* p. 67). Then there are the scene-changing "ticks" in *Thief of Time,* which, when time stops, vanish from the text with a *Ti* (Pratchett, *Thief,* p. 231) and only return (once time has started up again) with an *ick* (Pratchett, *Thief,* p. 335).

The interesting thing about the Discworld is that while the people don't admit that they are characters in stories, they do actively admit the power of stories in their lives. As *The Science of the Discworld II:*

One. Changing the Story

The Globe explains: "The Discworld runs on magic, and magic is indissolubly linked to Narrative Causality, the power of story. A spell is a story about what a person wants to happen, and magic is what turns stories into reality. On Discworld, things happen *because people expect them to*" (Stewart, Cohen and Pratchett, *Science*, p. 23). What exactly does that mean? It means that what "everybody knows" is probably right. (Probably, because Pratchett is very fond of throwing "probably" under the bus.)

In *Guards! Guards!*, a dragon attacks the city of Ankh-Morpork. Near the climax, three of the watchmen, Lance-Corporal Carrot Ironfoundersson, Sergeant Fred Colon and Corporal Nobby Nobbs are on the rooftop, discussing Colon's chances of hitting the dragon in its weak spot. After all, everyone knows that dragons have a "voonerable" spot. Everyone in our world knows this because of *The Hobbit* and Smaug's vulnerable spot. Thus, everyone in the Discworld, which is a reflection of our world, knows the same thing—though for them, it's just a fact, as opposed to something that many people know because of one book. The three guardsmen also know that million-to-one chances *always* work. So they decided to stack their odds in their favor so that Sergeant Colon can hit the dragon in its voonerable spot and thus save the city and the virgin, Lady Ramkin.

> Nobby put his head on one side.
> "It looks promising," he said critically. "We might be nearly there. I reckon the chances of a man with soot on his face, his tongue sticking out, standing on one leg and singing The Hedgehog Song ever hitting a dragon's voonerables would be … what do you say, Carrot?"
> "A million to one, I reckon," said Carrot virtuously" [Pratchett, *Guards*, p. 301].

However, despite everyone knowing that million-to-one chances always succeed, the watchmen fail. Colon *does* hit the dragon, "but Chance, who sometimes can overrule even the gods, has 999,999 casting votes. In *this* universe, for example, the arrow bounced off a scale and clattered away into oblivion" (Pratchett, *Guards*, p. 304).

Thus, the million-to-one chance is used and abused in the Discworld. The characters decide that it was an actual viable solution based on the fact that everyone knew that a million-to-one chance worked. No one in the real world would ever try and shoot a dragon in its voon-

The Tropes of Fantasy Fiction

erables on the idea that the last-ditch, million-to-one chance always worked in stories. The real world doesn't work like that. People may wish it does, but it doesn't. At least ... not most of the time. After all, there was probably a million-to-one chance of the Apollo 13 crew making it back alive. And yet they did.

The power of stories even works on things like the concept of the sun. It doesn't seem like there would be much story involved in the sun. It's just a great big ball of gas that the Earth revolves around. In the Discworld, though, the sun revolves around the Disc. Why? Because that's what makes sense. That's what it looks like. *Everyone* can see that the sun revolves around the Disc. It certainly made sense to most of the world hundreds of years ago, but, sadly for the Earth, just because it made sense didn't make it true. But, still, in the present-day real world, where science rules, there doesn't seem to be much in the way of story revolving around the sun.

In *Hogfather*, the protagonist, Susan, learns that it is necessary for people to believe in the Hogfather—the Discworld's Santa Claus equivalent. Her grandfather, Death, tells her that if they don't the sun won't rise. After she does save the Hogfather, she asks Death what would have happened.

WHAT WOULD HAVE HAPPENED IF YOU HADN'T SAVED HIM?
"Yes! The sun would have risen just the same, yes?"
NO.
"Oh, come on. You can't expect me to believe that. It's an astronomical fact."
THE SUN WOULD NOT HAVE RISEN.
"Really? Then what would have happened, pray?"
A MERE BALL OF FLAMING GAS WOULD HAVE ILLUMINATED THE WORLD.
They walked in silence for a moment.
"Ah," sad Susan dully. "Trickery with words. I would have thought you would have been more literal-minded than that."
I AM NOTHING BUT LITERAL-MINDED. TRICKERY WITH WORDS IS WHERE HUMANS LIVE" [Pratchett, *Hogfather*, p. 335].

The "everybody" in "everybody knows" are, in fact, the readers themselves. Readers familiar with fantasy tropes and stories, that is. If a reader isn't familiar with *The Hobbit*, they wouldn't be one of the "everybody knows." While they may just think it's an interesting fact about dragons, that they have a "voonerable spot," and it wouldn't inter-

One. Changing the Story

rupt their enjoyment of the story, it won't reach the same level of humor as it would for an informed reader familiar with fantasy tropes.

In fact, Pratchett uses the reader's knowledge of the metatexual to turn various tropes on their heads. As Jessica Tiffin says in her book, *Marvelous Geometry:* "Pratchett's awareness of genre allows him to invoke and explore an apparently disparate series of narrative traditions, held together firmly by the sword and sorcery tradition" (Tiffin, *Marvelous,* p. 159).

Everybody knows that Radagast the Brown is kind to animals and talks to them. Ridcully the Brown, the Archchancellor of Unseen University, also talks to animals. But Ridcully tends to say things like, "Winged you, yer bastard!" (Pratchett, *Moving Pictures,* p. 12).

Everybody knows that Conan the Barbarian is a young, hefty, broad-shouldered man with enough testosterone to fuel an army. His Discworld equivalent, Ghenghiz Cohen, aka Cohen the Barbarian, is an old man who is skinny, though he's very good at not dying because that's how a barbarian survives to be in his nineties.

Everybody knows that the long-lost prince raised by someone else returns to the kingdom of his birth and overthrows the tyrant. Captain Carrot, who may be the missing heir of Ankh-Morpork's throne (it's never been officially said out loud) instead decides that Havelock Vetinari, the tyrant, is doing a good job and leaves him to rule while Carrot stays working as a watchman.

Everybody knows that elves are nice and caring, at least if the Tolkien version of elves, which are usually used by Pratchett. So the Discworld elves are terrific, as in, they cause terror.

Because these changes in tropes and expectations aren't always used for comedic effect, it keeps them from being parodies of the tropes Pratchett is subverting and allows them to become their own characters or menaces. "Pratchett comments that in his adaptation of the 'Tolkien-type imagery' involves a deliberate attempt 'to treat it as if the characters are real,' in defiance of the numerous 'bad copies of Tolkien' which are saturating the popular market'" (Tiffin, *Marvelous,* p. 159, citing Pratchett's interview on "Loose Ends," BBC Radio 4, 27 Nov. 1993).

Sometimes the narrativium of the Discworld does try and fight the "everybody knows" such as the "an ugly man becomes a lovely women" trope. In *Jingo,* Nobby Nobbs has to dress up as a woman in a harem outfit. This is a problem because Nobby is often described in terms of "*probably* being human"; not even Death knows what he is exactly.[3] And if Death doesn't know what you are, then there are serious issues.

Since everybody knows that about ugly men becoming attractive women, it makes sense that Nobby and his indeterminable species would turn into a beautiful woman and yet

> "Corporal Nobbs' appearance could be best summarized this way.
> One of the minor laws of the narrative universe is that any homely featured man who has, for some reason, to disguise himself as a woman will apparently become attractive to some otherwise perfectly sane men with, as the ancient scrolls say, hilarious results.
> In this case, the laws were fighting against the fact of Corporal Nobby Nobbs, and gave up" [Pratchett, *Jingo*, p. 325].

While most people in the Discworld depend on what "everybody knows" to determine the way the world works, a few characters are able to actively put it into words and to use it to their advantage. They realize what the power of stories is in their world and how it can help them win battles. When they try for the million-to-one chance, they *will* hit that dragon in the voonerables.

Two such incidents happen in *The Last Hero* where Cohen and his Silver Horde decided to return fire to the gods with interest as a one last hurrah and bang for their lives. They want it to be their final adventure. Of course, since this will cause the entire world to burn away to a crisp, the rest of the world has every interest in stopping them. Lord Vetinari and others develop a plan to stop them which involves throwing a flying ship off the edge of the Disc so it can loop around and crash into the gods' mountaintop home. Rincewind the Wizard (whose hat spells the word "wizzard") is one of those people whom adventure happens to. However, he would rather spend his time having a boring life with potatoes and rocks. Knowing this about his life, he goes to Lord Vetinari and the others who are planning on how to stop Cohen, and the Horde to say that he doesn't wish to volunteer. This stumps the Patrician, as it would most people. When he asks for an explanation, Rincewind says,

> "Oh, but they will, sir, they will. Someone will say: hey, that Rincewind fella, he's the adventurous sort, he knows the Horde, Cohen seems to like him, he knows all there is to know about cruel and unusual geography, he'd be just

One. Changing the Story

the job for something like this." He sighed. "And then I'll run away, and probably hide in a crate somewhere that will be loaded onto the flying machine in any case."

"Will you?" [asked the Patrician]
"Probably, sir. Or there'll be a whole string of accidents that end up causing the same thing. Trust me, sir. I know how my life works. So I thought I'd better cut through the whole tedious business and come along and tell you I don't wish to volunteer" [Pratchett, *Hero*, p. 39].

There's no reasonable reason for this to happen to Rincewind; after all, in the real world, he could just go into his room and lock the door and nothing should happen to him. But on the Discworld, the narrative *requires* him to end up on the ship. Rincewind is the guy who gets dragged reluctantly onto adventures no matter what.

Then later Captain Carrot faces off against Cohen and his horde of six. They're threatening him when one of them points out that they should double-check what was happening.

"The horde could calculate the peculiar mathematics of heroism quite quickly.
There was, there always was, at the start and finish, the Code. They lived by the Code. You follow the Code, and you became part of the Code for those who followed you. The Code was it. Without the Code, you weren't a hero. You were just a thug in a loincloth.
The Code was quite clear. One brave man against seven ... won. They knew it was true. In the past, they'd all relied on it. The higher the odds, the greater the victory. That was the Code.
Forget the Code, dismiss the Code, deny the Code ... and the Code would take you" [Pratchett, *Hero*, p. 143].

The Horde knows the power of story and of narrative in their world. For them it's called the Code. It's how they survived all these years. It's how they defeated five armies with only eight people in the climatic battle of *Interesting Times*. In a sense, they realize that they are in a story, or that at least they can use the rules of stories to their advantage. Their world works that way. That is the power of narrativium.

And that is how Pratchett plays with the meta-text. He knows that readers have certain set ideas of how fantasy stories should go. The books "simultaneously comment self-consciously on the popular genre of fantasy from a position *within* the generic ghetto defined by Ursula Le Guin... Thus, an awareness of the working of classic fantasy continually and ironically weaves through the Discworld, but as a facet of the author's awareness of the far older traditions of the marvelous" (Tiffin, *Marvelous,* p. 160). Pratchett knows that readers were weaned on Tolkien, thus taking their expectations and twisting them. He turns the expectations into something more realistic and less ethereal. He takes the stories we tell ourselves and turns them into a world where they are actually the rules of the universe, as opposed to us just wishing they were. It would be nice, however.

Traditions

The Discworld plays around with narrative expectations by using the idea of "everybody knows" that X should happen. People who live on the Disc truly believe this to be so, and the world will sometimes be helpful—by providing light-giving fungus to any adventurers who stumble into the underground caverns[4]—or be unhelpful by locking up prisoners in a room where they couldn't use anything in it to escape.[5] But the narrative is mostly a passive force, rather like light or atoms. It exists but in most cases doesn't try and do anything (unless it has to deal with the idea of Nobby being considered an attractive woman). Generally speaking, however, it doesn't have a mind of its own. There are people who can manipulate it to their own ends—such as heroes who follow the Code—but the narrative itself doesn't want or do anything.

In the *Tales of the Five Hundred Kingdoms* series by Mercedes Lackey, the characters face a different and yet similar issue with the power of stories and expectations. While on Discworld people who live there can force things into the stories they want to have happen (in some cases) because everybody knows that's how things go, an outside force called the Tradition causes these things to happen in the *Tales of the Five Hundred Kingdoms* series.

The Tradition acts like a forceful and rather conceited matchmaker who takes any person or thing that could possibly resemble a character or story item and forces it into one of the known fairy tales or stories. In *The Fairy Godmother,* it's explained thus:

"You see, whenever there is a person whose life begins to resemble a tale—the brave little orphan lad, the lovely girl with the wicked stepmother, the princess with the overly protective father—something begins to happen, and that something is *magic*. ... Magic begins to gather around them, you see, and in fact there are even certain people to whom that begins to happen to them the moment they are born. The magic tries to force their lives down the path that their circumstances most closely resemble, and the longer it takes for that to happen, the more magic begins to gather around them" [Lackey, *Godmother*, p. 56].

Thus, the main character, Elena, who has a wicked stepmother and two wicked stepsisters, would be forced down the path of Cinderella. However, circumstances conspire against her. She is twenty-one at the start of the book, while her prince is just a child of eleven. There is no way for her "happily ever after" to happen as things are set up. The Tradition doesn't care and would still probably try to force her to marry the prince in some fashion, so long as it fits the story.

To counteract the Tradition—because for every happy ending, there are often many unhappy endings that precede it—are the Fairy Godmothers and their helpers. For example, there is the Ladderlocks tale, or, as most readers know it, Rapunzel. Before the girl can be rescued by her prince, others must try and get to her first, others who fail and fall to their deaths or are caught in the bower of thorns around the tower before the appropriate prince arrives. And even then the lucky prince himself may end up blind or worse. Obviously, this is a story with a barely triumphant happy ending, what with it having wrought so much death beforehand. Never mind the fact that the girl herself will have been kidnapped by an evil witch and forced to live in a tower away from her family. Elena wonders, when she learns about this, why some of the girls don't go mad themselves. "Some of them do," Madame confirmed. "I know of one who hung herself with her hair" (Lackey, *Godmother*, p. 164).

What the Fairy Godmothers do is try and steer the Tradition to less tragic paths. In *The Fairy Godmother*, there is a girl who is supposed to become a Ladderlocks. To prevent this, Elena and Madame Bella shift the Tradition toward the Tender Princess (or "The Princess and the Pea," as most readers know the story). Thus, not only is the girl saved from living without her family and from being raised by an evil sorceress, but all the young men were saved from their deaths as well.

In many ways, the Tradition acts as the authorial imperative—the writer trying to force their will upon the characters of the world they have created. Many authors will often complain about writer's block or that they couldn't get a scene to work because it seemed like the characters were protesting the actions. They refused to do what the author tells them to. It's only after the author changes the course of the story that the characters become more pliant and no longer act out of character. Characters will often seem to take on a life of their own and change the direction of the story, contrary to how the author originally saw it. To go back to Terry Pratchett, he originally saw Vimes as a character who would introduce Ankh-Morpork to the reader before Carrot arrived. However, Vimes ended up becoming the main character of the guard subseries instead of Carrot.

But this is what happens in the universe for the people of the Five Hundred Kingdoms. They rebel, not against the author, Mercedes Lackey, but instead against the Tradition and the force of tragedy and clichés that it lays over the world. They do this by exploiting *their* knowledge of the traditional tales. They know that during a Quest in which three siblings are sent out, the eldest two will always fail and the youngest will succeed. The Fairy Godmothers set up the tests so that they can make sure the Questers—as they're called—are sent to the right places for the proper story to unfold.

They know that the Tradition doesn't care if a sorceress is evil or not, as long as she has the trappings of evil: a fondness for black clothing, a gloomy tower, and bats. So they will find a sorceress willing to do such a thing, or has a tendency to do such a thing, without actually being evil, or they will take on the role themselves, as Godmother Lily did in *The Sleeping Beauty*. The Tradition satisfied, they can move to make the story the girls and boys are caught up in into something more reasonable to their wants.

Also, they will exploit the Tradition to their own ends so that they can get rid of an evil sorceress or wizard. This happens frequently in *One Good Knight*. First, the Fairy Godmothers use the loophole of a barrier preventing any man from entering by sending a female knight, Georgina, to rescue Princess Andromeda from being eaten by a dragon. Then the princess prevents herself from falling in love with Georgina—whom, at the time, she thought was a man—by making the two of them blood siblings. Later on, they need to turn a group of girls that has no

One. Changing the Story

fighting abilities into a force that could take the kingdom back from Andromeda's mother, so they turn to several tales at once to force the Tradition to help them. First, they become "the Ragged Company." This tale involves a champion gathering a group of untrained peasants and training them into a force capable of invading a castle. Georgina knows that the Tradition likes unlikely heroes; she figures that the gaggle of girls will be the most unlikely of heroes and thus the Tradition will help them. To push their case even further, she has the girls of noble blood swear off their nobility and become sisters with the non-noble girls, thus drawing them closer to the original story path. This allows the girls to pick up fighting skills much quicker than they normally would be able to do.

> "Now," said Gina [Georgina] with a grim smile, "I am going to prove to you that this has already worked."
>
> She crooked her finger and summoned Dita, possibly the least likely fighter of them all, from the back of the group. She picked up one of the two fighting staves she had at her feet, and handed it to the girl, who held uncertainly. Then she herself took the second stave, looked off nonchalantly into the distance, then suddenly whirled and executed a lighting three-strike attack on the girl, holding nothing back.
>
> The others gasped, squealed or screamed. Dita herself yelped.
>
> But her hands moved surely and of themselves. Crack, crack, crack. All three attacks were met. And countered" [Lackey, *Knight*, p. 308].

While the girls aren't going to be able to attack the castle right away, they now have the advantage of only needing a training montage to get them into fighting shape, as opposed to years of training, like Georgina had.

Many characters in *The Tales of the Five Hundred Kingdoms* are similarly genre-savvy. In *Fortune's Fool*, the father of one of the main characters, Sasha, acts in public as if he dislikes and is disappointed with his youngest son—the seventh, who is supposed to be the Fool—but in private treats him with care. In return, Sasha plays the part of the Fool in the public eye and is able to choose the particular path of the Fool he wishes.

They are basically doing what many readers often feel or wish they could do themselves when reading traditional fairy tales and stories. The reader sees the cliché-archetype character and wishes that they were something else, that the author's imperative didn't turn the person into a Chosen One because they were an Orphan Who Happens to Find a Mystical Object, because that's what happens in Quest Stories.

While other stories may have characters realize that they're in roles similar to fairy stories, they are unable to do anything about it, something that happens in books like the *Discworld* series, especially in *Witches Abroad,* when Granny Weatherwax's sister firmly believes that she's the Good Witch and Fairy Godmother because she invokes the traditional stories. But while in the Discworld, things happen because everybody knows this is how the world is supposed to be (everybody knows that toy makers are supposed to whistle while they work) (Pratchett, *Witches Abroad,* p. 86). The world runs on narrative causality; the world of the Five Hundred Kingdoms runs on *bendable* narrative causality. They are able to tell the "author" they're not happy in the story they're in and wish to be in a different story.

Technically, the characters aren't breaking the fourth wall at all. They don't acknowledge that they're in a book being written by an author. However, they do recognize that they are in a story, or at least that their lives deliberately resemble a story. While in the *Thursday Next* stories, the characters only realize they're in a book or are a certain kind of character when they are BookWorld characters, the everyday people of the Five Hundred Kingdoms can realize that such a thing exists because that's how stories are and that's how their world works. They aren't characters in a story being written by any particular author; yet, at the same time, they know that they are characters being forced into roles they can defy, subvert or agree to go along with.

In this way, they become more like readers and authors themselves, engaging in the text of a story. They know how the story is going to end, so they decide to rewrite the ending, something that many people often wish they could do with many published works. Readers wish that characters would fall in love with different characters—Harry and Hermione from the *Harry Potter* series is a popular pairing—or that a different character would win or that certain people wouldn't die. When a person writes fan fiction, they're engaging the text in a meta-textual manner because they are trying to fix what they don't believe should be there. They want to change the story to how they feel that it should be. They want to add elements that would make the story or world more appealing to them. They want to make their own versions of "happily ever after."

One. Changing the Story

And this is what the Fairy Godmothers and other protagonists of the *Tales of the Five Hundred Kingdoms* series do. They write fan fiction about the stories of their lives. However, unlike the reader, whose piece will have no impact on the actual work, the people in the Five Hundred Kingdoms are literally rewriting their destinies. With careful work, they can knowingly change their destiny.

This is something unusual in many fantasy stories. Most of the time, when a character is given a Quest and a prophecy, the outcome is usually given. Sometimes, the prophecy will say, "if X happens, then Y will happen," which will allow for a certain outcome, but all the possible outcomes are written out in the prophecy. The prophecies in the *Sword of Truth* novels and the Dragonic Prophecy in the *Eberron* campaign setting work like this, for example.

But in most cases the prophecy is given and then is fulfilled. It's one of the reasons why the Evil Overlord's List includes "#47. If I learn that a callow youth has begun a quest to destroy me, I will slay him while he is still a callow youth instead of waiting for him to mature" (*Overlord*). The Fairy Godmothers and others, however, can say, "Oh, I see this person's life is going to follow this tale, so I will push it in another direction." Or, "I will do something so unexpected that the Tradition will not know what to do and thus leave me alone." They grasp their destinies and don't let prophecy stand in their way of their desired ending. In some cases, they may *want* the desired ending, but if they don't, they have the ability to change it.

Prophecy and the authorial imperative have no sway over them. They are, despite the fantasy world they live in, able to control their lives much as the readers can. They no longer become characters in a tale—the Ella Cinders or the Ladderlocks—but instead become whomever they wish to be. They disagree with the text and create their own meta-text.

Into the Stories: A Brief Aside

Fan fiction, as mentioned above, is a way for the fans of a work to engage the stories and create their own text on a meta-textual level. Not all of fan fiction is good. In fact, a great deal of it is bad, but the writers are more interested in creating their meta-text instead of accuracy. Thus, they create inaccuracies in the worlds of their stories—things like it taking only a few days to get to the Mines of Moria in the *Fellowship of the Ring*, instead of forty days, or their own Mary Sue or Gary Stu characters creating ten members of the Fellowship, instead of nine. While for some readers this may just be irritating and others may not care, there was a group of authors who created an odd meta-textual response to these bad fan-fiction stories by writing fan fiction that took place within the stories of the bad fan fiction.

As fan fiction is a response to canon stories, these meta-fictional fan-fiction stories were a response to these inaccurate and poorly written fan-fiction stories. There were two versions of this. One was called the PPC, or the Protectors of the Plot Continuum, and the other was a Fan Fiction University. The PPC was a collaborative storytelling effort. Multiple authors worked within the shared world of the PPC and could interact with each other in crossovers, but they also ran their own stories. "Agents" of the PPC would go into the fan-fiction stories and destroy the non-canon elements, thus returning the canon world to its original textual state. Agents were usually original characters or characters rescued from bad fan-fiction stories. The agents were aware that they were going into fictional stories and dealing with fictional characters. Much like the *Thursday Next* books, they, as well as the world around them, were affected by poor punctuation, grammar and spelling. Their own awareness of their own fictionality was left up in the air to the various authors of the PPC stories.

In the Fan Fiction Universities—the first being the Official Fan Fiction University of Middle Earth (or OFUM), by Camilla Sandman—a different approach was taken. There, fan fiction authors were pulled into Middle Earth and forced to go to university to learn how to write good fan fiction. They were taught how to keep characters in character and the importance of proper grammar, by the characters of Middle Earth. While the fan-fiction authors were made up, Camilla would use fans of the story as names for minor characters. Thus, the fans of the fan-fiction story as well as the original canon text were able to interact with both versions of the story.

The PPC and the various Fan Fiction Universities even crossed over a few times, creating a massive collaborative work that commented on the nature of the text, the ideas of the meta-text and the fourth wall all within a fictional context that never actually admitted to breaking the fourth wall, much like the *Five Hundred Kingdoms* and the *Discworld* novels.

Thus, the fans discovered one of the marvelous things about fantasy fiction: its ability to comment on the nature of the story and storytelling without breaking the fourth wall. Instead, it is able to create a world where such things are part and parcel of everyday life. This makes the commentary feel more natural, as it's not breaking apart the action to turn and wink at the reader, stopping the flow and pulling the reader away from the story.

CHAPTER TWO

A Matter of Perception

> Mr. Praline: Never mind that, my lad. I wish to complain about this parrot what I purchased not half an hour ago from this very boutique.
> Owner: Oh yes, the, uh, the Norwegian Blue... What's, uh... What's wrong with it?
> Mr. Praline: I'll tell you what's wrong with it, my lad. 'E's dead, that's what's wrong with it!
> Owner: No, no, 'e's uh ... he's resting.
> —Monty Python, the Dead Parrot sketch

Perception of any given work is a tricky subject. A single subject can elicit different interpretations. The important thing to realize when reading or viewing any story is that no one interpretation is incorrect.[1] It's all how the reader interprets the information given to him, both from the text itself and what others tell him.

Imagine, if you would, the following scene:

> An older man stands under the window belonging to a young girl he'd like nothing more than to murder. But he doesn't want to do so just yet. He wants to get to know her. To get her to want to be killed by him. No one is home right now. Not the girl—she's with her friends—and not the girl's father. He's at work.
> The man tests the window.
> It opens, but when he moves it, the hinges creak loudly and noticeably.
> That would never do.
> From a bag, the man pulls a can of WD-40. Carefully, he oils the hinges until they open as smoothly as the girl's sighs.
> The man smiles to himself and leaves as quickly as silently as he came.
> Later that night, the man returns to the girl's window. Standing in the shadows, he can see her silhouette as she moves around her room. When she gets ready for bed, he can watch her pull off her shirt. And, though her silhouette barely changes, the knowledge sends a thrill down his spine.
> Finally, the lights turn off.
> The man waits a few minutes more, so that he's certain that she's asleep.

Two. A Matter of Perception

Only then does he slowly open up her window. Every breath he takes is one of held action. Will she hear him? Will she wake up? She doesn't. He's able to slip into her room.

His gaze takes in everything quickly, but settles on her sleeping form.

A small smile flits onto his face as he takes the lone chair in the room. Entwining his fingers, he sits through out the night and watches her sleep. When the sun begins to rise, he slips back through the window and carefully shuts it. As the light fills the sky, he slinks off into the dark back to his own home.

That is most definitely an unsettling scene. It would readily be at home in any psychological horror novel. It might even occur in mystery novels before the girl is found murdered. And yet it is an event that happens in a book that is considered by its fans to be one of the most romantic series to have come out in the mid–2000s to late 2000s. Edward, the main love interest in *Twilight* by Stephenie Meyer, watches a girl sleep, a girl that he admits wanting to kill. Not only that, but he admits doing such a thing to the protagonist, Bella. In the famous meadow scene, where Edward reveals to Bella that he is a vampire, he says that when he first saw her,

> "It took everything I had not to jump up in the middle of that class full of children and—" He stopped abruptly, looking away. "When you walked past me, I could have ruined everything that Carlisle has built for us, right then and there. If I hadn't been denying my thirst for the last, well, too many years I wouldn't have been able to stop myself…. And then, as I tried to rearrange my schedule in a pointless attempt to avoid you, you were there—in that close, warm little room, the scent was maddening. I so very nearly took you then. There was only one other frail human—so easily dealt with" [Meyer, *Twilight*, pp. 269–270].

Later on that day, after that confession, Bella invites him home, and this is when he admits to sneaking into her bedroom and watching her sleep.

> "You spied on me?" But somehow I couldn't infuse my voice with the proper outrage. I was flattered.
> He was unrepentant. "What else is there to do at night?" [Meyer, *Twilight*, p. 292].

His reasons for doing so were out of jealousy. "That was the first night I came here. I wrestled all night, while watching you sleep, with the chasm between what I knew was *right*, moral, ethical, and what I *wanted*. I knew that if I continued to ignore you as I should, or if I left for a few years, till you were gone, that someday you would say yes to Mike, or someone like him. It made me angry" (Meyer, *Twilight*, p. 303).

The book is also peppered with Edward warning Bella that he is dangerous, that she should stay away from him, that he could kill her, and that he's barely restraining himself from doing so. It's important to note that he does not want to kill her, because he is a vampire. It's because of a desire to possess her. Her smell, and the fact that he can't read her mind, attract him to her initially; his jealousy makes him want to keep her. These sorts of things could and do happen in stories where there isn't even a single supernatural element. Edward's motives and behavior could be at home in a *Law and Order* or *CSI* episode.

In fact, a great deal of the *Twilight* saga is about the psychological effect that Edward has on Bella, about how he makes her emotionally dependent on him. Edward has realized that Bella is in need of emotional attention because of her low self-esteem and so he gives it to her, drawing her into needing him as an emotional crutch. In *New Moon,* Bella has become so dependent on him that when he leaves her to go up to Alaska—for her own good, apparently—that eight pages of the book are left utterly blank except for the words "October, November, December and January." Without Edward, Bella has absolutely nothing in her life worth mentioning. He has become her one and only thing to think about, know about, or care about.

Her obsession with him turns into suicidal tendencies. She deliberately puts herself into danger so she might be able to hallucinate his voice or see him. She wants to die to be with him. By asking him to turn her into a vampire, she is giving up her human life to death. Nothing else in her life is worth staying for. "Life holds little value for Bella without Edward. While watching a scary movie with friends, she concludes, 'It was depressing to realize that … my story was over'" (Meyer, *New Moon*, p. 106). "With Edward gone, she feels she has no future" (Melissa A. Click, Jennifer Stevens Aubrey and Elizabeth Behm-Morawitz, *Bitten by Twilight: Youth Culture, Media & the Vampire Franchise,* p. 126).

Bella wants to give everything up to be with Edward, her family, her friends and her future. After all, becoming a vampire is dying and, through that, forever leaving everything behind (even if the *Twilight* vampires don't actually die when being transformed, they still give up

Two. A Matter of Perception

their old life for the new one). Bella agrees to marry Edward in exchange for becoming a vampire. Though she says that she is irrevocably in love with him, her main goal seems to be to become a vampire so that she won't get old and become unwanted by Edward.

She would rather die than lose him.

This utter dependence that Edward has created in Bella and the way he treats her—from stalking her to preventing her from seeing friends by ruining the engine of her car—has caused some critics of the books to claim that Edward is abusing her. They have even used the domestic violence checklists to prove their claim. An article in *Psychology Today* by Wind Goodfriend, titled, appropriately, "Relationship Violence in Twilight," summarizes several points for these claims for both Bella and Edward. The first is Bella's lack of self-esteem. "When Edward shows interest in her, Bella's low self-esteem puts him in a position of power over her; he can treat her however he'd like, because she perceives that he's out of her league and is lucky to be the dirt on the bottom of his shoe (or the blood on the bottom of his fangs, I guess)" (Goodfriend, "Relationship Violence"). The second is an attraction to men who are forbidden; that would be Edward, who constantly tells Bella that he's no good for her and that she should stay away from him, and then later Jacob, when he says that he can't see her anymore. Third is an attraction to violence. "Bella is simply excited by violence, aggression, and danger; she finds it all *thrilling*. Bella's attraction to anything dangerous is clear in many cases through her human life. She rides a motorcycle because it's dangerous. When Edward tells Bella that he'll literally kill anyone who tries to hurt her, she's attracted to his violent nature. And, as anyone on 'Team Jacob' will note, she's only interested in Jacob after she learns that he's a violent werewolf who might rip off her face" (Goodfriend, "Relationship Violence").

For Edward, the symptoms include "his control over Bella and his attempts to isolate her from others. Abusers often use this tactic as a way of ensuring that their victims have no way to escape[,] should they attempt to do so" (Goodfriend, "Relationship Violence"). Then there is "the use of coercion to accelerate the development of closeness," which Goodfriend calls "another common warning sign of abuse. If an abuser can get full commitment from his (or her) victim as early as possible, this basically 'locks in' the victim and cuts them off from escape." And then there is Edward's severe jealousy; he cannot stand anyone else giving attention to Bella. This is shown in examples like the one above, when he tells her why he decided to watch her sleep.

All of these aspects, given to someone unfamiliar with the series, will more than likely give him the impression that this is not a romance series but instead a horror series.

And yet a great deal of people consider it an exceptionally romantic series, a romance that is somehow on par with the love of Romeo and Juliet, Westley and Buttercup, or Tristan and Isolde. It is *the* great love story of the modern generation. Why is that? Because, among other reasons, Meyer's books follow a great many of the romance fiction tropes and stereotypes, especially the ones found in the supermarket book aisle with names like *Captured by the Highlander* (with a cover of a bare chest man in a kilt), *Subtle Destiny, Subtle Lovers* and *Her Heart for the Asking*.[2]

So what makes a romance novel a romance novel?

The basic thing about a romance is the focus on the relationship of the two main characters. Will they or won't they get together? With the happy ending, they will. "Today, *romance* is usually understood to refer to a fictional account of passionate love prevailing against social, economic, or psychological odds, but any plot that revolves around love can now be characterized as a romance" (Ross Murfin and Supryia M. Ray, *The Bedford Glossary of Critical and Literary Terms*, p. 346). It also fulfills the basic romantic myths that a great deal of people have been brought up believing: love at first sight, finding that perfect someone and being together with them forever. This is expressed in almost everything, especially in most Disney movies where relationships happen within a few hours and last forever. One date, one meeting is enough for the characters to realize that they were meant for each other and don't need anything else. They will be forever happy and have someone to take care of them ... or someone for them to take care of. They will no longer be alone.

Never being alone is a very powerful motivator. Being with someone who completely understands them enough to be the perfect companion is very tempting and very desirable. This perfect companionship is demonstrated the best with the werewolves (or shapeshifters) and their imprinting. "The wolves claim that this was not inherently a romantic love, yet in all cases, imprinting occurs among heterosexual

Two. A Matter of Perception

couples whose long-term goal is a romantic relationship. When the wolves imprint on babies and toddlers, the initial connection is not romantic, but they imply that it will eventually lead there"; "Bella questions whether Claire would have a choice in the matter, and Jacob replies, 'Of course. But why shouldn't she choose him, in the end? He'll be her perfect match. Like he was designed for her alone'"; "Both vampires and wolves, then, view instant attraction as the foundation for lifelong romantic relationships" (Aubrey Click and Behm-Morawitz, *Bitten by Twilight*, p. 123).

The readers are being given a relationship that they are told is second only to the perfection of vampire romance, one that will not fail or falter. Quil, the audience is told, is so dedicated that he is willing to wait until Claire is sixteen or so. Jacob Black need only wait for seven years, as half-vampire Renesmee Cullen ages at a different rate than humans and so will be physically seventeen at the age of seven. Both are presented as so in love with these babies that they won't even think about looking elsewhere.

A great deal of the *Twilight* books focus on non-sexual relationships. Bella and Edward don't have sex until the fourth book, only after they're married. But the books are charged with romantic and sexual imagery, nonetheless. Sitting next to Edward in science class, Bella feels an overwhelming need to touch Edward, "a crazy impulse to reach out and touch him, to stroke his perfect face just once in the darkness, nearly overwhelmed me.... I tried unsuccessfully to relax, but the electric current that seemed to be originating from somewhere in his body never slackened.... The overpowering craving to touch him also refused to fade" (Meyer, *Twilight*, p. 219). A short while later, when Edward walks Bella to class, "he raised his hand, hesitant, conflict raging in his eyes, and then swiftly brushed the length of my cheek bone with his fingertips ... I walked into the gym, lightheaded and wobbly" (Meyer, *Twilight*, p. 220). All of this breathlessness comes from Bella just wanting to touch or be touched by Edward.

Imagine meeting someone who is so attractive and desirable that even a touch of the person could send you into a post-orgasmic state! And that person feels the same way about you! The readers can get all the passion and desire for sex without ever actually needing to perform the act. They don't even have to feel guilty for the desires, because wanting to hold hands with someone is a lot less controversial for women than wanting to have sex with a man and being the one who initiates it.

Then, of course, there are all the traits that Edward possesses that increase his so-called perfection, beyond his godly, Adonis-like looks. Edward is *that* cool kid in high school. The one that all the girls want. He's rich, he's handsome, he's strong, he's attentive, he's smart, he's mature and he's paying attention to that one girl in class that a lot of girls and women feel they are: the awkward, uncertain-of-herself girl in the back of the class who apparently has trouble making friends and who will forever be stuck in nothingness. When Bella first sees Edward in the school cafeteria, she asks her dining companion, Jessica, who he is. "That's Edward. He's gorgeous, of course, but don't waste your time. He doesn't date. Apparently none of the girls here are good-looking enough for him" (Meyer, *Twilight,* p. 22).

Here, Edward, *the* guy that no one can get, is immediately attracted to the new girl. The quiet girl. He's so attracted to her that he can't stay away from her. He can't get enough of her. Edward rescues Bella from would-be attackers, both mortal and vampiric. She is so important to him that he's willing to break laws to be with her and to kill himself if she dies ... or if he even *believes* that she's dead.

Edward is willing, we're told but never shown, to fight against his own monstrous nature to be with her, to become a better person to be with her.

Helping the audience to interpret this as a romance is the fact that Bella herself sees it as one, as she is our narrator and our point-of-view character. She tells us that she is flattered by Edward's attention. That she is attracted to him. That he's a wonderful person. And, since she is the point-of-view character and this is her story, it seems that the readers should accept her view of how the book should be interpreted.

While this is a hotly debated topic for many people, what exactly does it have to do with fantasy fiction and tropes? This is an easy question to answer. It is a good example of the dichotomy of people's reactions to the series. It is one book and yet people are completely divided on how it should be interpreted based on who is reading it, what they're told about the book beforehand, and their own life experiences. Their metafictional reactions are different based on what they know and what they're told.

Two. *A Matter of Perception*

Is it bad that a book has such disparate views?

One could argue that it is because it might go against the author's vision of how the book should be viewed. The author had a specific idea in creating her book and anything counter to that is a misinterpretation. After all, she should know what it is she is writing about; it came from her mind and she directed it.

Yet it could be argued that if the author had properly written the book, then there wouldn't be any confusion or such radically different interpretations on how the book should be read. The character's actions and the narrative would support each other and not contradict each other. There wouldn't be a meta-textual conflict. The reader would be in sync with the author's intentions. The possibility of other interpretations would be there, but the other interpretations wouldn't be over such huge things as "is the story a romance novel" or "was one of the characters abusing the other."

It's the author's job to be as precise as possible when crafting characters, story and worlds. Their *intention* should be moral ambiguity. The author should be able to create the work in such a way that it can stand on its own without his input and still get his idea across. This is the problem with Meyer's writing. By creating an inconsistent narrator in Bella, Meyer creates a serious fiction vs. metafiction conflict. Bella is unreliable, even to herself. We can presume that she reports Edward's actions correctly (why would she have any reason to lie about the person she's supposedly in love with telling her that he wanted to kill her?), but we *can* wonder about her reactions, which are emotionally disconnected from the reality she presents. One would assume, if she were properly connected to reality, that Edward's actions would frighten and horrify her. Yet she is so disconnected, or so willfully oblivious to the meaning of his actions and words, that she presents both words and actions to herself—and to us—as desirable.

If Bella were to admit to herself that Edward's actions were frightening or that he was dangerous and yet she was still attracted to him, the fiction vs. metafiction conflict in the narrative wouldn't be as obvious. After all, Edward is presented to be the paragon of good looks (despite the sparkling), and Bella is a teenage girl who hasn't had anyone pay attention to her or think that she's worthy of attention. Or so she thinks. The narrative proves otherwise. Several human boys do express interest

The Tropes of Fantasy Fiction

in her, as does a young werewolf later on. But to Bella they don't count. She's not allowed to feel attraction or notice them because Meyer is setting up Edward to be her one-and-only true love. She can't have a one-and-only if she is attracted to other people.

The people who feel the book is a romance will accept the story from Bella's point of view as true. They are probably typical romance readers whose "reading is fueled by dissatisfaction; female readers seek a kind of care and tenderness that they are unlikely to experience in traditional, patriarchal marriages" (Click, Aubrey and Behm-Morawitz, *Bitten by Twilight*, p. 120). Since these readers are already familiar with the romance genre, they can pick up on the romance tropes more easily. In the *Smart Bitches, Trashy Books* review of the book, the reviewer points out that "Meyer definitely taps into the dark, mysterious tortured hero, one of my personal favorite archetypes" (sb Wendell) and that Bella "subsumes her identity" (sb Wendell). This subsuming is one of the ways that Bella is a blank slate. With no personality to speak of (because she gives it up to make everyone happy), the readers can project their own personality onto her.

Readers who aren't usually into romance but who picked up the book to see what the fuss was about are likely to be the ones who are drawn into the actions of the characters and book events, the meta-text, and not Bella's interpretation of them. Because they're reading the secondary narrative, they're unable to allow themselves to be swept up in the romance of the characters. From the same review, Wendell touches on the idea of Edward watching Bella sleep: "Former Angsty Sarah can see why that's incredibly seductive, especially when one is feeling lonely and without anyone who truly understands. Currently Adult Sarah, who is a lot older and one would hope marginally wiser than F.A.S.[,] is majorly squicked out" (sb Wendell). Here, she points out the personality divide between someone who would be caught up in *Twilight* and someone who wouldn't be.

Blondes Have More Fun

As mentioned earlier, the *Twilight Saga* isn't a possible horror series because Edward is a vampire and because there are werewolves, but

Two. A Matter of Perception

because of the way the story is told. The idea is the same, but Meyer has told the story unclearly and so leaves plenty of room for interpretation. A more obvious example of a single idea leading to two vastly different interpretations is *Buffy the Vampire Slayer*. The premise of *Buffy* is fairly simple: instead of being the one who gets killed by the vampires, the cheerleader is the one who *kills* the vampires. A role reversal story. The execution of the movie and the television show couldn't be more different.

Both of them were created by Joss Whedon, but the movie was taken in a direction he didn't quite approve of. It focused more on the comedic aspects of the idea—a cheerleader destined to hunt vampires instead of the horror aspects—than of vampires hunting and killing people. The television show reversed this, focusing more on the horror aspects with vampires trying to destroy the world. Though the show is more serious and darker in tone than the movie, it still does have its comedic elements, as if it hasn't forgotten the ridiculousness of its idea.

What this shows is that it's not the idea that makes a genre but the execution. Here, though, there is no confusion as to the genres of the television show or movie. The characters' actions match their descriptions of what they're supposed to be. There's very little room for alternative character interpretation. Buffy's actions, in both the television show and movie, are those of a slightly ditzy teenage girl stuck between the life she wants and her duties as the Slayer. The Buffy in the movie is shallower than the one on television but, since the television show happens after the movie, it could be explained as character growth.

Just a Little Change

But what about when a book is turned into a movie? The movies are (usually) a result of the director's vision and his take on the source material. The writers and directors constantly add scenes or remove scenes; they combine characters or exorcise them completely depending on their own personal vision. To go back to *Twilight,* Bill Condon, the director of *Breaking Dawn Part 2,* inserted a scene at the end where it appeared that the Cullens and the Volturi fought, leading to a massive amount of death and destruction on both sides, but revealed this was a vision Alice Cullen showed the Volturi, illustrating why the two sides shouldn't fight. This upset quite a lot of fans when they saw it, and yet others said that it brought much-needed tension and a climax to the story.

In the book *Breaking Dawn,* the two vampire sides spend whole chapters poking at each other with their powers and expecting violence to happen as they wait for the Volturi's decision in how they're going to deal with Renesmee when everything just falls apart. Somehow Alice finds another half-vampire that proves that Renesmee is harmless—even though such a thing was supposedly impossible—and thus saves everyone without anything really happening. The expected battle breaks up with no bickering and no physical combat. The problem is solved.

This isn't to say that the book should have ended with a huge combat sequence, but instead the vampires opposing the Cullens give up too easily after all their tension and threats. Not one of them violently protests Aro's decision. Not one of them, having built up adrenaline and anger for many pages, tries to fight anyway to take out their aggression on the others for perceived slights. Which seems highly unrealistic, but in a way consistent with Meyer's writing.

Does this deviation make Condon's interpretation wrong? No. The story was given to him. It was his decision to go in the creative direction he did, much like the two different directions of the *Buffy the Vampire Slayer* idea.

A more striking example of genre issues from adaptations can be found in the case of *Ella Enchanted.* The movie made quite a few big changes to the story so that it feels like, at times, it is only *Ella Enchanted* in name. The only thing that is truly the same is the obedience curse/blessing that Ella has. Whereas in the book the main conflict comes from Ella trying to break her curse and survive the torments brought upon her because of the curse—from having to obey her stepsisters and stepmother to being afraid to marry Prince Char because of what might happen if someone in the court found out about the curse and made her hurt him—the movie adds in the additional and unneeded plot line of Char's evil uncle, Sir Edgar, trying to take over the kingdom and assassinate Char. The movie's world has very little in common with the book's as well. For example, it has stylized malls with escalators, even if the escalators are run by men turning cranks, instead of open markets, and

Prince Char has fangirls, complete with a fan club much like any movie star. Even the way Ella breaks the curse is different and creates an entirely different moral to the story.

In the book, Ella could only break the curse in order to prevent hurting someone she loved: "I had been able to break the curse myself. I'd had to have reason enough, love enough to do it, to find the will and strength. My safety from the ogres hadn't been enough; zhulpH's rescue hadn't been enough, especially not with guards about; my slavery to Mum Olga hadn't been enough. Kyrria was enough. Char was enough" (Levine, *Ella*, p. 228). But in the movie, she is able to break the curse by ordering herself to not be obedient (*Ella Enchanted* movie). While one is about doing something to protect a person that you love more than your own life, the other is about trickery and loophole abuse. She didn't break the curse through her will by *not* obeying; she just made herself obey. It was not a selfless act but a selfish one. True, she was still trying to save Prince Char, but ordering herself to be disobedient was an easy way out. She didn't have to struggle to obey that command. Also, it's entirely possible that since she's still cursed, someone could command her to be obedient again.

So was this movie a proper adaptation of the book? Did the writers and director create an acceptable version of this book? No. Unlike the case of *Breaking Dawn Part 2*, they only took the germ of the idea and ran off with it in a completely different direction. If the names of the characters had been changed in the *Ella Enchanted* movie, then no one would have likely realized where the story came from. The writers and director didn't understand the core concepts and ideas of the book. While the *Buffy the Vampire Slayer* movie and television show were quite different in tone, they still had the same story and the same idea and the same spirit—as proven by the fact that the television show kept the movie's story as its back story, if modified slightly to take out the sillier elements.

Melding Matters

It is important to remember that the problem with *Twilight* fiction vs. metafictional content is not that it's a mixed genre (which would be

The Tropes of Fantasy Fiction

Supernatural/Paranormal Romance, like the Anita Blake series). Instead, it's trying to be one thing but has a bit of a split personality. There is too much room for character interpretation.

The book *Warm Bodies*, by Isaac Marion, is a romance where one of the love interests, R, is a zombie. A zombie is possibly a worse love interest than a vampire, considering its generally deteriorating state. (Though that also depends on the kind of vampire used in the story. Most vampires used in romance novels aren't the icky kinds.) Since a zombie is used, *Warm Bodies* pulls itself into the horror genre, which is mixed with a bit of post-apocalyptic fiction since it does take place in the future, and then, of course, it's a romance.

However, in *Warm Bodies,* the characters' actions and the text describing them are consistent. Throughout the narrative, R knows that his behavior is strange and wonders why he does it. He knows his actions are strange and so do the other characters. In fact, it's this behavior that drives the story forward. No one excuses it. No one ignores it. Everyone wants to know why it's happening. The romance comes slowly and not until the very end. It's built into the characters—R and Julie—learning about each other and what is going on.

Had this been the *Twilight Saga,* there would be an instant attraction from Julie to R. She would never question his actions or the fact that he's different than the other zombies. She would also try and stay with him. R would still require and eat human flesh and she would not be appalled by this, despite the fact that everyone else is. She would also *want* to become a zombie, even though they're created by a deep apathy, something the human race created. "I think we crushed ourselves down over the centuries. Buried ourselves under greed and hate and whatever other sins we could find until our souls finally hit the rock bottom of the universe. And then they scraped a hole through it, into some … dark place…. We released it. We poked through the seabed and the oil erupted, painted us black, pulled our inner sickness out for everyone to see. Now here we are in this dry corpse of a world, rotting on our feet till there's nothing left but bones and the buzz of flies" (Marion, *Bodies*, p. 221). Obviously, this is not a thing to strive for and yet in a way this is what Bella strove for. She strove to become a vampire, and yet the readers are supposed to take it as her striving for life.

Hence the fiction vs. metafiction conflict.

Which *Warm Bodies* fortunately lacks. Through R's thoughts, from the very beginning, we see a man who wants to better himself. He wants to become more than what he is. He doesn't know how, but his search for things like a name and memories shows the reader this. And when he meets Julie and starts to consume the brain of her boyfriend, Perry, he finds a way to do such a thing. So the book acts as a cohesive whole with no contradiction.

Sticky Bits

This cohesiveness is something that an author must strive for when creating his stories. While the genre of a story isn't necessarily important, it does help a reader interpret the kind of story it's supposed to be. Since authors have certain ideas of what they want the story to be and how it's supposed to be read, they must make sure that they hit all the correct buttons. This removes the need for the author to explain what the story is about, allowing it to stand on its own legs. An author shouldn't need to say that this is a romance or this is a horror story; the story itself should make it evident. Genre writing is not like abstract art or literary writing where the nature of a great deal of things is left up to the audience. To be of a certain genre, a story needs to follow certain rules—*rules*, and not clichés. A portrait requires a figure to be the main focus of a picture if it is to be called a portrait; that is a rule, not a cliché.

It's not that authors have to make sure that their story doesn't mix and mingle with any other genres but that the genre they wish it to be should be the main focus. With *Twilight,* the focus should be on the romance with the supernatural elements being used to enhance it, but too many other distracting factors remove it from the romance genre. While this might not be a bad thing, it's not what Meyer wishes, and therefore *Twilight* fails as what it's supposed to be.

Chapter Three

The Power of Stories

> Agatha: Obviously, there's some sort of hidden room. If I'm reading the map correctly[,] it should be here-ish.
> Tarvek: Oh[,] great. So all we have to do is figure out where an insane evil genius would put a secret room.
> Agatha: True. Well, let's try to think like a diabolical, paranoid, amoral megalomaniac.... where would you put it?
> Tarvek: Oh. Well, here[,] but—<button is pushed and the door opens in to the secret room>
>
> —*Girl Genius*

In 2010 and 2012, the Sherlock Holmes mythos got two modern-day remakes with the BBC's *Sherlock* and CBS' *Elementary*, respectively. Both series take the detective and his doctor sidekick and put him into the modern world. *Elementary* even goes one step further in its updating and makes Doctor Watson a woman—Joan—and moves Sherlock to New York City instead of keeping him in London. Both of the Sherlocks are consulting detectives and use their deductive abilities to solve crimes. Both televisions shows also have one unusual situation that isn't found in most other Sherlock Holmes adaptations. Both of them exist in a world where the *Sherlock Holmes* stories and novels by Arthur Conan Doyle were never written. They can never reference the series having existed. And yet at the same time, Sherlock Holmes is a very big part of our popular culture. Without it, there wouldn't be the Disney animated movie *The Great Mouse Detective,* in which a mouse lives in Sherlock Holmes's apartment and has a parallel life; *Detective Conan* where the protagonist models himself after Sherlock; and several episodes of *Star Trek: The Next Generation* where Data himself plays Sherlock. *None* of these things can exist in the *Sherlock* and *Elementary* universes because Sherlock Holmes didn't exist until these characters were born. So, naturally, since those comic books, television episodes, and movies were created before these two shows were made—thus, the Sherlocks weren't old enough to become consulting detectives and gain a reputation—they can't exist. There is no Sherlock Holmes popular-culture mythos.

Theoretically, Doyle could have created the same character but given him a different name—say, Theo Sammeth—but then people would say to the two Sherlocks that they were acting just like Theo Sammeth or, "Who did they think they were? Theo Sammeth?" And that doesn't even begin to cover all the minor characters and cases that they would run into. It's highly unlikely that a "real person's" life would mimic a fictional character's life so exactly. Even though the *Elementary* series doesn't follow the original series precisely, there are still characters with similar names. *Sherlock* would have this problem more than *Elementary*.

It's hard to imagine a world where Sherlock Holmes—as written by Conan Doyle and using those names—couldn't exist and yet by necessity Conan Doyle's stories and characters don't exist in those two television shows. The Sherlock Holmes mythos has such a strong hold in today's popular culture that almost everyone, even people who have never even read the books or seen the movies and television shows are familiar with him and what he does.

In many ways, urban fantasies and stories involving monsters such as zombies face a similar problem. Popular culture has spread knowledge about creatures like zombies, vampires, werewolves, and so on to such an extent that characters are practically *required* to know about them. Authors can deal with this problem in several ways. They can ignore it, they can use it, or they can have the information that "everyone knows," from books, TV and movies, to be wrong.

A Zombie Apocalypse?

Ignoring the references in popular culture is fairly easy; authors just don't mention the works involving the creatures the characters face or flat-out state that such works don't exist. This happens a lot in modern-day zombie fiction ... despite the proliferation of zombies in pop culture, to the point that the CDC has a zombie section on their website. (Their reasoning for it is that "if you are generally well-equipped to deal with a zombie apocalypse, you will be prepared for a hurricane, pandemic, earthquake, or terrorist attack" [CDC].) Readers are expected to go with the conceit that zombie fiction doesn't exist in the worlds where the zombie stories take place ... at least fiction about the zombie that is found in popular culture, the usually shambling undead creature that craves brains, as opposed to the one found in the Voudon faith. This becomes exceptionally hard in worlds that are similar to our own in almost every other aspect.

One way around this is that the fiction exists but that the characters can't believe that they're in a zombie apocalypse because it only happens *in* fiction. This level of denial allows the characters to have moments where they're not "genre savvy" and can do stupid things, things that a person who is familiar with zombie fiction wouldn't do. This also creates moments of humor when one of the characters will say that the creatures can't be zombies/vampires/werewolves and another will answer back with, "If they're not zombies/vampires/werewolves, how come they're acting like them?" This happens in movies like *Shaun of the Dead* and *30 Days of Night*.

In Seanan McGuire's *Newsflesh* trilogy (written under the pen name Mira Grant), this is played with. During the initial outbreaks of the Kellis-Amberlee virus that causes zombification of anyone who dies, the traditional news media refuses to believe that the victims were zombies and instead called it some sort of plague. However, the bloggers and "geeks" of the world, those who were steeped in popular culture, knew that the zombies were zombies and took appropriate steps right away to protect themselves.

> "George Romero didn't mean to save the world any more than Dr. Alexander Kellis meant to almost destroy it, but you can't always choose your lot in life. Most people wouldn't have had the first idea of how to deal with the zombies if it weren't for the lessons they'd learned from Romero's movies. Go for the brain; fire works, but only if you don't let the burning zombie touch you; once you're bitten, you're dead. Fans of Romero's films applied the lessons of a thousand zombie movies to the reality of what had happened. They traded details of the attacks and their results over a thousand blogs from a thousand places, and humanity survived" [Grant, *Feed*, p. 98].

By doing this, McGuire places the world of the *Newsflesh* trilogy into our own, which gives the readers reference points as to how they should act and the idea that the people of the fictional world are just as smart as the readers. After all, the readers who have been exposed to the fiction would do the same thing. What they know tells them how to deal with zombies. This creates a link between the reader and the story and makes it more personal. Recognizing who her audience is, McGuire references things like San Diego Comic Con, the largest convention in the world relating to popular culture, from comic books to movies to video games, an event that she travels to regularly. There is even a short story that takes place within the convention itself involving *Firefly* fans. There are also references to *Buffy the Vampire Slayer*—one of the characters is nicknamed Buffy because she is "cute, blonde and living in a world full of zombies" (Grant, *Feed*, p. 23).

The connections draw the reader into the story as he tries and see how his world changes because of a zombie outbreak. He recognizes the references; he recognizes the world. And so he is now a part of this world-to-be, thirty years in the future. He can think to himself, "I too wouldn't be fooled by the newscasters saying it wasn't a zombie outbreak. I would be right, just like the others."

It's All There in the Book

The Dresden Files is full of popular culture references. The main character and others make references to everything from *Harry Potter* to *Star Trek,* Beowulf to Mozart. Harry has a *Star Wars* poster in his apartment and plays *Dungeons and Dragons.* Within the series, there are also vampires (four kinds) and werewolves (also four kinds), demons, dragons, angels, Knights Templers, fairies of all sorts and even zombie dinosaurs. And wizards. Considering the amount of pop culture references that are sprinkled through the series, it would make sense for the characters to try and use what they know from the books and movies in fighting against the various bad guys they come across.

And they do.

In fact, some of our popular culture items were even created to be handbooks *to* know how to fight these monsters in the night. One of the four kinds of Dresdenverse vampires are the walking-corpse kind; they form the Black Court. At one point in *Grave Peril,* one of the characters mentions that said court's numbers had been drastically reduced in recent years because of "too much publicity" (Butcher, *Grave Peril,* p. 251). "Stoker published the *Big Book of Black Court Vampire Slaying*" (Butcher, *Grave Peril,* p. 251). Harry, and everyone else, knows how to deal with these kinds of vampires because they've read or seen fiction depicting how to deal with them. The novel *Dracula* doesn't help them with the other vampire courts—except that the Red Court can't enter a home uninvited—but now everyone in the world knows how to deal with the Black Court. In fact, the book was published at the behest of one of the other vampire courts.

The characters of the Dresden Files use the modern-day tools available to them. Even the bad guys do it. In *Proven Guilty,* Harry has been kidnapped. He is wanted by more than several parties in the supernatural world. So what does his capturer do? Sell him on eBay.

> "His phone buzzed again. He stepped away and spoke quietly, his back to us. After a moment he snapped his fingers and said, "Glau, get on the computer. The action is closing in five minutes and there's always a last second rush. We'll need to verify an account." He turned back to the phone. "No, unacceptable. A numbered account only. I don't trust those people at PayPal."
> "Hey!" I protested. "Are you selling me on eBay?" [Butcher, *Proven Guilty,* p. 275].

By doing this, Butcher sets the world of the *Dresden Files* into the real world. He answers questions like, "Why wouldn't the villains use the modern day tools at their disposal? Why wouldn't the good guys just shoot the bad guy? Or the bad guys just shoot the good guys?" And actually, thanks to one of the Seven Laws of Magic, it's against the law of the White Council for a wizard *to* use magic to kill someone. It's the First Law, (Butcher, *Storm Front,* p. 85), so wizards *have* to use guns and other non-magical weapons to kill their human enemies in combat situations unless they want to potentially end up dead themselves. It's this sort of practicality that permeates the *Dresden Files* universe. They often use mundane and practical solutions to their problems, much like the reader might do in their situation. After all, while a magical ceremony and building up of huge amounts of power to destroy your foes is pretty impressive, sometimes it's just more effective to shoot the guy.

Interestingly, there is a tabletop role-playing game for the *Dresden Files* universe. The book is written "in-universe," as if Harry and one of

Three. The Power of Stories

his allies, Will Borden, are writing it. They're writing it to be used as a manual for others to know how to fight the things that go bump in the night, much like *Dracula* was written so people could learn how to deal with the Black Court vampires. Throughout the book are scattered notes written by Will, Bob (a spirit of intellect who, for most of the series, functions as Harry's arcane computer) and Harry, commenting on the contents as if it's a draft copy. The writers even poke fun at Harry's life by using him as a character being created by a guy named "Jim B." Harry constantly points out that Jim is doing a horrible job playing and creating him. At one point, Harry says that Jim should "[R]OLL BETTER, when I'm hip-deep in crap, ok"? (*Dresden Files RPG*, p. 58). While being both amusing and a good way to learn how to play the game, the comments also give a good idea of how the *Dresden Files* universe works and how the characters think, which is interesting and useful for the fans of the world, who are always interested in getting more information and tidbits about the series. Also, since the book is written as if the readers were in the *Dresdenverse*, it creates a meta-textual moment for the readers as they go through the book, making them feel like the characters are actually real, even though they know that they're not.

This is also part of the point of role-playing games in general: creating a situation where people can pretend like they're in another world or situation that's not their own mundane life.

But this is what a person who is steeped in popular cultural lore would do. They would know that stories teach people even if they don't realize it. Now everyone knows that garlic harms vampires or silver hurts werewolves. So, to protect other people, they would create something that people would use to gain new knowledge. Admittedly, it wouldn't work with people who don't read pop-culture books and game manuals, but the people who are into pop culture are also the sort that tend to write books and movies which then slip out into the world's broader culture.

It's sort of the opposite of the modern-day Sherlock problem. Whereas in those adaptations they *can't* reference Sherlock Holmes, in *The Dresden Files,* it's almost required that characters reference other works and modern-day things because that is how the characters see the world around them, especially since it's told in first person. If Harry didn't reference how to deal with things that went bump in the night by pointing out various books or even using his own narration as a handbook, then he wouldn't be consistent with his established personality as a protector. This is a way for him to protect people.

Vampires Don't Sparkle!

Of course, a problem arises if a character is too well-steeped in popular culture: it makes it easier for them to prepare for and deal with the problems they're about to face. Sure, vampires are problematic, but if you never invite someone in, then you've never got them coming into the house. Or you can always carry holy water, garlic, or a gun to protect yourself. But at that point it becomes a "if a character doesn't do X, then they're intentionally being an idiot," and that's not very much fun for the reader. Characters should be smart and learn from the world around them.

What an author can do to prevent this is to change the rules. The world and fiction within the world could be the same; it's just that the fiction writers—like Stoker—got it wrong. Perhaps they never dealt with real vampires or they thought something else was a vampire-like creature.

This is what happens in Stephenie Meyer's *Twilight* series. Several of the main characters are vampires, including the main love interest, Edward. Early in the book, Bella does an online search on vampires. She eventually finds a website that discusses various vampire myths, but it's not helpful.

> Overall, though, there was little that coincided with Jacob's stories or my own observations. I'd made a little catalogue in my mind as I'd read and carefully compared it with each myth. Speed, strength, beauty, pale skin, eyes that shift color; and then Jacob's criteria: blood drinkers, enemies of the werewolf, cold-skinned, and immortal. There were very few myths that matched even one factor [Meyer, *Twilight*, p. 135].

While that wasn't explicitly true based on what she described a few paragraphs earlier, she isn't finding any information about vampires that matches what she knows about the Cullens. In fact, the vampires of *Twilight* sparkle. "His skin, white despite the faint flush from yesterday's hunting trip literally sparkled, like thousands of tiny diamonds were

Three. The Power of Stories

embedded in the surface" (Meyer, *Twilight*, p. 260). With this ability to sparkle, Meyer has created a type of vampire that no one has been able to prepare for because none of the internal world mythology appears to discuss it. Everything written about vampires is a red herring to those that actually exist. They can't go out into sunlight not because they'll turn to dust but because they'll sparkle and let everyone know they're not humans. They do still drink blood, but that's immaterial to the one big difference that everyone familiar with the vampire genre before *Twilight* would point out and have pointed out: the vampires sparkle. This causes a problem only for the readers who have trouble accepting sparkling vampires.

Of course, the types of readers who *do* have problems with vampires sparkling are probably not the intended audience. Meyer has said in interviews, such as one with *Entertainment Weekly*, that she had little exposure to vampire fiction before writing the books and continued to avoid it afterwards, "But I can't read other people's vampires. If it's too close [to my writing], I get upset; if it's too far away, I get upset. It just makes me very neurotic" (Gregory Kirschling, "Stephenie Meyer's 'Twilight Zone,'" EW.com, posted July 5, 2008, http://www.ew.com/ew/article/0,,20049578,00.html). Instead, she wanted the books to be more about the relationship between Bella and Edward. The fact that he is a vampire is almost secondary to the romance. Because of this, it's not important to the story and the world that he doesn't match up with what people traditionally think of as vampires.

However, in-world, the vampires not matching up with the mythologies has given those vampires a leg up on staying alive. In fact, the older vampires use the wrong mythologies to keep the fledging vampires in line, as was shown in Meyer's novella, *The Short Second Life of Bree Tanner*. While trapped in a cave to avoid the daylight, Bree and Diego spend some time discussing how the vampire mythologies are wrong compared to what they know about themselves. Eventually, Diego says, "What if the stories are exactly that? Made up?" (Meyer, *Bree*, p. 41).

While there is no actual explanation as to why the "sparkling vampire" wouldn't make it into the human mythologies, considering all the other different kinds of vampires there are in human mythology, by managing to keep the fledglings ignorant of their true nature, somehow

The Tropes of Fantasy Fiction

(because it would make sense that the vampires would sparkle in artificial sources as well) the senior vampires can keep them from running out of control. Of course, this doesn't explain why they can't just go somewhere else during the night and slowly leave the area, but that's not the important fact here. Riley and the other older vampires know the mythologies and the truth and so use it against the newborn vampires as a control mechanism. Perhaps the truth of what vampires really are has been suppressed in the *Twilight Saga* or perhaps Meyer didn't think it completely through. Either way it creates a way for people to be faced with vampires which can't be handled in the traditional manner.

In the Stories

A rather interesting example of knowledge from stories happens in the Web comic *Girl Genius*. It's a Gas Lamp fantasy where mad scientists run amuck, creating things from monstrous and malevolent buildings to tiny miniature mammoths, huge zeppelins fly in the skies and SCIENCE![1] is how all of the crazy stuff works. At one point the heroine of the series, Agatha, has been kidnapped by the evil prince and a rescue party has been formed to save her. The rescue becomes stymied due to a huge lighting moat preventing entrance into the castle. So, one of the characters, Lars, suggests that they'll have to go and look for the secret passage. Why? Because "they're in all the stories" ("The Rescue Party at Work," *Girl Genius*, http://www.girlgeniusonline.com/comic.php?date=20060410). While the others in the group look at Lars like he's gone insane, they decide to try it and it turns out he's right! Why? Because they're in all the stories. And in a world where the mad scientists reign, it does make about as much sense as anything else. While there's no reason for Lars to be correct, logically speaking, the world is built in such a way that the people who built such a castle *would* put in the secret passageways. Possibly because that's what they read in a story and thought it would be a brilliant idea to build. Life imitating fiction imitating life.

This works within the world of *Girl Genius* because the people that populate it possess enough absurdity that it would make sense that someone would eventually do such a thing. If they could make calming pies, why not build a castle with the same specifics found within stories?

Modifying Reality

But this—the appearance of monsters or magic from stories in the character's world—is something writers need to keep in mind when they are writing of such things in a world where most people only know of their existence in stories. Stories are what drives society, telling it what it knows is right and wrong, real or fake. The monsters and magic have a hidden place in many of these worlds just discussed, but they still exist. So there must be modifications. Without the modifications, the fantasy elements would seem tacked-on, as if the characters are unfamiliar with the world around them, living in some cave in the middle of nowhere without access to any story form of information.

Even if the character isn't initially familiar with a monster or an idea, which is entirely possible—after all, there are people who are unfamiliar with *The Lord of the Rings* or *Star Trek*, beyond knowing their titles—they should be able to become familiar with the topic easily enough with all the technology available to modern-day people, even if they just do a Google search or go to the library. This is what an intelligent individual would do. In stories not set in the modern era, it would be difficult to gain information because of the lack of ability to spread it around easily. Today, finding something out about Washington, D.C., from Los Angeles is a few clicks of the mouse or a phone call away. Even thirty years ago, it could take a couple of days to get the information. The internet and telephone have completely changed the way information is gathered and disseminated. Stories written in today's time and place have to reflect this.

Is it possible to have characters in our world not be familiar with our modern-day pop culture and make it believable? Yes. At first.

This is what happens in the Harry Potter books and the Wizarding World. Rowling's wizards have very little contact with the Muggle world. This is shown several times throughout the series: Mr. Weasley collects plugs; during the Quidditch World Cup Tournament, when wizards were

The Tropes of Fantasy Fiction

told to dress like Muggles, old men ended up wearing women's pajamas; and they have completely different children's stories. In *Harry Potter and the Deathly Hallows*, Ron, Hermione and Harry end up discussing *The Tales of Beedle the Bard*, a book that Hermione received from Dumbledore's will. Much to Ron's surprise, it's full of stories that neither Harry nor Hermione are familiar with, because they were raised by Muggles.

> "Come off it!" sad Ron, looking in disbelief from Harry to Hermione. "You must've heard of Babbitty Rabbitt—"
> "Ron, you know full well Harry and I were brought up by Muggles!" said Hermione. "We didn't hear stories like that when we were little, we heard 'Snow White and the Seven Dwarfs' and Cinderella'—"
> "What's that, an illness?" asked Ron [Rowling, *Deathly Hallows*, p. 135].

As Ron wasn't raised in the Muggle world, it would make sense that he's not familiar with the stories of non-wizards. And yet, at the same time, it's mentioned throughout the books that there are witches and wizards—like Hermione—who come from non-wizarding families. They're the first in their line to have magic, and they tend to marry into wizarding families. Also, some wizards don't marry wizards themselves so half-blood witches and wizards are born. Both of those factors should have brought Muggle stories into the wizarding world. It's not as likely as wizard stories would have flowed the other way, as they are very careful to keep their existence a secret. There is no reason, however, for Muggle stories to be kept secret from wizards.

While it makes sense that Hermione—the Muggleborn wizard—wouldn't be familiar with Beedle's Tales, there is little reason for Ron to be unfamiliar with Cinderella. This would be a bigger problem if the characters needed to know Muggle stories as opposed to wizarding ones.

Characters and people do not exist in a vacuum. When the writer remembers this and includes the world, the stories and the culture around them, then the books become more believable and more engrossing. When writers don't do this, if the writing isn't done well, then the readers end up wondering why a character doesn't know such a thing, a thing that everyone else in the "real world" would know. It makes their characters seem ignorant, dull, dumb and not at all worth reading about. A teenager in today's world should know what a computer is, how to use email and probably have half a dozen or more social media accounts. If they don't, then there has better be a good explanation for it. The explanation must be given; otherwise, the story is sloppy, lazy and unbelievable, which is something that no writer should want to write and no reader wants to read.

Chapter Four

Magic of Fantasy, Fantasy of Magic

> Magic is probably the key element that separates fantasy from other genres. Although to be fair, if you write the kind of artsy, literary book that eggheads (who would never admit to reading something as lowbrow as fantasy) like to read, you may get away with the label "magical realism."
> —Brent Weeks, "Writing Fantasy: Tools and Techniques" at brentweeks.com

Terry Goodkind insists that his *Sword of Truth* series, with wizards, dragons, sorceresses and magic, is not a fantasy series and to call it that is an insult. Essentially, he is saying that even though it walks like a duck, sounds like a duck, and has the DNA of a duck, it is, in fact, actually a stegosaurus. While birds are believed to be descended from dinosaurs, a duck is still a duck, and is most definitely not a stegosaurus. Even though *The Sword of Truth* series is a fantasy, that doesn't stop it from being something else as well. After all, there are many different kinds of ducks in the world, and it being a fantasy isn't a bad thing.

However, it does bring up a bit of a point: what makes a book a fantasy novel? The magic. After all, one of the defining characteristics of fantasy is magic. It's what separates it from science fiction and regular fiction. But is magic actually necessary for a book to be a fantasy novel? It seems to be. Looking at the fantasy section of the bookstore, every book appears to have magic in it.

And yet there are a few anomalies found within.

Four. Magic of Fantasy, Fantasy of Magic

Plain Old Dragons

One of the more interesting anomalies is the *Temeraire* series by Naomi Novik. These books follow the adventures of Captain William Laurence during the middle of the Napoleonic War. His adventures as captain of a *dragon*. A dragon large enough to carry a crew of at least twenty people who climb and crawl over his back. Laurence is part of the British aerial corps, which is staffed by dragons. Intelligent dragons who are capable of speaking English and other languages, reading and doing higher mathematics like geometry. Despite all of this, there is no magic in this version of history.

There are dragons.

But no magic.

Magic is never once mentioned or considered as a real possibility. Dragons are as natural a beast as a horse. Some of them are capable of breathing fire and others are able to spit acid. The title character dragon is able to create large bursts of air with a roar which is called "the Divine Wind." But all of it is brought down and considered to be biological. Exactly what the biology *is* isn't explained; it's just glossed over. But draconic abilities are still just considered to be natural functions like a skunk's stink or a viper's venom.

As it takes place in the Napoleonic Wars, the series is an alternate history. Indeed, quite a lot of history has changed from what we know of it. Napoleon was able to land on British soil and nearly take over England. Several of the African tribes that were raided for slaves lead a successful war to push out the various Western colonies and then to make their way over to South America and make alliances with the Inca kingdoms there. The United States' history looks to be quite different as well, with more of a mixing between Native American and colonist cultures.

But there are plenty of other alternate history books out there without magic that aren't considered to be fantasy and instead fall into the science-fiction category. Harry Turtledove writes quite a few of them, for example. It is the presence of dragons that makes the *Temeraire* series fantasy. That is the one nail that changed all of history. Perhaps if the dragons were aliens, the series might be considered science fiction.

However, since dragons are so linked in culture to fantasy and magic, their sheer presence marks the books as fantasy, despite the lack of any other magic in the setting. Dragons are not realistic creatures that exist on Earth any more than aliens do, after all.

Perhaps, then, it's the fact that the dragons—creatures that do not exist in real life—are considered native to Earth that makes Temeraire's world fantasy. They are from our history and mythology, but they aren't "real" as far as we know. So, even though dragons are completely and utterly unmagical in this series, they are part of fantasy because they remain things from stories and not possibilities.

Inconceivable!

What about stories without magic and without any sort of dragons or things of that nature? *The Princess Bride*, by William Goldman, is definitely considered a fantasy or fairy tale. The story does take place within the fictional countries of Florin and Guilder, which according to the author in his introduction, really do exist. Even when he's discussing the creation of the movie *The Princess Bride*, he keeps up the pretense. "Alas, Morgenstern invented it all," he writes, "and I must be contended with the fact that my abridgement (though *killed* by all Florinese experts back in '73—the reviews in the learned journals brutalized me; in my book-writing career, only *Boys and Girls Together* got a worse savaging) at least brought Morgenstern to a wider American audience" (Goldman, *Bride*, p. vii). But there are plenty of books out there as well that have fake countries in them. Agatha Christie's novel *The Secret of Chimneys* takes place in "Herzoslovakia," the television show *The West Wing* had "Qumar," while *24* had "Islamic Republic of Kamistan."

Then again, the books do take place in the past in a time before Europe and after America, which is even more wibbly-wobbly than any good time travel story makes it. The story also takes place after jeans were created. But that could be just the satire.

However, there is one event that happens within *The Princess Bride* that does touch upon the edges of magic. After Westley, the Man in Black, is killed by Prince Humperdinck, Inigo and Fezzik take his body to Miracle Max, who declares that Westley is only sort of dead. And since he is only sort of dead, Miracle Max can bring him back to life with a resurrection pill. With that pill, Westley is brought back to life.

Four. Magic of Fantasy, Fantasy of Magic

There's not magical in the scene in itself; in fact, it is downright mundane as the pill takes effect.

> Fezzik worked at the dead man's mouth a while, got it the way Inigo said, tilted the neck perfect the first time, and Inigo knelt directly above the cavity, dropped the pill down, and as it hit the throat he heard, "Couldn't beat me alone, you dastards; well, I beat you each apart, I'll beat you both together" [Goldman, *Bride*, p. 288].

That's it. There's no place for a swelling of triumphant music as if this had been a movie.

In fact, in the movie itself, when they bring Westley back to life, it's treated as if they were slapping him awake, exactly as it happened in the book. There isn't music at all. When Aragorn returned to Helm's Deep in Peter Jackson's *The Two Towers* movie, it was directed as a dramatic event. Pushing open the doors to see King Theoden, Aragorn is back lit as he shoves them open like a man returned from hell, signaling that he is still alive and still ready to kill some orcs.

These mundane actions don't feel magical at all and don't act magical, even if they are magical: bringing a man back to life after so long after taking a pill. If it's not treated as magical, does it make it any less magical? Could it be just some long-forgotten form of CPR or an ancient form of the chest panels used to restart the heart?

If it doesn't feel magical, does it mean that it's not magic?

It's a hard question to ask, because it seems to go against everything that a person considers to be fantasy.

It's a miracle, but is it magical?

And if it's not magical, is the story a fantasy?

People would say yes because of the other elements within the story that make it a fantasy. As the grandfather says in the movie, it has "fencing, fighting, torture, revenge, giants, monsters, chases, escapes, true love, miracles…." (Goldman, *The Princess Bride* [1987]). It has all the aspects of a fairy tale, which are most definitely fantasy. Tolkien in his essay *On Fairy-Stories* says "the definition of a fairy-story—what it is or what it should be—does not, then depend on any definition or historical account of elf or fairy, but instead upon the nature of *Faerie*: the Perilous Realm itself, and the air that blows in that country" (Tolkien, *Tolkien Reader*, p. 38). That is, if it has the structure of a fairy tale even if it doesn't have any fairies in it, it is still a fairy tale. Thus, even though *The*

The Tropes of Fantasy Fiction

Princess Bride or the *Temeraire* series don't have any fairies or obvious magic, they are fantasy because they take place in this Perilous Realm.

Real Worlds

But what about the *Sword of Truth* series? Is it fantasy? Everything says it is, and it seems to be easy to just let it go at that. The author's point of view must be considered, however. After all, everything that is written is filtered through the author's point of view. Some critics, especially New Critics, would say that this isn't true, that the text is the text, and everything can be gleaned from it, and that the author has no bearing on the story. Once it is written and printed, nothing else matters. And yet the author clearly has a serious influence on his work. His ideas are the ones that are placed on paper. The things he wishes to communicate are expressed throughout every word. If they weren't, then Goodkind's Objectivism and Ayn Rand favoritism wouldn't be splashed all over the sixth book *Faith of the Fallen*. There, Richard proves to the people in the heart of an Evil Empire and the Evil Overlord's domain that they can think and do for themselves. That it was better to think of themselves first and foremost and not give everything away to other people. That they needed free will and not just go along with what the government told them to do.

So, with that in mind, it would make sense if the author said that the book wasn't true fantasy but instead a novel, because "I'm really writing books about human beings" (Goodkind Web archive). People should keep that in mind because that is how he wishes it to be interpreted. But at the same time this is, of course, ridiculous. There are plenty of "novels" that aren't books written about human beings and plenty of fantasy books that are. Terry Pratchett's books are most definitely about humans.[1] Meanwhile, Nicholas Sparks's books could be considered novels and at the same time rehashes of the same story over and over again.

In fact, as the series progresses, Goodkind's characters become less and less human, turning into spokesmen for his Objectivist ideals. The transformation happens in *Faith of the Fallen* with Richard creating a statue so beautiful and captivating that everyone just gives up on their socialist tendencies and embrace the ones he was espousing. Thus, they are no longer human and are instead flat cardboard characters who have nothing else to do in life except be the mouthpieces for Goodkind.

Confused Reality

One of the more interesting things about the *Thursday Next* novels and the idea of magic for fantasy are, despite the complete and utter—what we would call—fantastical and magical things happening, magic is never brought up. It seems like it should be used on a fairly everyday basis considering the unusual things that happen such as Spike Stoker capturing a Supreme Evil Being, or an SEB. They're common enough that there's an SEB transportation service and a containment facility for them. In *Lost in a Good Book,* Spike says that capture of them is the main job of his Spec-Ops division and that, "Quite how there can be more than one Supreme Evil Being I have no idea. Every SEB I ever captured considered itself not only the worst personification of unadulterated evil that ever stalked the earth, but also the only personification of unadulterated evil that ever stalked the earth. It must have been quite a surprise—and not a little galling—to be locked away with several thousand other SEBs, all pretty much the same, in row upon row of plain glass jars at the Loathsome Id Containment Facility" (Fforde, *Lost,* p. 255). There is something called the Dark One, but he is made out to be less something to speak about only in bright sunlight with a knocking on wood or even not named at all (like Voldemort as He Who Must Not Be Named) and more like an evil CEO. It's not treated as magic as much as an everyday quirk of life, like coffee shops seeming to be on every other corner in Seattle.

Perhaps it's the utter absurdist nature of the *Thursday Next* series that takes it away from the fantasy section in book stores and into the literature section. After all, these books definitely are in Tolkien's "Perilous Realm," with the BookWorld functioning as the Land of Faerie for the series and Thursday the hapless mortal who stumbles into it, and yet for some reason people (i.e., those in charge of classifying books) don't feel like they are fantasy fiction.

Which possibly leads into the idea of Magical Realism.

Potato Potahto

Magical realism is a strange creature. It is basically fantasy written by people who don't wish to admit they're writing fantasy but instead say that they're writing literature. Of course, they abhor the idea that fantasy could be literature.

The term was first used in the 1920s to describe a style of painting found in Germany. The term is credited to art critic Franz Roh who introduced the term "to refer to a new form of post-expressionist painting during the Weimar Republic.... He coined the term that is translated as 'magical realism' to define a form of painting that differs greatly from its predecessor (expressionist art) in its attention to accurate detail, a smooth photograph-like clarity of picture and the representation of the mystical non-material aspects of reality" (Maggie Ann Bowers, *Magic(al) Realism*, p. 9). Eventually, the term became mostly associated with Latin American writers, though there are, of course, non–Latin American Magical Realist writers.

The common thread between these writings designated as Magical Realism is that they supposedly take the fantastic as an everyday thing. "The ordinariness of magical realism's magic relies on its accepted and unquestioned position in tangible and material reality" (Bowers, *Magic(al)*, p. 24), and "it relies upon the full acceptance of the veracity of the fiction during the reading experience, no matter how different this perspective may be to the reader's non-opinions and judgments" (Bowers, *Magic(al)*, p. 4).

But how does this relate to fantasy fiction? Bower's statements can be found on any kind of writing, no matter the genre: "Amaryll Beatrice Chanady distinguishes magical realist literature from fantasy literature (the fantastic) based on differences between three shared dimensions: the use of antinomy (the simultaneous presence of two conflicting codes), the inclusion of events that cannot be integrated into a logical framework, and the use of authorial reticence. In fantasy, the presence of the supernatural code is perceived as problematic, something that draws special attention—but in magical realism, the presence of the supernatural is accepted. In fantasy, authorial reticence creates a disturbing effect on the reader; it works to *integrate the supernatural* into the natural framework in magical realism. This integration is made pos-

Four. Magic of Fantasy, Fantasy of Magic

sible in magical realism as the author presents the supernatural as being equally valid to the natural. There is no hierarchy between the two codes" ("Magic Realism," *Wikipedia*).

This seems to say that magical realism tells a story with "fantastical" elements but doesn't bring attention to the fact that they're fantastical and not found in every day life. That they're perfectly ordinary and mundane. There are, however, plenty of fantasy books that do the same thing, from Novak's world where dragons are everyday and Fforde's world where cloning dodos are perfectly reasonable. But even in traditional fantasy there are stories where the fantastic is taken as mundane. Brandon Sanderson's book, *The Rithmatist*, takes place in a world where chalk drawings can come to life and eat people. No one in the book questions the fact that this happens, that certain kinds of chalk lines can stop these said chalk drawings, or that there can only be a certain number of rithmatists alive at any one point. The fascination of the main character, Joel, with the world of rithmatists is one born from spending time with his father, who studied them with great passion. Joel loves the theory of rithmatics, but never questions their existence. In this world, the story of Mary Rowlandson's capture and captivity by Native Americans still exists, but instead of being captured by the Native Americans, she's captured by the chalkings. Here, the supernatural—the chalk drawings either coming to life or being living organisms in their own right—are as equally valid as the natural world: that of *the Rithmatist*'s alternate 1900s-era America.

Meanwhile, in *The Very Old Man with Enormous Wings*, by Gabriel Garcia Marquez, the magical element is that of an old man with wings who washes up on the shore one stormy night. Even after learning that he might be an angel, the people who find him throw him into a chicken coop. In most stories, angels are treated with some sort of awe or reverence. In this one, he is kept in a chicken coop and turned into a spectacle instead of a person. They try to feed him mothballs for some reason—as if feeding any living thing mothballs makes perfect sense— and throw stones at him to try and make him move. And those are the merciful ones. The ones that aren't shoving a branding iron onto his side. The couple whose chicken coop he lives in grows very rich through people coming to see him and "[w]ith the money they saved they built a two-story mansion with balconies and gardens and high netting so that crabs wouldn't get in during the winter, and with iron bars on the windows so that angels wouldn't get in" (Garcia Marquez, "Wings"). The angel, who brought them this prosperity, still lives in the chicken coop. And they only clean it out once in a while to get rid of the smell. Eventually, the angel flies away, and the only reaction that Elisenda (the wife of the couple) has to this event is that "he was no longer an annoyance in her life" (Garcia Marquez, "Wings").

Throughout the story, things like a girl who got turned into a spider (and becomes another freak show—the only food she gets are meatballs), or a woman who counted the number of her heartbeats but has run out of numbers, are presented as asides. Things just thrown in. They have little to no bearing on the story, beyond the spider girl taking away all the attention from the angel.

While things like that are obviously magical, the question becomes, what is the realism? It is certainly not in the way people act towards the angel. If this were a realistic representation people would most certainly not put him into a chicken coop and be able to keep him there for so many years. There would be a rush of religious people, from Judaism, Christianity and Islam, to the town, not just the local priest, unless men with wings are a commonplace thing. But the text does not seem to indicate that. The church asks questions like how many of him can fit on a pin. The government would have more than likely taken him away.

DC Comics' *JLA* treated angels in a much more realistic manner than *The Very Old Man*. In issue no. 25, General Eiling orders his men to fire upon the Justice League member Zauriel, an angel. His lieutenant reports back to him that some of the men are reluctant to fire upon the angel for religious reasons. While the men are used to fighting people in brightly colored tights, they still feel that firing upon an angel would be sacrilege. The response is that "our intelligence says that the angel wears mortal flesh, which makes him fallen—you tell that to your boys from the Bible belt" (*JLA*, issue 25, p. 4). This motivates the men into firing. This is a much more realistic representation of people encountering an angel. Even though the citizens of the DC universe are used to things like aliens and magic, they still feel a sense of worry for their souls in the face of an angel. In fact, the feeling is probably heightened, because they have physical proof that God exists.

The *Welcome to Night Vale* podcast, which could be described as

Four. Magic of Fantasy, Fantasy of Magic

"the *Prairie Home Companion* for *The Twilight Zone,*" also has the same sort of throw-it-in strangeness, like the dog park no one should go into; Wednesday being canceled; and the acknowledged existence of the sheriff's secret police. Night Vale, too, has angels, and their angels are treated with a certain amount of realism[2]: the realism of denial and uncertainty of trusting the government and trusting what people say and see.

Perhaps, then, what is meant by "realism" is the utter pathos and inhumanity shown by the people in the story; their complete lack of caring toward a fellow creature; or in how they turn into monsters when faced with anything caged. That is often mistaken for realism. Or maybe the lack of Other Creatures, like elves or dwarfs, in the world. But there are clearly creatures in the world, even if they aren't from any particular mythology. They aren't traditional fantasy creatures; perhaps that makes them more realistic.

The fact that Magical Realism has fantastic or magical elements puts it strictly into the fantasy category, like many other great works, such as *Beowulf,* Shakespeare's *The Tempest,* and *Sir Gawain and the Green Knight,* as well as more modern fantasies from Tolkien, C.S. Lewis and Neil Gaiman. This isn't a *bad* thing. Some people associate fantasy with swords, endless quests and vampires hanging out in bars being sexy, which is what the fantasy genre market is currently full of. It is quite reasonable for people not want to be associated with such things. However, if by using the definition stated in the introduction, a work has some sort of magic—something that can't exist or happen in today's world—it *is* fantasy.

They are, in many ways, what Terry Goodkind says that he wishes his novels were. By not invoking the tropes, Magical Realism stories remove themselves from the traditionally troped fantasy genre and linger in the in-between space of the literary story and the traditional fantasy story. It allows people who wouldn't normally dare to read fantasy a chance to read fantasy but pretend that they're not. The tone and style of the stories puts Magical Realism in its own side bubble. Readers are comforted by the fact that there isn't anything traditionally found in fantasy, so it can't actually *be* fantasy. Because everyone knows that real fantasy has elves, dragons, quests, and things like that. But they forget that fantasy is more than just those things; it's the existence of magic and the creation of something that isn't there. It doesn't need elves, as

The Tropes of Fantasy Fiction

magical realism proves; it just needs magic—magic which is used to create situations and opportunities that cannot exist in the real world. It's used to tell stories from different perspectives in different ways.

So the question returns. Is magic necessary for fantasy?

Yes, it is. However, just because a story is fantasy doesn't mean that limits what kind of story can be told with it. Instead, the magic opens up endless possibilities. Because of that, it shouldn't be shoved off into a corner as something to be mocked. Instead, it should be celebrated for anything and everything it can do.

Chapter Five

Not What You Think It Is

> 29. I will dress in bright and cheery colors, and so throw my enemies into confusion.
> —The Top 100 Things I'd Do If I Ever Became an Evil Overlord

Thanks in part to Peter Jackson's *Lord of the Rings* and *Hobbit* movies, when people think of what a fantasy world looks like, they tend to think of New Zealand. The long journeys walking through beautiful endless landscapes, and walking and walking and walking on their quest to stop the Dark Lord. And there are a lot of Dark Lords that need to be stopped on these quests. As the *Tough Guide to Fantasyland* notes in its entry on "Journey": "No discovery or action can take place in Fantasyland without a good deal of travelling about. This is in the Rules" (Jones, *Tough Guide*, p. 104). This has caused, and quite rightly so, a lot of complaints by both fans and critics of fantasy, leading to the oft-repeated cry, "All fantasy is the same!" As discussed in the introduction to this book, this is one of the important strengths and weaknesses of the fantasy genre: the taking of the same idea and running over it in different ways.

Sometimes, however, an author will do something completely different and change an idea that seems to be required in fantasy fiction. They say, "It can be done in this other way and still be fantasy." Admittedly, a great many of the fantasy tropes are there, but there are certain ideas that a reader thinks are part of the fundamental make-up of fantasy that are changed into a different kind of magic system.

Rolling the Dice

An easy example of this is actually found in the *Dungeons and Dragons* role-playing game systems. Created in 1974 by Gary Gygax and Dave

The Tropes of Fantasy Fiction

Arenson, it was a mix of many different fantasy world elements. Many of its races—those you can play and those you can fight—borrow heavily from Tolkien's worlds. The dragons came from earlier fantasy war games, and the magic systems were based on a story by Jack Vance. The rules and systems of what makes a *Dungeons and Dragons* game had been set—perhaps seemingly—in stone. Then in 2004, *Wizards of the Coast* published a new campaign setting, the first setting published and created for the *Dungeons and Dragons* 3.5 edition rules. Called Eberron, it was the first new setting created in over ten years.

And Eberron changed several ideas that were considered fundamental to the concept of *Dungeons and Dragons* for the past thirty years, both mechanically and in the flavor of the worlds. One of those was the importance of alignment. In 3.5 and earlier editions, there were nine possible alignments: lawful good, neutral good, chaotic good, lawful neutral, true neutral, chaotic neutral, lawful evil, neutral evil and chaotic evil. The various alignments restricted what sort of spells a cleric and other divine spell casters could cast and what gods they could worship. *The Player's Handbook* says that "a cleric's alignment must be within one step of his deity's (that is, it may be one step away on either the lawful-chaotic axis or the good-evil axis, but not both)" (*Player's Handbook,* p. 31), and in regard to choosing spells, "a cleric can't cast spells of an alignment opposed to his own or his deity's (if he has one). For example, a good cleric (or neutral cleric of a good deity) cannot cast evil spells" (*Player's Handbook,* p. 33).

Looking through the *Monster Manual* reveals a whole assortment of creatures that have their alignments marked as "always this sort of alignment," be it a red dragon, which is "always chaotic evil" (*Monster Manual,* p. 75) or an angel, which is "always good (any)" (*Monster Manual,* p. 12). The monsters are essentially forced into their alignment, no matter what their circumstances may be.

In the Eberron campaign setting, there is a paragraph in the very front of the book that describes the tone and attitude of the setting and has a particular point to say about alignments: "Alignments are relative gauges of a character or a creature's viewpoint, and not an absolute barometer of affiliation and action; nothing is exactly as it seems. Alignments are blurred, so that it is possible to encounter an evil silver dragon or a good vampire. Traditionally good aligned creatures may wind up opposed to the heroes, while well-known agents of evil might provide assistance when it's least expected" (*Eberron Campaign*, p. 8).

Why is this? In an editorial about Eberron and alignments, Keith Baker, the creator of the Eberron setting, says that, "There's a place for clear-cut struggles between good and evil, and it's why we have forces like the Emerald Claw in Eberron. However, in my home games, I've always preferred to challenge the players to think about their actions—to have things be less clear-cut than 'We're good, they're evil, beating them up is the right thing to do.' From the start, film noir was called out as a major influence of Eberron, and a noir story relies on a certain level of moral ambiguity and shades of gray. It shouldn't always be easy to decide who the villain is in a scenario ... or if killing the villain will solve a problem" (Baker, "Dragonmarks 4/4: Good and Evil," keith-baker.com, posted on April 4, 2012, accessible at http://keith-baker.com/dragonmarks-44-good-and-evil/).

This allows good clerics to cast evil spells and vice versa. It creates an entirely new form of trouble for the players in the fact that now they don't really know who to trust. Older players have been conditioned to believe that meeting a red dragon automatically means "run away in terror" if they don't think they have the resources to fight it, and a gold dragon automatically means "we're okay." Now, in Eberron, these things have changed. The players are unable to use their meta-knowledge of years of playing *Dungeons and Dragons* in other settings to judge who is friend and who is foe. Their certainty in meeting that gold dragon—who, previous gaming experience tells them, *should* be friendly—has been tossed into the trash bin. Should they run screaming? Should they try and talk to it? Even if it *is* friendly, will it betray them? They cannot know. While dragons are always dangerous, the inability to count on alignment, something that players tend to unconsciously do, creates even more danger, more tension and more excitement.

Another thing that the Eberron setting does that subverts the traditional ideas of classic *Dungeons and Dragons* is how it presents several cultures for races. Mostly notable are the elves and orcs. Traditionally considered to be savages, "[o]rcs believe that to survive, they must conquer as much territory as possible ... their deities teach them that all other beings are inferior and all worldly goods rightfully belong to the orcs, having been stolen by the others. The chief orc deity is Gruumsh, a one-eyed god who tolerates no sign of peaceability among his people" (*Monster Manual*, p. 204). Clearly, these are monsters to be reckoned with, very much like the orcs found in Tolkien's *Lord of the Rings* trilogy.

The Eberron Campaign setting describes a different kind of orc culture: "The orcs have always been more spiritual and attuned to nature than their goblinoid cousins. They have always lived as barbarians, embracing the energy and vitality of the wilds. When the hobgoblins were building the Dhakaani Empire, the orcs were learning druidic secrets from the dragon Vvaraak... Orcs are typically deeply religious creatures with little interest in adapting to the modern world" (*Eberron Campaign*, p. 305).

These orcs don't sound at all like the orcs from the regular monster manual. These orcs are interested in peace and keeping the world safe. They're not interested in expansion. They just want to live in harmony with nature.

In fact, they sound just like the elves from the *Monster Manual*. "Elves believe that independence and freedom for the individual are more important that the ridged structures of civilization, so they tend to live and travel in small bands... Elves live in harmony with nature... Treasures such as elven music and crafts disguise the fact that elves are dedicated warriors determined to check the spread of evil in the forests" (*Monster Manual*, p. 102).

So, this begs the question—if the orcs of Eberron are in tune with nature, what are the elves of Eberron like? There are three kinds of elves in Eberron: those that live within the cities and distance themselves from the other two kinds; those that belong to the nation of Valenar; and those that live on the island of Aerenal, the ancestral home of the elves.

"The Valenar elves have no interest in peace," the handbook says. "The Valenar elves slowly seek to expand their territory, but are more interested in battle than land." In fact, "few people trust the Valenar elves or are comfortable hiring them in large numbers" (*Eberron*, p. 210). One of their chief exports is their warriors. These ideas are similar to what the *Arms and Equipment Guide* says about orc mercenaries: "Orcs make superb shock troops, diving into any fray with ruthless abandon. If the pay is right, they will happily fight whomever they're told to" (*Arms*, p. 71). Warmongering is hardly the traditional elf ideal.

The Aerenal elves are more interested in worshiping their ancestors, and some of their greatest desires are to become the deathless, a form of undead that uses "positive" energy instead of negative energy, as typical undead do. The deathless are sustained by the worship of the living elves: "For the elves, death is not something to be feared; instead, it is embraced and ultimately welcomed" (*Eberron*, p. 216). There are some elves that even believe "that their souls are being unfairly trapped in mortal flesh" (*Eberron*, p. 218). Becoming deathless is one of an Aerenal elf's ultimate goals. They also live in highly structured societies and huge cities, which is a far cry from the elves that live in small bands and ignore the ways of civilization.

Finally, there are the elves who have lived in Khorvaire for many generations and aren't newcomers like the Valenar elves. While they are generally no different than other citizens of the continent, there is one line of elves that has developed a dragonmark, a magical "tattoo" that appears on some people and mechanically gives player characters extra benefits. This is seen in the world as a manifestation of the dragonic prophecy. Elves have developed the Mark of Shadow and have two houses that specialize in espionage and assassination. They act as entertainers and spies for most of the nations in Khorvaire.

Spies and assassins? It's hard to imagine any of Tolkien's elves doing such things.

With changes to things that most players considered being fundamental to the game, Eberron subverts and yet at the same time shows what the game could be. Even if the players or dungeon master don't set the campaign within Eberron, it helps open the box on possibilities beyond what Tolkien has set forth.

Dark and Evil… But Still a Good Thing

In the course of many books, as mentioned earlier, there are many evil Dark Lords who do evil Dark Lord things for evil Dark Lord reasons. This means, of course, that their reasons for doing things don't always make sense. This is especially true when the villains are more powerful than the average person of the land, with godlike powers. Then their motives tend to be heavily obscured and tend to seem like they're doing evil just because they're evil.

The Tropes of Fantasy Fiction

It often leads to conversations that look like this:
"Minion! Bring me puppies and kittens to sacrifice!"
"Why, Master of All Evil and Darkness?"
"Because I'm evil!" Dark Lord zaps Minion horribly.

Sometimes when the dark lord's manners are discussed to give them depth and reasoning, the conversations can look like this:
"Minion! Bring me puppies and kittens to sacrifice!"
"Why, Master of All Evil and Darkness?"
"Because I need their pure and innocent blood to help raise a demon to take over all the world and crush all those who defy me under my heel and watch the blood splatter. For I was horribly abused as a child and now I want to take it out on everyone as a take that." Dark Lord zaps Minion horribly.

In either case, the Dark Lord is unquestionably evil and his reasoning for doing evil is rather one-sided. Sauron from *Lord of the Rings* falls into this category, as do Orannis of the *Old Kingdom* series by Garth Nix and any of the hundreds of demons or devils out there in fiction. The Dark Lord in the *Wheel of Time* series is actually called the Dark One. They want to destroy things because ... they want to destroy things.... And they're evil. No other motive is given to them. They are merely the ultimate obstacle the hero needs to destroy in order to save the world.

The term "Dark Lord," as it is being used here, is the figure or individual that the hero of the story must destroy. He or she is often a purveyor of chaos and death and wanton destruction. When writers try to make it seem like the Dark Lord, especially one on a godlike level, isn't exactly evil, he or she is often portrayed as merely the force of chaos which their opposite number—some form of order—has put down or trapped and now is leaking into the world. Thus, the hero must stop them and plug up the hole. In any case, to save the world, the Dark Lord must be stopped and ultimately destroyed.

But what if this was not the case?

In Brandon Sanderson's *Mistborn* series (not including *The Alloy of Law*, which takes place some three hundred years later), the main characters discover that killing off the Dark Lord was actually a bad idea. The first book in the series, *Mistborn*, comes off as a typical caper/destroy the bad guy adventure. The heroine, Vin, along with

Five. Not What You Think It Is

Kelsier, her mentor with their gang, come up with an elaborate plan to take out the Lord Ruler, a man who has set himself up as a god and has ruled with an iron fist for a thousand years. But once they have killed him, Vin discovers that the Lord Ruler was actually holding the world together and preventing it from being destroyed.

On his website, Sanderson says that he wanted to "write a story about a world where the good guys lost. I wanted to take the standard fantasy story I'd read a dozen times that of a young peasant hero who went on a quest to defeat a Dark Lord and turn it on its head. What if the Dark Lord won? What if, in the final climactic moments, he killed the hero and took over the world?" (Sanderson). In this case, the good guys are *not* the protagonists of *Mistborn,* but instead the individuals from a thousand years ago, one of whom turned into the Lord Ruler.

There is a dark and malevolent force called Ruin that exists in the land that the series takes place in. Ruin appears to have read the Evil Overlord's List, a compellation of things that any genre-savvy Evil Overlord should keep in mind when trying to take over the world[1] and from which this chapter's quote comes from. What Ruin does is to take the prophecy of the Hero of Ages and uses it to create his own Hero, who will release him from his prison. He does this by rewriting the prophecies to his own purposes, pointing them toward people he could influence and who would have the power needed to free him. "The alterations are slight. Clever, even. A word here, a slight twist there" (Sanderson, *The Well of Ascension,* p. 760). Only things written on metal are incapable of being corrupted by him, and this is how the protagonists of the series learn the true prophecy and how to save the world that was being destroyed by Ruin. Everything about Alendi, the first supposed Hero of Ages, fit the prophecies.

The man who became the Lord Ruler a thousand years prior prevented the first supposed Hero of Ages from "stopping Ruin" by entering the Well of Ascension instead of Alendi and taking the power for himself, instead of releasing it like the prophecies now said.

Thus, the man who took power for himself and killed the hero, like most Dark Lords wish they could do, was actually saving the world. By killing the hero, he became a hero himself. However, the power he gained was nearly unlimited, so he made a few mistakes in trying to help the world. He accidentally brought the world too close to the sun, so he created the ash mounts and their ash to protect people. Then, since this blotted out most of the sun, he made it so that people could breathe the ash-clotted air and plants could survive without much sunlight.

The fact that ash is constantly mentioned throughout the series but no one has any trouble breathing it is something that most readers won't notice. It's not something that is part of their day-to-day lives; while they know intellectually that ash should make it hard, if not deadly, to breathe, since the book doesn't mention it, it's completely forgotten. No, it's not even completely forgotten; it's just not even thought of. Breathing normally is something that is taken for granted, after all.

And then Sanderson pulls out a brilliant moment of meta-text vs. text moment. In several of the many epitaphs through *The Hero of Ages*, he discusses the fact that the Lord Ruler physically changed people so that they were able to breathe the ash-laden air. At that moment, the reader is pulled out of the story and he realizes, "Oh, yes, people *aren't* supposed to be able to breathe in ash-filled air." At the same time, the reader is given a completely reasonable and logical reason that works within the world's rules as to how this could be. It makes the reader contemplate all the previous things that he had just taken as is and realize that there were reasons for them to be as they were. There's also the delight of knowing that this thing that he probably didn't think about but was rather important was thought about by the author and given a good reason for existing. Which is quite unusual for many, many fantasy books.

Another way that the *Mistborn* series subverts the traditional fantasy series is the fact that technology marched on. In most fantasy series that take place over a long period of time, the world does not advance noticeably in a technological sense. Mercedes Lackey's *Heralds of Valdemar* series takes place over a span of 600 years, and yet technology and society change very little. There is the loss of the Heralds that can use the gift of magic in the *Last Herald Mage* trilogy, which only shows up again in the *Mage Winds* trilogy, which takes place six hundred years later. But despite the lack of mage gift, very little changes in Valdemar's society and its relationships with the various kingdoms. Even technology hasn't changed. A person from Vanyel's time (during *The Last Herald Mage*) wouldn't find much out of place in the *Mage Winds* time period.

Meanwhile, in the *Mistborn* universe, they evolve from medieval-

Five. Not What You Think It Is

level technology, for the most part—canning and the ability to make pocket watches exist, but even then watches haven't changed much: "Pocket watches—another Khlenni appropriation—that were made in the tenth century of the empire were nearly identical to those made in the first" (Sanderson, *Hero of Ages*, p. 243). But those were all controlled by the Lord Ruler. Trains and skyscrapers arrive in *The Alloy of Law* once people were freed of the stasis. Sanderson says in the introduction to *The Alloy of Law* that he "wanted to move away from the idea of fantasy worlds as static places, where millennia would pass and technology would never change. The plan the was for a second epic trilogy set in an urban era, and a third trilogy set in a futuristic era—with Allomancy, Feruchemy, and Hemalurgy being the common threads that tied them together" (Sanderson, *Alloy*, p. IX).

Progress was intentionally stopped in the *Mistborn* books to stabilize the realm and protect the people from Ruin. Once Ruin was no longer a threat and the world was healed by the true Hero of Ages in *The Hero of Ages*, the world could continue its technological progress with nothing impeding its people anymore.

Bringing technological advancement into any world with magic is very difficult because the writer must deal with the question of, "How does magic affect the development of everything?" In many ways, magic should make development easier because it creates things that normal people can't on their own. They can't blow things up with fire or create things out of nothing or change people into frogs, but magic lets them do so. Mining would be a lot easier if the owner of a mine could hire someone who could blast things or move the rock with magic. Even in worlds were magic is more subtle and isn't widely used, nothing should stop the rest of the populace from creating and inventing technology. Instead, the worlds are allowed to stay in stasis. It is, admittedly, a lot easier than having to figure out how the world would have changed and progressed.

When in Rome

While most don't bother moving their stories technologically forward, they also don't tend to take them out of the European medieval

The Tropes of Fantasy Fiction

setting either. Fantasy is swords and sorcery with kings, knights and castles. In many cases, it seems like it really *is* just Europe, with some dragons, dwarfs and elves attached. They use the terms, rules and societal structure from that time period or around then. Everyone dresses in similar fashions. This is pretty much expected when a person picks up a fantasy novel.

Jim Butcher's *Codex Alera* series is obviously very different, because it's based on Roman society. It was written because of a bet between Jim and another writer about how, even if you took a tired old cliché, if it was written correctly, you could get a good story. He was given two terrible story ideas—"lost Roman Legion" and then "Pokemon"—and made a bet that he could write this story. The result was the idea of the lost Ninth Spanish Roman Legion, who ended up in a different world where they learned to control and cultivate these spirits of the land the original Pokemon are based on—that they called furies (SDCC interview, https://www.youtube.com/watch?v=ylKRYe0ZWH).

Two things make this series different. One is the setting itself—based on Roman society, or the people who were in that particular Roman Legion—and the main character himself, Tavi.

When reading through the *Codex Alera,* you get the sense of things that are both familiar but, at the same time, a bit alien. The familiarity comes from knowing things about Roman culture and society. The use of numbers as names in Tavi's family—Octavian, Septimus and Primus, and, Sextus—are familiar in that the reader will usually recognize that they're numbers. And yet they are unfamiliar in that they might not recognize that "Tavi" is short for "Oc*tavi*an," and thus not realize his relationship to the Emperor of Alera. Butcher is counting on this for the reveal later on in the series when Tavi himself learns that he is the First Lord's grandson. And those people who recognize it earlier gain the satisfaction of knowing that they were clever enough to see through the subterfuge created by Tavi's mother, and Butcher himself.

Another use of familiarity and names comes with the place names found throughout the series. Like most societies and implants in new places, the original legion named the places around them with things from home. Thus, they have the Gaul and Tiber Rivers, the former named for the region that is now modern day France and Belgium and the latter one of the main rivers of Rome. One of the cities is named

Five. Not What You Think It Is

after the goddess Ceres, though the existence and worship of the Roman deities appears to have been lost.

Butcher throws in things like legions instead of armies; a Tribune Logistica instead of a logistics officer; and citizens and freeholders who hold public debates much like those in Rome, instead of court. All of these things lend to the world of Codex Alera that unfamiliar and alien feeling. The world is a society that the readers have not explored before. Thus, they are left in a lurch and must push on through the story to pick up what is going on.

And then there is the protagonist, Tavi. Unlike many protagonists who, in the first book, discover their magical abilities which set them apart and require them to learn how to control their awesome abilities that are completely different from and clearly better than everyone else's, Tavi doesn't have any magic whatsoever. While this may not seem like a big deal, it is, because everyone in Tavi's society has some ability to furycraft. They may be small or weak, but everyone can call a fury except for him. With everyone having some sort of magical ability, it becomes an aversion when Tavi starts off in the series not having any at all. It's not until the last pages of *Cursor's Fury*, book three of the series, when Tavi finally gains the ability to manipulate and call upon furies. And even then, it's expressed as him being able to turn a lamp on and off as opposed to some massive explosion of ability that causes damage and awe and wonder for everyone else around him. That particular bit comes near the end of *First Lord's Fury* at the climatic battle.

However, since everyone else has the ability to furycraft, Tavi's lack of ability gives him one distinct advantage: it forced him to learn how to do the same things without crafting. He's learned to think outside of the box. This comes in very handy throughout the series, because it allows him and others to create effects that people who are used to furycrafting wouldn't expect. In *Cursor's Fury*, to prove that he can furycraft, he uses a magnifying glass lens to reflect light and create a fire. Later on in the book, he has his Knights Aeris do the same thing.

> "Thirty knights all together raised a far-viewing craft of the kind normally used to observe objects at a distance. Instead of forming only between their own hands, however, this crafting was massive, all their furies working in tandem to form a disk-shaped crafting a quarter of a mile across directly above the wall where they stood. It gathered all that sudden sunlight, shaping

it, focusing it into a fiery stream of energy only a few inches across that bred down directly upon Max.... The searing point of sunlight flashed across the bridge and where it touched, raiders and ritualists screamed as skin blackened and clothing and fury instantly burst into flame" [Butcher, *Cursor's*, p. 492].

If Tavi had furycrafting, then he would have never needed to learn how to create a flame using a magnifying glass. If he never learned how to do that, he wouldn't have come up with the idea to create a massive one to burn down the much larger army attacking them.

Another interesting thing that Butcher does within the Codex Alera series is using unusual wildlife. While there are horses, cows, and other domestic livestock that were brought with the Legion, there are also animals that aren't usually found within any sort of fantasy series. There are herdbane which "looked like a bird—if a bird could be eight feet tall and mounted on a pair of long powerful legs, thicker and stronger looking than a racing horse's, and tipped with wicked claws. Its head sat on the end of a long, powerful, flexible neck, and sported a hawk's beak, enlarged many times, sharp-looking and viciously hooked. Its feathers were colored in all dark browns and blacks, though its eyes were a brilliant shade of gold" (Butcher, *Calderon*, p. 57). This is a rather good description of a Terror Bird, a large bird that lived in South America about "60.2 million years ago... They could tower up to 3 metres in height—far larger than an ostrich—and had huge, hooked beaks for gouging their prey" (Helen Pearson, "Big bird had swift legs," Nature.com, posted October 25, 2006).

These creatures aren't typically found in fantasy stories; not even dinosaurs are typically found in fantasy stories. And yet they aren't completely alien either. By mixing the familiar and untraditional in the world of the *Codex Alera,* Butcher takes one of the common storylines of fantasy—that of the farm boy who discovers that he is a prince and then saves the world—and turns it into something different, in flavor, if not in structure.

Winter Is Coming to a Head

In the middle of *A Game of Thrones,* by George R.R. Martin, a most strange incident happens: someone gets their head cut off. This isn't

Five. Not What You Think It Is

particularly horrible, considering what happens throughout the rest of the series. No, what makes it unusual is who gets beheaded: Ned Stark, the man the readers thought was the book's protagonist. Ned is first introduced as a man who believes in carrying out justice by his own hand, not leaving it to minions, as he tells his son: "We still hold to the belief that the man who passes the sentence should swing the sword. If you would take a man's life, you owe it to him to look into his eyes and hear his final words. And if you cannot bear to do that, then perhaps the man does not deserve to die" (Martin, *Thrones*, p. 16). He is also an outsider and honorable, which is why the king seeks him out in his northern castle. King Robert wants him to come to court and be the hand of the king, his duty being to help ferret out problems in his court because Robert doesn't trust anyone else there. He knows that Stark, an old friend, will place honor and honesty above everything else and will always do the right thing.

Unfortunately, this becomes a huge problem. When he discovers that King Robert's children aren't his own but are instead those of his wife's twin brother, Ned Stark tells Queen Cersei that he knows this but that no one else does. While up until this point he was fairly aware that things were going to go badly, so aware that he didn't think he should go down south to be with King Robert, this is probably one of the more foolish things he could do. It leads to a chain of events with the king dying and then getting himself captured. Which culminates with the following:

> "Prince Joffrey ... no, King Joffrey ... stepped out from behind the shields of his Kingsguard. "My mother bids me to let Lord Eddard take the black, and Lady Sansa has begged mercy for her father." He looked straight at Sansa then, and smiled, and for a brief moment Arya thought that the gods had heard her prayer, until Joffrey turned back to the crowd and said, "But they have the soft hearts of women. So long as I am your king, treason shall never go unpunished. Ser Ilyn, bring me his head!" [Martin, *Thrones*, p. 726].

What has just happened? The character the readers have been led to believe is going to be the protagonist of the series has just been killed, in a situation that usually, in many stories, involves a last-minute rescue or reprieve. To this point, *A Game of Thrones* was a highly political and interesting, if typical low-fantasy novel. And then the hero up and gets his head cut off by a spoiled brat who should have, in theory, if this book had followed the traditional paths of things, gotten a lesson on how to be a good king and lived happily ever after. Sadly, Joffrey never gets this lesson.

Contrast this with Mercedes Lackey's *Arrows of the Queen* trilogy. There, Talia, the protagonist, is brought to court to be the Queen's Own Herald. She was brought up in the border lands with absolutely no contact with the outside world. Her people, the Holderkin, were severely patriarchal and against women doing anything except getting married and having children. Thus, she has absolutely no experience with court or political intrigue. She also has been asked to help tame "the Brat," the queen's only daughter who has been spoiled rotten and expects everyone to do what she says. If she doesn't learn how to change her behavior, the daughter may not be chosen and thus will not be able to become queen.

Talia manages to do this. She helps regain vital information that might have been lost. She gains the trust of the council and straightens out "the Brat" so that, in later books, Elspeth can be chosen. She even reveals the traitor who has been feeding information to Valdemar's enemies and serves him justice.

Even though the courts of Westeros and Valdemar are exceptionally different, and the *Arrows of the Queen* trilogy and *Game of Thrones* are completely different kinds of books, both Ned Stark and Talia's story purpose is that of the outsider brought into a court to bring a new perspective.

Another thing that Martin does is destroy the idea of the Chosen One: the child born of prophecy. Daenerys, the daughter of the last "true" king of Westeros, was driven into exile as an infant and has never truly known her home kingdom. She is married off to Khal Drogo, the head of a *khalasar*, one of the clans of the Dothraki, a nomadic nation of people that are expert horsemen and raiders. Her brother hoped to gain an alliance with Drogo and then use the 40,000 warriors in Drogo's *khalasar* to retake his kingdom. Eventually, Daenerys becomes pregnant, and Dothraki prophesies that she carries "the stallion who mounts the world." He is "the *khal* of *khals* promised in ancient prophecy, child. He will unite the Dothraki into a single *khalasar* and ride to the ends of the earth, or so it was promised. All the people of the world will be his herd" (Martin, *Thrones*, p. 496).

Here, the readers are being lead to believe that Daenerys's child

Five. Not What You Think It Is

would become, as the prophecy says, a great leader—perhaps the one who will reclaim Westeros' throne from those who took it from her family. This, too, is a fairly standard trope: the exiled prince returning home in triumph with armies at his back.

Yet this doesn't happen.

After someone tries to kill Daenerys, Drogo resolves fully to commit himself to an invasion of Westeros. As he gathers his resources and men, he is injured in battle and eventually, because the wound festers, starts to die. Daenerys tries to save him with magic, but, by doing so, accidentally sacrifices her unborn child. Her unborn child: the stallion who mounts the world. The child of prophecy. Thus, this character and storyline have been destroyed, much like Ned Stark's character and storyline as the outsider who cleans up the court.

By doing this, Martin sets the stage and tone for the rest of the *Song of Ice and Fire* series. He lets the readers know that anyone can die—even the characters that readers were sure were protected by their statuses as archetypes.

Therefore, either the reader ends up reading because of the complex characters that Martin creates and a desire to know what happens to them even if they are afraid that their favorite characters may end up on the headsman block, much like Ned Stark did; or the reader will not want to read the books because they feel like they cannot get attached to any characters. What would be the point of attaching themselves to a character if he or she might not live through the series? While the characters of the series are fascinating, some readers are afraid to get invested in them. And if readers aren't invested in a work, then they aren't likely to be interested in continuing through the series. This is one of the more dangerous aspects of completely breaking the typical fantasy story tropes, especially in such a brutal manner. While everyone can die in horrible and random manners in the real world, it isn't often so in fantasy. So, depending on readers' desires for reading fantasy and general outlook on the world, they may or may not be pleased with such outcomes for their favored characters. A review of the third book in the series, *A Storm of Swords,* from the *Inchoatus Group* comments that "every good thing that this world has seems to be taken away and people who were once joyous become creatures of pain. These books are tremendous. People should read them. But if this absence of joy is going to trouble you or you're looking for something more affirming, then you should probably seek elsewhere. If there is going to be joy in this series it's probably another three books or so off (Inchoatus Group, web)." As of *A Dance with Dragons*, the fifth book, this joy has yet to be found.

Still, by forcing readers to take the chance that their favorite characters, even characters that they assumed to be the protagonists and those they could hold onto throughout the series, Martin subverts and changes the romantic idea of fantasy as being a place of joy and happy endings.

Balancing the Scales

In an episode of the television show *Angel,* the protagonist Angel and one of his cohorts get into a discussion about who would win in a fight: a caveman or an astronaut. Neither of them were able to come to an agreement, one declaring that the astronaut's better technology would give him an advantage while the other saying that well, if he didn't have any technology he'd be out of luck. This is, in a way, similar to how magic and technology are treated. This doesn't include worlds where magic is used instead of technology to gain the same effects, such as in the earlier-mentioned Eberron, but instead in worlds where the two of them are quite separate and yet exist in the same world. Many times, these kinds of worlds are in urban fantasies. There seems to be a need to prove which one—magic or technology—is better or more effective.

Is magic better because the characters can be walking arsenals whose death curses can destroy entire lives or they can turn people into frogs? Is technology better because it's a lot easier to kill someone with a gun than with a sword, and indoor plumbing is a good thing?

Technology took the upper hand in the episode of *Buffy the Vampire Slayer* titled "Innocence." Buffy and her friends were facing down a demon known as the Judge, a demon that could not be killed by any technology known to man, during the fourteenth century. An entire army tried to destroy him, but the best that they ended up doing, with a serious loss of life, was to dismember him and spread his pieces about the Earth.

Five. Not What You Think It Is

Buffy did not have an entire army at her disposal; however, what she did have was modern-day technology. She figured that since the Judge was destroyed in the fourteenth century, he couldn't have known about advances in warfare. So she used a rocket launcher, which blew the Judge up with remarkable efficiency. Here, technology won over magic.

In the Harry Potter books, however, magic wins over technology. While the wizards do use things like cars and radios, magic has made them better. They use Portkeys to travel to places, thus bypassing annoying things like airports and airline security. And the wizarding world's tents would be quite desirable by any camper who likes camping but dislikes all the issues that come with roughing it. This is what one of the tents used in *The Goblet of Fire* looks like on the inside.

> "We'll be a bit cramped," [Mr. Weasley] called, "but I think we'll all squeeze in. Come and have a look."
>
> Harry bent down, ducked under the tent flap, and felt his jaw drop. He had walked into what looked like an old-fashioned, three-room flat, complete with bathroom and kitchen. Oddly enough, it was furnished in exactly the same sort of style as Mrs. Figg's house: There were crocheted covers on the mismatched chairs and a strong smell of cats.
>
> "Well, it's not for long," said Mr. Weasley, mopping his bald patch with a handkerchief and peering in at the four bunk beds that stood in the bedroom [Rowling, *Goblet,* p. 80].

A three-room apartment in a place that looks from the outside like it can only hold two people? This is something technology has yet to be able to do and probably will not be able to do for many years. In this case, the magic clearly wins over the technology. While the Muggles may have invented things like photos and candy, the wizards have vastly improved upon them. They have taken the base and mundane and made it into the fantastic.

In Garth Nix's *Old Kingdom* trilogy, the fight between magic and technology is given an interesting spin. Neither one is allowed to get the upper hand, but each has its own importance and strength, depending on where the characters are. There are two countries in the books. One is that of the Old Kingdom, where magic is of the norm, and the other is Ancelstierre, where technology levels and society are equivalent to England in World War I. The two of them meet up at a location known as the Wall, the Old Kingdom to the north and Ancelstierre (and other nations) to the south. Despite being right next to each other, the two countries are actually in separate worlds, according to Garth Nix on his website's FAQ, which explains the disparities of cultures and abilities.

These two worlds have one interesting property in common: their greatest strength doesn't work in the other side. Magic, which is what makes the Old Kingdom function, doesn't work in Ancelstierre unless you're right near the Wall. Technology—manufactured things like guns and cars—don't work in the Old Kingdom. They will jam up and fall apart. Manufactured clothing and paper will deteriorate. Even pens will malfunction, as Nick, one of the characters from Ancelstierre, discovers to his dismay.

The Ancelstierre government pretty much denies the existence of magic, and there is very little known about it. In a letter to Sameth, the prince of the Old Kingdom, Nick says that "[the Old Kingdom] never gets mentioned in the papers, either, except obliquely when Corolini is raving on in the Moot about sending 'undesirables and Southerlings' to what he calls the 'extreme North.' ... Everything about the Old Kingdom seems to fall under a conspiracy of silence..." (Nix, *Lirael*, p. 383). Despite this, the soldiers at the Wall have quickly realized that magic does exist and causes problems with their equipment, so they've learned to take precautions. "Due to the unreliably of technology, the Ancelstierran soldiers of the Perimeter garrison wore mail over their khaki battledress, had nasal and neck bars on their helmets and carried extremely old-fashioned sword-bayonets in well worn scabbards. Shields, or more correctly, 'bucklers, small, perimeter garrison only,' were carried on their backs, the factory khaki long since submerged under brightly painted regimental or personal signs. Camouflage was not considered an issue at this particular posting" (Nix, *Sabriel*, p. 31).

Clearly, it seems that magic has the upper hand. And this is quite true, up close to the Wall, but the further south people go into Ancelstierre, the harder it is to use magic, until it's impossible to do so. "Not for the first time, Touchstone wished that he could reach the Charter and draw upon it for strength and magical assistance. But they were five hundred miles south of the Wall, and the air was still and cold" (Nix, *Abhorsen*, p. 2). While Touchstone is a formidable warrior in the Old Kingdom, capable of going into massive rages that allow him to perform feats of strength that shouldn't be possible, here in the south he is ren-

Five. Not What You Think It Is

dered just an ordinary man. Sabriel, the Abhorsen, a powerful Charter Mage who is charged with keeping the dead quiet and defeating rogue necromancers and Free Magic mages, is left with only a gun to protect herself. While she does have a sword, a sword does very little good in the middle of a gun fight.

This is the crux and subversion of the series. In many books and stories, Sabriel and Touchstone would still be able to use their magic. It wouldn't be limited to just their world, and they could use it to protect themselves from attempted assassinations or other such problems. By taking their magic away, Nix brings them down to ordinary levels. He makes them like everyone else in Ancelstierre, possibly even lower. Touchstone, who grew up in the Old Kingdom, is unfamiliar and uncomfortable with the trappings of technology, so he could stumble as he falls back on long-ingrained habits of using magic. He is at a serious disadvantage now. While he knows how to use a gun, he isn't proficient in it in a way that someone who uses one every day would be because there's no way for Touchstone to learn how to do so. He must rule the Old Kingdom; he can't take time away from such duties just to go several hundred miles to learn how to use a weapon that would have barely any use for him.

So Nix has created a balance where neither magic nor technology can have the upper hand. Both are powerful in their own lands, but once removed from there, they aren't good for anything beyond wishful thinking. While the series mostly takes place in the Old Kingdom and thus magic taking precedence, the few scenes that do happen in Ancelstierre show the strength of technology in its own right. Neither is considered better or worse, just what is needed in its own world.

When writers create subversions, they bring attention to what has gone before and what can happen in the future. They have to acknowledge what has been done to show what they are doing differently and thus bring to light the original structure or idea. It creates a conversation between the reader and the writer where they can see if they agree with the subversion, determines if the subversion needs to exist, and find a new way to enjoy those things they thought couldn't change. In short, it makes the reader think about what he knew and what he can know, opening up paths to different worlds and different possibilities. Once the subversion is in place, other authors can build upon it, slowly creating an entirely new branch on the fantasy-trope tree. Eventually, that subversion will become its own trope and will open up ways for new paths and new ideas, an endless spiraling chain that helps fantasy grow as a genre. It helps keep fantasy fresh, destroying the idea that everything has been done before and there's nothing new to be done. If this were true, then no subversions could exist and no new ideas could happen. But instead writers take that idea, that well-worn trope and say to themselves, "Yes, this is how it's been done … but what if…?" And it's the "what if?" that is one of fantasy's greatest strengths.

CHAPTER SIX

Heroes and Protagonists, Villains and Antagonists

> *Heroes*: These are mythical beings, often selected at birth, who perform amazing deeds of courage, strength, and magical mayhem, usually against huge odds. The Rule is that the Hero is always Out There. If you get to meet a so-called Hero, she/he always turns out to be just another human, with human failings, who has happened to be in the right place at the right time (or the wrong place at the wrong time, more likely). Tourists, too, may perform amazing deeds and quite normally end up SAVING THE WORLD, but cannot qualify as Heroes because they are not Out There.
> —Diane Wynne Jones, *The Tough Guide to Fantasyland*

One of the big problems that arises in discussing characters in fantasy is the word "hero." In literary criticism, the term "hero" refers to the chief character of the work in question and is often interchangeable with "protagonist" and "main character" (Murfin and Ray, *Bedford*, p. 156). In most situations, this is fine. Even when talking about a morally questionable main character, calling them a hero is acceptable as they are the hero of their own story. Christopher Booker calls such characters the "hero as monster." indicating their position of hero in their own story and as the main character. The problem arises in fantasy stories because the word takes on a second connotation that is quite separate from that of "main character," that is, of the heroic or hero archetype. These two things are quite different, but can become easily confused within a fantasy story.

This is because in fantasy the main character-hero is often a hero archetype-hero. Heroic archetype characters are charged with being a force for good in the world. They are the rescuers of people in need, the slayers of monsters and the doers of great deeds. King Arthur, Sir

The Tropes of Fantasy Fiction

Gawain, Beowulf, Wonder Woman, Luke Skywalker, Superman, Captain America, Luïthien Tinuïviel are all heroes. They are the people whom sagas are written about and children wish to be like. They are role models. This is true for people in the story and readers alike.

Yet the hero as a lead character, as mentioned above, may not necessarily fall into this hero archetype; he or she may be an evil character or the villain. This character archetype is the one that creates the monsters or even is the monster itself. These characters are the beings that cause innocent people to tremble in fear, to bar their doors and not go out at night. They stand for everything the hero is fighting against. They are what creates the need for the hero as archetype.

However, stories also have another character dynamic beyond that of the hero and the villain relationship, that of the antagonist and the protagonist. This is relatively simple to define, compared to the dynamic between a hero and a villain. A protagonist is the person the story's point of view follows or is about; the antagonist is the person (or thing) who is the opposing force.

The protagonist and the hero are not always the same thing. This is easier to see in books that don't take place in a fantasy setting, where the reader doesn't expect to have a noble hero. No one would call Gregor Samsa, the guy who got turned into a cockroach in Kafka's *Metamorphosis*, a heroic archetype, but he is most certainly the protagonist. Nor would you call the titular Moby Dick a villain, but the whale is most certainly the antagonist.

And yet the term "hero" is often used for the main character, no matter what sort of people they are. In Christopher Booker's book *The Seven Basic Plots*, he says that one of these plots is the Hero as Monster—as part of the tragedy plot. He calls characters such as Richard III a hero despite the fact that "we have little difficulty recognizing him at once as a 'monster.' Indeed, Richard of Gloucester, as portrayed by Shakespeare, is one of the most explicitly monstrous figures in all of storytelling" (Booker, *Seven*, p. 181). However, the fact that Richard can be called a monster automatically disqualifies him as being the hero. He is most certainly the *protagonist* of the story, but he is not a hero. Richard's actions disqualify him as being a hero, expect perhaps to himself.

In fantasy, the reader *expects* the protagonist to be the hero, and

Six. Heroes and Protagonists, Villains and Antagonists

most of the time, the protagonist *is* the hero. The textual and metatextual problems arise when the protagonist is supposed to be the hero but doesn't act in a heroic manner. It's important for a character designated as the hero to act in a heroic manner, so that even if we were reading a story told from the villain's point of view where the hero is the antagonist, the reader can still be able to tell that he or she is a heroic character. An excellent example of such an idea is in the *Batman: The Animated Series* episode, "Almost Got Him." In this episode, the Joker, Two-Face, Poison Ivy, the Penguin and Killer Croc meet in a bar to play poker and end up discussing how each of them almost killed Batman. Each is the protagonist of his or her story, but Batman is still the hero as he's trying to stop them from carrying out their criminal plans. While they may see themselves as heroes, and they may *be* heroes as monsters, this term becomes too confusing when discussing fantasy, where the idea of the archetypal hero is so important to the genre. This is why it's necessary to make the distinction between hero and protagonist and villain and antagonist.

Down the Fine Lines

Before continuing, further distinction of the definition of hero and villain/ protagonist and antagonist must be made regarding the hero-villain dynamic. For starters, there is a difference between a hero and a heroic character. *Heroes* are the characters that seem to shine and do good because it's the right thing to do. Captain Carrot from the Discworld and Superman are examples. They are larger than life and have the charisma, the code of honor, and the willingness to do good no matter what. It is nearly impossible to make them do an evil act. And when their code of honor forces them to kill a villain, it must be done as "an observation of due process, but the execution must take the form of sword point or a bullet to the villain's chest, not to his back" (Roger B. Rollin, "Beowulf to Batman: The Epic Hero and Pop Culture," *College English* 31, no. 5 [Feb. 1970], p. 438).

Meanwhile, *heroic* characters are more like Commander Vimes or Batman. They'll go into the buildings on fire to rescue children as readily as a hero, but they have an edge to them. They're not as polished. They

The Tropes of Fantasy Fiction

break rules; they have a darker past that has taken away some of that shine. They aren't good for the sake of being good; they are good because someone has to hold back the darkness. Oftentimes, the hero character will be paired off with a heroic character to provide contrast and tension between the two working styles and to thus create conflict for the story.

Some heroic-hero pairs include: Harry Dresden and Michael Carpenter, Commander Vimes and Captain Carrot, Batman and Superman, and Han Solo and Luke Skywalker.

A heroic character allows the writer to create a protagonist that is still overall a good person even if sometimes their methods may be questionable or against the law. Robin Hood is such a character. He is a thief and an outlaw, which, by the very definition of the words, makes him a criminal ... but he steals from the rich and gives to the poor. That is a good thing, if we ignore the fact that the poor are being given stolen goods and could get into worse trouble for it later, because it allows the poor people to make their lives better.

The heroic characters are doing evil for the greater good. Their small acts of evil are okay because they lead to that greater good. This is something that many heroes may have issues with, as they feel that people should work within the law to create good.

Obviously, then, there must be an opposite of heroic character, and that would be the villainous character. They're the ones who are only "evil" because their mode of operation tends to go against society's way of doing things. They generally have a code of honor and may even work with the heroes in certain situations. A villainous character isn't evil for evil's sake. He does evil for selfish and personal reasons, and the rest of society doesn't agree with his methods.

The point of these kinds of characters is to create a moral dilemma for the heroes. The villainous character is definitely doing something wrong but he's often just skirting the edges of the law, or the heroes don't have any proof of it, or they're just too useful. He is in charge of the criminal organizations in the city and, if they leave, someone worse will take their place.

Two excellent examples of this type of character are David Xanatos from the *Gargoyles* animated series and Johnny Marcone from the *Dresden Files* series by Jim Butcher. Interestingly, as both series progress,

Six. Heroes and Protagonists, Villains and Antagonists

both men have started to move towards the heroic end of the spectrum without actually leaving their villainous routes.

Finally, there is the designated villain and hero. These are characters that the story tells us should be the hero or the villain ... but their own personal actions do not follow through on this. These are the characters that create the greatest textual and meta-textual dissonance. They are the characters that make the reader say, "What? No, that can't be right. I don't believe it," when it comes to their actions, for good or ill.

Within this category, there are two types: the characters that the author designates as heroes and villains, i.e., the characters that the author wants the reader to think are good and evil, and then the characters that the people inside the story designate as hero and villain. Sometimes the author wants the readers to believe that the character is a hero in an honest and non-ironic or subversive way and yet somehow manages to write the character acting in ways contrary to the definition of what it is to be a hero. Usually these types of characters are found in second-world stories where the main characters are supposed to be heroes, as opposed to being heroic. The in-story version of a designated hero is the character that individuals within the world are *told* is the hero. These are usually set up to be false heroes whose treachery is revealed at the end by the true heroes; other times, everyone knows that they're not heroes but the government (or something else) requires people to say that they are.

The author's designated villain falls into the same situation as the author's designated hero. We, the readers, are supposed to believe this character is a villain ... but none of his actions support it. Either we never see the character acting like a villain or what actions we *do* see him perform that are supposed to be villainous are, perhaps, just something that agents of a government would do, like putting down a rebellion but not doing anything else cruel to punish those living where the rebellion is.

The in-story designated villain is a bit harder to pick out. After all, being a villain, his actions have far more latitude than a hero's. Heroes are restrained by morals; villains are not. Most of the time, designated villains are the characters that the main protagonist dislikes. The protagonist designates them, in-story, as villains, even if they may not actually *be* villains. These types of characters are often bullies or obfuscating government officials. Sometimes the hero will declare a dislike for an individual; he just doesn't trust them on instinct, but none of the other characters believe him. If the character the hero distrusts turns out to actually be the villain, without anything to back up the hero's dislike beyond "the plot says so," then you have a case of the hero always being right, which is a sign of poor writing.

With all of these designations of character types, we end up with a spectrum that looks something like this:

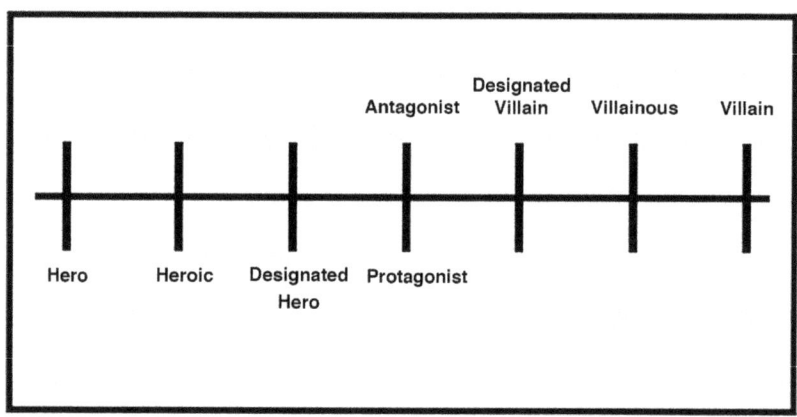

Hero and Heroic

Terry Pratchett's *Discworld* series gives us two very excellent examples of a heroic and a hero character. These are Commander Vimes of the Watch and Captain Carrot, also of the Watch, respectively. Vimes is first introduced in *Guards! Guards!*, lying drunk in the gutter. He is a man described as being two drinks shy of sober and full of cynicism at the world. Vimes is not afraid of violence and is the sort of man who will use anything in a fight and is not afraid of a dirty trick or three. As the series progresses, he gains more and more titles, eventually ending up as His Grace Sir Samuel Vimes, Duke of Ankh, Commander of the City Watch, Lord of the Ramkin Estate, King of the River, and Blackboard Monitor (the last being a title given to him by the dwarfs). In *Night Watch*, we learn that he sprinkles his house and grounds full of potential traps for thieves and assassins. He badmouths all the authority figures he comes in contact with.

Six. Heroes and Protagonists, Villains and Antagonists

However, Vimes is also known as incorruptible. Crime in the city goes *down* when he is out of town, because people are afraid of what he'll do if it's up when he comes back. The Assassin's Guild removes the bounty on his head out of fear. In *Thud!*, Vimes is possessed by an ancient evil that has been around since possibly the dawn of time and beats it from sheer force of personality. The Watchmen he has trained are in demand all over the Discworld.

The only reason that Vimes is a good man is because he forces himself to be good. It's a daily struggle for him and he is always watching the dark. He knows what the bad guys would do, because he would do it himself.

On the other hand, Captain Carrot is the paragon of the hero archetype. He practically radiates it, from his origins as an orphan child found in the woods and raised as a dwarf (and he is still considered one despite being over six-feet high) to his epic charisma that allows him to stop a potential riot by metaphorically shaking his finger at the potential participants and essentially telling them they were behaving badly and what *would* their mothers think? He stopped a war by arresting the people in charge of it and then got the two sides that had been at each other's throats to calm down sufficiently to play a game of football. Carrot also has a sword that is completely and utterly unmagical and very much a sword, to the point that it is probably more real than any other sword around. Considering the magical and narrative nature of the Discworld, this is a very important and unusual thing. As befitting a hero, he is also likely the heir to Ankh-Morpork throne; he even has a crown-shaped birthmark on his shoulder.

He also never lies and yet is able to get around that by being very cleverly obtuse. In *Men at Arms*, he was ordered to leave and not bother the clown guild if they wouldn't let him investigate. He told the head of the clowns that if the man didn't do what he asked, he'd have to carry out his orders, adding that he'd be very sorry if he had to carry them out. Since he was completely and utterly sincere and telling the truth, and everyone knew that he told the truth, the guild head let him do what Carrot wished so he wouldn't have to do what he was ordered to do ... without actually knowing what Carrot's orders were. As Sergeant Colon observed, "He'd seen people bluff on a bad hand, but he'd never seen anyone bluff with no cards" (Pratchett, *Men*, p. 258).

But the upshot of his character is that he is good. He is honest. He believes in the best in everyone. And he can take out a troll if need be (while apologizing to it later). Captain Carrot is a hero.

Villains and Villainous Characters

An excellent example of a villainous character is David Xanatos from the animated series *Gargoyles*. Xantaos is a man who always makes sure he always wins. Every plan has a positive outcome for him, whether he fails or wins. But what makes him a villainous character? For starters, he will do whatever it takes to reach his goals, whether buying an entire castle and moving it from Scotland to New York brick by brick, creating a robot duplicate of himself and breaking people out from prison to get his fiancée out on good behavior, stealing from himself so he can get a tax break, and looking good in the public eye for donating something valuable to the museum and then getting the item back without anyone knowing it's gone. He is willing to sacrifice his friends in pursuit of his goals of immortality and trying to gain the respect of his father.

The heroes of the series, Goliath and the other gargoyles, constantly work to thwart his plans and prevent him from possibly taking over the world. However, despite all of this, he is also perfectly willing to help the heroes when need be. When a spell turns people to stone during the night, he helps break it, even though he also helped cause it ("City of Stone"). Mostly, Xanatos is selfish and does things as long as they benefit him. Things change after he becomes a father; he starts becoming slightly more helpful, allowing the gargoyles to return to the castle. But this is still for his benefit, as they will help protect his son.

For a villain, one should turn to Lord Voldemort from *Harry Potter*. The example that best showcases his villainy takes place near the end of *Harry Potter and the Goblet of Fire*, when he tells Peter Pettigrew, aka Wormtail, to "kill the spare" after Harry and Cedric appear in the cemetery. Voldemort has complete and utter disregard for Cedric's life, not even bothering to taunt Harry about how he is going to kill him or allowing Harry to try and bargain for his life. Cedric is less than nothing to Voldemort, who just orders him killed out of hand with barely a thought.

It doesn't help Voldemort's character that the entire wizarding world

Six. Heroes and Protagonists, Villains and Antagonists

fears him to the point that they refused to say his name, calling him "He-Who-Must-Not-Be-Named" or "You-Know-Who." To say his name is to invite him to notice you. And for him to notice you is to court death. Even after he was supposedly dead for eleven years at the beginning of *The Sorcerer's Stone*, and throughout the rest of the series, people were still afraid to use his name. The wounds he left in the wizarding world were deep and slow to heal.

In book six, *Harry Potter and the Half-Blood Prince,* the readers learn about Horcruxes, objects—such as cups, diaries or animals—used to store bits of a person's soul away to create a form of immortality. The only way to create a Horcrux is by murdering someone: "By an act of evil—the supreme act of evil. By committing murder. Killing rips the soul apart. The wizard intent upon creating a Horcrux would use the damage to his advantage: He would encase the torn portion ..." (Rowling, *Half-Blood,* p. 498). The fact that Voldemort is willing to do this seven times, thus completely decimating his soul, shows that not only does he have complete disregard for other people's lives, but he also has complete disregard for his own as long as he gets what he wants.

In many ways, villains and heroes can be one-note characters. They're good or they're evil, and they have to stay on that end of the spectrum. This is more of a problem for villains than heroes, because a lot of times a villain's motivations seem to be "because I'm evil" as opposed to anything deeper-rooted. Being good for the sake of being good is a more socially acceptable ideal. It's generally thought that most people try to be good, as they don't necessarily think of themselves as evil.

A villainous character is given more dimensions because he's allowed to do things that are not strictly evil or bad. While he does things that often tend to be morally dark to meet his goals, he's just as willing to do good ones, sometimes because he wants to and sometimes because he needs to further a goal.

The same goes for heroic characters. Their lives run more on choices. They have more choices open to them because they're willing to do more things. Heroes know exactly what they will and will not do. And while they sometimes *may* do things that are wrong, these acts are often called out against them and will later come back to haunt them. This might happen to a heroic character, but they're more willing to live with this. Their lines in the sand are much fuzzier and are thus easier to cross. It's easier for the heroic characters to slide into darkness and for the villainous characters to climb out.

However, when a hero falls, it usually is pretty spectacular, even if it leaves him with the unfortunate tendency to wear black leather and grow a beard.

Designated Heroes and Villains

And now we turn to an example to further explain what a writer-designated hero is. Say, for example, a character ambushes a group of soldiers on their routine duty when the character could have easily avoided them, brutally slaughters them in horrible ways that include punching one of them through the chest with his fist, and finally chasing after the lone survivor and snapping the survivor's neck after he begs for mercy and surrenders. That character should be considered a villain, shouldn't he? And yet this is what Eragon and Arya do in the chapter titled "Mercy, Dragon Rider" in *Brisingr*. They are returning to the Varden—opponents of the main antagonist, King Galbatorix, and his empire—and spot a patrol of Galbatorix's soldiers over a half hour away with their superior elf senses. They have plenty of time before the soldiers reach them. Eragon has been shown previously using an invisibility spell in the chapter "Escape and Evasion," when he had less time to prepare than now, though the spell worked. They also mention in this chapter that they are trying to avoid notice. Since both Arya and Eragon are powerful spell-casters, it should be easy for them to at least create an illusion that they aren't there when the patrol rides by.

Given all of this, there is no reason why any encounter or conflict should happen.

And yet it does.

The reason for it is because, essentially, the writer says so. But even if they did have to encounter the patrol, they didn't need to kill any or all of them. Even if the patrol was cruel to Eragon and Arya, since the soldiers didn't know who they were, they could have just subdued them and tied them up. This is a common solution for heroes. They also could have removed the soldiers' clothing,[1] even if Arya and Eragon didn't

Six. Heroes and Protagonists, Villains and Antagonists

necessarily need to use the uniforms for disguise; stealing their clothes would prevent the soldiers from coming after them. But instead they forcibly killed the soldiers in a brutal manner.

> Four soldiers who had dismounted confronted him with drawn swords. They charged. Dodging to the right, he caught the first soldier's wrist as the man swung his sword and punched him in the armpit. The man collapsed and was still. Eragon dispatched his next opponents by twisting their heads until their spines snapped. The fourth soldier was so close by then, running at him with a sword held high, Eragon could not evade him
> Trapped, he did the one thing he could: he struck the man in the chest with all his might. A fount of blood and sweat erupted as his fist connected. The blow staved in the man's ribs and propelled him more than a dozen feet over the grass, where he fetched up against another corpse [Paolini, *Brisingr*, p. 183].

A little while later the, last solider, who begs for mercy but finds none, cries out, "Why are you doing this? You're a monster!" (Paolini, *Brisingr*, p. 185), right before Eragon suffocates him with one hand. Such actions are not those of heroes or even possibly heroic characters. This is not to say that heroes shouldn't kill, which is something that will be discussed later in this chapter. Eragon, throughout the series, is said to be a hero ... and yet he never acts like one. The author lauds Eragon's actions, and yet, in *Inheritance,* another character, one that is supposed to be a villain, is said to have done something similar.

> "Aye, that's the one. Anyway, so [Barst] goes to this village and orders all the men to join Galbatorix's army. Same story as always. Only, the men refuse, and they attack Barst and his soldiers."
> "Brave," said the deep-voiced man. "Stupid, but brave."
> "Well, Barst was too clever for them; he had archers posted around the village before he went in. The soldiers kill half the men and thrash the rest within an inch of their lives. No surprise there. Then Barst takes the leader, the man who started the fight, and he grabs him by the neck, and with his bare hands, he pulls his head right off!"
> "No."
> "Like a chicken. And what's worse, he ordered the man's family burned alive as well" [Paolini, *Inheritance,* p. 126].

The actions of both Eragon and Barst are heinous and, to me, comparable. However, Eragon is the character the readers are supposed to side with. There is nothing essentially wrong with Eragon's actions except that he's being asked to fill the hero's role in the story. If he wasn't placed in such a role, then his actions would be that of a heroic character or the protagonist.

On the flip side, to continue using the Inheritance Cycle as an example, the designated villain in the series is Galbatorix. At the start of *Eragon,* he has been ruling for at least a hundred years since the fall of the other dragon riders (Paolini, *Eragon,* p. 101). There are no real signs of hardship in his empire. Eragon's village lives without much interference besides the tax collectors. And Galbatorix has been keeping the supposedly evil race of Urgals at bay so they don't terrorize anyone. As one of the traders says, "Because the Varden's attacks have increased, Galbatorix has forced cities to send more soldiers to the borders, men who are needed to combat the Urgals" (Paolini, *Eragon,* p. 25). Cities such as Teirm appear to be prosperous without any overbearing presence of the king's men controlling things. In fact, the king even sends soldiers to help protect the city (Paolini, *Eragon,* p. 173). He isn't actively waging war against the dwarfs or the elves or Sudra (a region that supported the rebellious Varden rather than himself). The empire as a whole appears to be functioning without anything evil or horrible happening, except for the Urgals attacking. But their attacks have been on the rise because Galbatorix has to send men to fight the Varden. No one is dragged from their homes for questioning Galbatorix's rule. No one appears to be frightened of him or his soldiers. There is no known torture or hardship besides taxes … and this has been going on for at least a hundred years!

Yet we are constantly told that Galbatorix is evil by all the characters the reader is told are the heroes. He has done nothing visibly evil—and yet we are supposed to take the Varden's word that he is.

As a comparison, consider the evil empire and emperor in the *Sword of Truth* series. Ruled by Emperor Jagang and the High Priest of the Fellowship of Order, Brother Narev, the empire claimed that they ruled and controlled in the name of the Creator.

> They allowed their troops to murder, rape and steal from innocent people, saying that it was the duty of all to bend to the will of others in need. People were brainwashed with the promise of a better world after death and that their current life was worthless. Anyone who spoke out against these thoughts were [sic] quickly put to death, being accused of treason against the Creator ["Imperial Order," *Sword of Truth* Wikia].

Six. Heroes and Protagonists, Villains and Antagonists

Here, we are actively seeing the empire behave in a villainous and evil manner. Jajang is both the antagonist and the villain. Even if we were to see a story with the emperor as the protagonist, we would still believe him to be a villain and an evil character because of his actions. Nothing we actually see in the first couple of books leads us to believe that Galbatorix is evil. Temperamental, perhaps, but not evil. Characters who are actively working against him telling us that he's evil aren't enough, because of course they would villainize him.

The reader must see the good or evil acts being performed. Or to put it another way, "Show. Don't tell."

However, Galbatorix works fairly well as an antagonist because Eragon and the Varden wish to overthrow him, so he is working against the protagonists. This creates conflict, which should drive the story forward.

Another good example of a designated hero is Tristan from Robert Newcomb's *The Fifth Sorceress*. Tristan has all the earmarks of a hero: he is a prince, an able fighter, the Chosen One of prophecy, and attractive to all women. However, there are many other things that conspire against him being a true hero instead of a designated hero. The first is his attitude to doing his duty as prince and king.

The book starts with him about to be crowned king. His father is abdicating the throne to him, as is the custom of his people. Tristan complains a great deal about this. In fact, he downright whines. His attitude toward having to take the throne is that of a teenager who doesn't want to deal with responsibility. Shockingly, however, Tristan is in fact about to turn thirty!

Throughout his introduction, there are phrases like "*he also did not wish to be counseled by wizards for the remainder of his life*" (Newcomb, *Fifth*, p. 16), "*even his twin sister Shailiha, his most staunch defender of what some would call his recent disregard for his royal duties and responsibilities, had begun to criticize him about his romantic dalliances*" (Newcomb, *Fifth*, p. 23), and "*politics was not his strong suit, and he still had much to learn, with very little time remaining in which to learn it*" (Newcomb, *Fifth*, p. 24). Tristan is turning thirty in a few days and he's still having trouble learning politics.

Any sympathy for the man is washed away. He is an adult. Most people, by the time they're thirty, have jobs and responsibilities. While they may not like their jobs, they realize their necessity. Also, one would assume that by the age of thirty he would have reconciled himself to his fate and actively started working and learning how to be a king instead of running off into the woods to throw knives and play fetch with his horse. Here, he comes off as incompetent for, by the age of thirty, *not* learning what he needs to know about how to run a country. There's no way he could be prepared for everything, but it sounds like he's completely unprepared, especially when he talks about skipping out on lessons and then admitting that he should go to them *because* he's unprepared.

Tristan also constantly acts in the most idiotic of manners. During his coronation, the Minions of Day and Night attack and slaughter nearly everyone. Tristan and his family are captured. Kluge, the leader of the Minions of Day and Night, tells Tristan that he must kill his father by chopping off his head or the leader would do it himself. And then he offers Tristan a weapon.

Tristan has been given a weapon and the bad guy is standing there. What should he do? In theory, he should attack the minion.

Now, before we discuss what Tristan actually does, let us look at a similar example:

In *Skyfall*, the 2012 James Bond film, a similar situation occurs. The villain Silva has tied up the Bond girl Severine and placed a glass of whiskey on her head. He tells Bond that they are going to play a game of "Shoot the Whiskey Off the Girl's Head." Bond is surrounded by the villain's henchmen and severely out of shape. He shoots at the girl, deliberately missing her. The bad guy then shoots the girl dead, thus no longer leaving Bond an excuse to play it safe. Bond takes out the mooks, using their own weapons in incredible James Bond-style, and captures Silva just in time for the cavalry to arrive.

This does not happen in *The Fifth Sorceress*.

> "Good-bye, Father," he heard himself say, impossibly.
> Tristan gripped the heavy sword in both hands and raised it high over his head.
> I beg the Afterlife, let my aim be true, he heard a voice say. A voice that was distant, yet at the same time deep within himself.
> Tristan brought the full weight of his strength down with the dreggan, cleanly cutting the king's head from his shoulders. Blood erupted everywhere as the head rolled off the altar and onto the floor. Morganna screamed and collapsed.

Six. Heroes and Protagonists, Villains and Antagonists

> In a flash, he was upon Kluge with everything he had left, the blade of the dreggan swinging through the air directly at the monster's head. But again the larger man was too fast for him, neatly avoiding the swing while at the same time slamming the fist hard into the prince's stomach. Tristan went down hard, retching, and then simply lay there, crying, until the vomit came once again. The dreggan skidded violently across the blood-soaked dais, landing beneath one of the thrones [Newcomb, *Fifth*, p. 209].

Yes, Tristan would have likely been beaten just as badly if he attacked Kluge before killing his father. However, it would have been more heroic if he'd attacked Kluge first. It might have prevented his father from receiving a mercy killing, but once he had the weapon in his hand, Tristan could have tried to do something besides just cutting off his father's head. He could have tried to get his father out of the way. He could have tried to *do* something!

But standing around and not doing anything until attacked is something that Tristan is very good at. He allows a monster to monologue at him and waits until the monster is done speaking before attacking. This is after, of course, he asks, "*And just what is it you intend to do... Talk me to death?*" (Newcomb, *Fifth*, p. 260). These sorts of incidents follow Tristan throughout the book. He is presented as being an intelligent, heroic man, but instead he comes off like an idiot. And since this book and these characters are not being presented as a parody, it makes it hard for the reader to take them seriously.

Another thing about designated heroes and villains is that it's easy to create alternative character interpretations for them to cast them on the other side of what they should be.

Mary Sues and Gary Stus

In discussing heroes and villains, it's important to bring up the concept of Mary Sues and Gary Stus. They're important to the discussion of the ideas of the designated hero and the heroic archetype.

The term "Mary Sue" was first used in Star Trek fandom to apply to a certain kind of female character. It came from Paula Smith's parody story, *A Trekkie's Tale* (1973), where the main character was named Lieutenant Mary Sue. A Mary Sue "often has thigh-length hair, violet eyes or eyes that change color depend on her mood, and is so incredibly

The Tropes of Fantasy Fiction

beautiful that the hero (or heroes) immediately falls completely in lust with her; he cannot form complete sentences until the completion of an incredibly flexible and fantastic NC-17 scene, and maybe not even then. She enters the story and not only absorbs all of the male protagonists' time, but she drives the plot as well. This usually entails the OFC [Original Female Character] saving the world with skills that only she possesses, and dying heroically in the process. In other words she's beautiful, she's smart, she's courageous, and everyone is so in love with her that grown men are reduced to puddles of goo as soon as they are gifted with her presence" (Anne Kustritz, "Slashing the Romance Narrative," *Journal of American Culture* [2003], p. 380).

As fan fiction became more and more accessible over the Internet, the term spread like wildfire and became a derogatory term used by fans for any Original Female Character. Less frequently used is the term "Gary Stu" for the male counterpart, if only because they're either rarer or not considered as threatening, in that it's all right for men to be perfect and get all the designated love interests, but for women, it's not. Another issue is that Gary Stus aren't male replicas of Mary Sues. Gary Stus usually involve power fantasies rather than love fantasies. Gary Stus frequently have all of the money, the political power, the gadgets and technological toys, the magic, the special bloodlines and, of course, harems of women. If this sounds very much like a lot of mainstream and genre fiction featuring uber-powered male protagonists, that's the point. Some people may argue that there's no such thing as a Gary Stu. However, they are definitely out there.

It's commonly thought that there are no Mary Sues in published stories; after all, the entire point of a Mary Sue, or of a Gary Stu, is to be a character inserted into a canon work to act as an authorial avatar. This is a way for the fan fiction writer to engage in a power fantasy and be with the characters he or she admires. The fan fiction Mary Sue is a combination of both daydreams and desires to interact with the story's setting. The writers want to have adventures with the strong heroes and heroines found in the books, movies or television shows. However, the characters in such worlds—especially the fantasy-based ones—are so powerful and fantastic that, to keep up with the main cast, the writer must create a character that is more powerful than he or she—the writer—would normally be. Their original character must have pow-

Six. Heroes and Protagonists, Villains and Antagonists

ers or skills that the writer could never have. And, since usually the original characters are teenagers, they have skills, like being able to use a sword or magic, which they gain easily so that they can quickly join the adventure. They have to be able to show that they are worthy to be with the canon characters. Unfortunately, the result of this is that the original characters end up—in their writer's desire to be noted by the canon characters—possessing abilities that shouldn't be, or can't, be found in the canon world.

Basically, when the original character *breaks the rules* of the setting, they become a Mary Sue (or a Gary Stu). In *Harry Potter* fan fiction, you get characters that are half-elf; in *the Lord of the Rings* fan fiction, you get characters that are able to resist the lure of the One Ring and help Frodo along his quest; in *Star Wars* fan fiction, you get characters who become Jedi Masters within a few years of being picked up by the Jedi temple.

And thus the point:

It is the context of the world and the characters involved that make the Mary Sue.

Out of context, Batman, for example, could be seen as a Mary Sue. He's incredibly rich; he has a tragic back story; he has all sorts of gadgets and training that allows him to compete in a world that has characters like Superman in it. However, this is the point. In the DC universe you have Superman, a nearly invulnerable alien who has all sorts of powers; you have Wonder Woman, a woman made from clay who embodies the essence of Truth; you have the Green Lanterns, space cops who have magic rings that allow them to create green constructs that can do almost anything as long as the ring bearer has the will to make it. All of these characters are highly fantastic and ridiculous when you don't suspend belief and look at them from a logical point of view. When you have a world where such characters are ordinary, then a character such as Batman fits into it. There is nothing in the world so ridiculous that it can't fit into the DC Comics universe. Thus, even though Batman has Mary Sue traits, the fact that everyone in his canon has similar traits means that he is, by default, not a Mary Sue. He's not an exception to the rule.

When you have characters, however, who learn how to fight with a sword so quickly that within a couple of months, they are considered a master swordsmen, and when you have characters who, for no explainable reason, are able to do things contrary to established, in-universe rules of magic, *then* you have a Mary Sue.

When the canon characters break the rules, they become the Mary Sues—not when they have ridiculous back stories or are overpowered.

Consider Rand al'Thor from the *Wheel of Time* series by Robert Jordan or Vanyel of the *Last Herald Mage* series by Mercedes Lackey. Both characters have traits that could be considered to be those of a Mary Sue; however, only one of them interacts with the world in such a way as to *be* a Mary Sue.

Rand starts out as a young farm boy pushed into extraordinary circumstances where he finds that he is the Dragon Reborn, the destroyer and saver of the world, as well as being *ta'veren,* someone who can affect the world around him and change people's destinies. Kingdoms bow down to him and he will lead the world through Armageddon. From what is told in the books, he is the most powerful person the world has seen and is slowly going mad; unfortunately, he also appears to be a Mary Sue.

It is not his great power that makes him a Mary Sue, for great power alone, as mentioned, does not make anyone a Mary Sue. The character who comes with the power, and how the character is used, make the difference between Mary Sue or not.

Rand defies reality in several ways beyond his powers. Consider his ability with the sword. At the beginning of the series, he is not even a novice, having never handled a sword at all. By *Lord of Chaos*, he is considered a sword master, and by *A Crown of Swords,* he is able to defeat groups of men by himself. The thing that must be noted is that all these books take place within a span of two years; *A Crown of Swords* takes place in the same winter in which *Lord of Chaos* ends. It took Inigo Montoya, of *The Princess Bride,* close to twenty years to become a sword master, yet Rand defies the natural order of things by becoming one in two years. This is similar to the fan-fiction Mary Sue's ability to be the best sword fighter despite being fifteen years old and not having the experience necessary to be the best sword fighter. After all, knowing the forms is all fine and good—but experience still counts.

Another trait of Rand's Suedom is his ability to defy the laws of common sense. Common sense would say that a man traveling alone on foot would be easier to catch up to than a man traveling alone on a

Six. Heroes and Protagonists, Villains and Antagonists

horse, especially when he's being tracked by people on horses and one of those people is as experienced a tracker as one of his allies, Lan, is supposed to be. Yet, in *The Dragon Reborn*, Rand *does* elude them. Perhaps this is meant to be mysterious, but it's really just a dysfunction of reality, much like what happens when the Mary Sue author makes it take only two weeks to a couple of days to reach the Mines of Moria instead of the forty days that it is supposed to.

Then there is the Mary Sue flaw that he suffers from. The Mary Sue flaw is an imperfection that the Sue author gives her creation to grant it the semblance of being a real, three-dimensional character. These flaws given are not hindrances to the characters or even real flaws. Such things as being "too nice" or "too pretty" are Mary Sue flaws, things to which the Mary Sue author can point to and say that yes, her character isn't perfect. Another form of the Mary Sue flaw is something that has no impact on the narrative, such as not being able to sing, which gives the Mary Sue something to agonize over without actually allowing the Mary Sue to be hindered by anything.

Rand's Mary Sue flaw is his view of women. He has the idea that they should not fight and die in battle. Despite seeing that the Aiel Maidens are perfectly capable warriors and that the Aes Sedai have been fighting and manipulating wars for thousands of years, he still refuses to let them battle. Every time that a woman dies and is somehow connected to him, he puts that woman on his mental list. He repeats this list to himself, never letting them go, never changing. It is this lack of change, the fact that he keeps this list going through the books instead of adapting his views and changing his position, that makes it a Mary Sue flaw. If he were to change his views on women, to grow accustomed to the fact that they are human and not something special as the books moved forward instead of keeping his position static, it would not be a Mary Sue flaw.

Rand's character stays the same throughout the series. He doesn't seem to learn from his experiences; the world around him doesn't affect the way he thinks. It's not that he resists learning; things just seem to go over his head as he trundles along towards his destiny. While this could be called stubborn, it is also unrealistic. He should change, just like any real person does. By staying in the same position, he becomes two-dimensional and a Mary Sue.

On the other hand, Herald Vanyel in Mercedes Lackey's *The Last Herald Mage* trilogy displays many Mary Sueish traits. He is the most powerful Herald Mage in existence and has a tendency toward angst and drama. He is also extremely good-looking, and he selflessly sacrifices his life so that others may live, something that was once thought to be the supreme identifying trait of a Mary Sue, especially since he left his beloved behind to cry and sing about his greatness.

Looking at the arc of the trilogy, the first and last books are the most important in regards to his Mary Sueish traits. However, these traits are mitigated somewhat. For example, if Vanyel was a complete Mary Sue he would have gotten access to his powers much earlier in the first book, or he would have been chosen for his sheer untapped potential. But he is not. He does not even get into the Bardic College. Instead, he plays the snob as he tries to fit in with court life.

When he does find love, it is like a Mary Sue's love: a true love, a life-bonding even, with Herald Trainee Tylendel. This is something that every Mary Sue wants and usually gets (even if it isn't a homosexual relationship). But a life-bonding is also a known thing in the Heralds' universe and, while not exactly common, isn't unheard of. The relationship, however, is doomed, first by the fact that they can't let anyone know that it exists and then by the fact that Tylendel actually does die, leaving Vanyel suicidal and alone after only being in the relationship for several months.

Despite this drastic turn of events, Vanyel eventually finds love once again, though it takes him many years to do so. During those years, he is alone and aloof, afraid to get close to anyone lest they, too, die on him. But once he does find love again, it is not just anyone, but the reincarnation of his first and only love, Tylendel. Once again, it is a bittersweet romance because Vanyel still feels afraid to love the Bard Stefan (Tylendel reincarnated) and, once they really get beyond that, Vanyel sacrifices himself to save Valdemar. This would be completely Mary Sueish, except for the fact that Vanyel genuinely does block and fend off everyone's attentions, including Stefan's, as opposed to a Sue, whose attempts at blocking off attentions usually last no longer than the love interest saying, "Hello" (or something to that effect), even when she has vowed never to love again.

Another thing that keeps Vanyel from becoming a complete and

Six. Heroes and Protagonists, Villains and Antagonists

total Mary Sue is that when he is chosen, and when he does get his powers, he does not automatically become the best Herald Mage that ever was. In fact, he rejects the idea of becoming a Herald once he becomes coherent enough to think about such things. He rejects and fails to understand throughout much of the book how a person could *want* to be a Herald. He is too self-involved to think about the greater good. Unfortunately, instead of eventually learning about becoming a Herald Mage and learning to become unselfish, he has a somewhat unbelievable epiphany when people look to him for protection from a sorcerer and he is all alone. It happens so suddenly and is such a 180-degree turnaround from his previous position that it seems to be almost forced upon him by the author. It is as if the author wanted to make him a Herald but didn't want to have to go through all the necessary steps to take him from spoiled brat to Herald trainee.

Those sorts of moments, as well as his overall character—the overly pretty, powerful, angsty man—cause Vanyel to keep straying into the land of the Mary Sue. But the fact remains that there are reasons for these things and that he does not always lose himself in his angst, nor does his need to find love or be the best Herald Mage drive him. He is a human being and fallible.

Which brings back the point of this digression about Mary Sues and designated heroes: not all Mary Sues are designated heroes, but a Mary Sue has a greater tendency to become one. The point of a Mary Sue is to be bigger and better than everyone else, and the designated hero is often such a character so that readers will know that he or she is supposed to be the hero. If he or she weren't the hero, how could he or she kill a hundred and ninety men in one battle and come out nearly unscathed, after all?

The Monster as Protagonist

Earlier, it was discussed that there cannot be a monster as hero, but that doesn't mean that there can't be a monster or villain as *protagonist*. They can even be as interesting, if not more interesting, than a typical hero protagonist; after all, people do find villainous characters enticing and fascinating, sometimes more than the hero. And the villain can even go on a "Hero's Journey," as discussed by Joseph Campbell, though it would end horribly wrong.

In the *Fallen Moon Trilogy*, author K.J. Taylor set out to create such a protagonist. Arren (later called Arenadd) goes through the Hero's Journey; however, his journey leads him to become the Dark Lord that Erian, the character who fits most of the archetypal hero characteristics, must defeat. Arenadd shows that a character may follow the same path as a hero; only a few tweakings to the mythology and archetypes send him down the dark side. In an email conversation, Taylor said that she made deliberate choices to make Arren the villain of the story despite his going on the same path as the hero. She said,

> I just drew on other stories in general. You will notice, though, in traditional fantasy stories evil things always seem to come out of "the cold North." Well, hell—in The Hobbit[,] Smaug is described as "a fire wyrm from the North," or something like that. And I'm pretty sure Sauron, etc. are Northerners in the LoTR universe—correct me if I'm wrong, I never looked very far into that. So of course Arenadd had to come from the North, where it's cold, hence the pale complexion.
>
> Black robes are also very traditional "evil" clothing, and black hair and eyes are very traditional. Black hair's become a bit more mainstream now (Harry Potter had it, after all), but I don't know of any heroes with black eyes. It's harder to read facial expressions on people with black eyes..., (this is one reason why people who meet Arenadd think of him as dispassionate).
>
> I did give him long, thin fingers because of Voldemort, though. That was a direct influence. And I was drawing on Star Wars a bit by giving him a tragic backstory [Taylor].

The entire first book can be seen as Arren's call to adventure. In this case, the call is to retake the Northern Kingdom back from the southerners and free his people from slavery. His death at the climax of *The Dark Griffin* leads to the moon goddess making him her champion. From there, he breaks all ties to his old life by, instead of just leaving, burning them all irrevocably. There is no turning back for him. He cannot return after having completed his quest. He is not granted the ability to just live freely. Instead, bits are taken from him as the trilogy progresses until he no longer remembers the man he was and he is completely the moon goddess's creature.

At her behest, he travels north, encountering more and more of his enslaved people and liberating them. However, instead of freeing them

Six. Heroes and Protagonists, Villains and Antagonists

in a way that would have kept the Southerners alive, he advocates killing them. His march to freedom is covered in blood. His march to the north is rather like the conquering armies of many villains, from the Death Eaters in *Harry Potter* to Jagang's armies in the *Sword of Truth* series. People flee in terror of him.

Because of all of this, Arenadd fits Booker's idea of the Monster as Hero and the Divided Self. He is "in some situation that does not give ease or satisfaction, which cries out for change" (Booker, *Seven,* p. 173), and for Taylor, this means making him a "ticking time bomb: others distrust him from the outset, his father disapproves, and he's constantly picked on for being a Northerner" (Taylor). With this setup, he is able to fall and fall hard.

CHAPTER SEVEN

No Man Is an Island

> About three things I was absolutely positive. First, Edward was a vampire. Second, there was a part of him—and I didn't know how potent that part might be—that thirsted for my blood. And third, I was unconditionally and irrevocably in love with him.
>
> —*Twilight*

Characters do not exist by themselves. As in the real world, they live in a world populated by people they have to interact with, even if "interaction" means just passing someone on the street or killing them. They have parents, even if they don't know them; they have peers, even if they don't talk to them; they have people that they're against and people they're for. There are the random people of the villages, and the kings and queens whom they serve or take down. The protagonist's interactions with the world and with the people and creatures within the world tell us a great deal about a character. However, unlike the real world, every interaction that a character has is planned and every action has a purpose of some sort. It might be as mundane as buying food for dinner or as grand as toppling the evil dragon ruler demon. Random encounters don't exist within a story, unlike in real life. Even those that seem random show purpose of character.

If a person were to see, in real life, someone in a fancy blue dress and heels run into a Panda Express, order take-out and then run out, it would certainly be something of mild note but nothing explicitly of importance. If it were to happen in a story, it would be a chance for the characters to show how they respond to supposedly random acts. Do they just ignore it, thus showing a disinterest in the strange or random things around them? Do they mention it with bemusement? Do they speculate on what the woman could be in a hurry for? The conversation

Seven. No Man Is an Island

leads to character development. Everything a character says and does leads to development, even if it's unexpected.

Sometimes, an author will intend one sort of character development and end up with something completely different, because of who the character is and what the reader's expectations of them are. If a character is a king, the reader will have a different expectation for how he acts and how he responds to things than if the character is a street child. And if a character is a good king, the reader will have different expectations than if he is a bad king. The author's job is to show who he is through his words and actions. However, writers must be sure that a character's actions and words show what the writers intend them to show.

At one point in Paolini's *Inheritance,* Eragon encounters Orik, king of the dwarves. Orik is sitting by himself making an Erôthknurl, which is a ball of mud made into a stone. The purpose of the scene is to show Eragon and Orik bonding, to learn a bit about dwarven culture, and to show how Orik is dealing with being king. It is this last part that is important. Throughout the series, Paolini has been trying to show that Orik is a good king, that he wants the best for his people and wishes to succeed in the battles to come. However, in the conversation between Eragon and Orik, Orik says something that makes it seem like he's not such a good king after all. When Saphira (Eragon's dragon) says that he must have a lot of responsibilities now that he's king, he replies, "I have nothing I must needs do at the moment. My men are ready for battle, but there is no battle for us to fight, and it would be bad for them if I were to fuss over them like a mother hen. Nor do I want to sit alone in my tent, watching mine beard grow... Thus, the Erôthknurl" (Paolini, *Inheritance,* p. 218).

The problem here is that he has nothing to do because his men are ready for the battle and he has no battle. Kings have much more to do than just preparing their men for battle. He still has things relating to his kingdom that must be done. There are petitions and rulings and laws that must be made. He still has to rule. He still has to provide for his people. Being a ruler is not easy. It leads to sleepless nights and far too much paperwork. It's the price of power.

Saying that he has nothing to do means that his kingdom has suddenly frozen in time and won't need anything done until he gets back, that he has an evil vizier, or that he's neglecting his duties by thinking that the only thing that needs doing is prepping his troops for battle. For example, it's highly likely that there are a great deal of dwarfs unhappy with working with the Urgals. Even within the camp, that would be causing problems that he would need to fix.

The intent of the scene is to show how lonely it is for Orik to be at the top, as he says a few lines later that his friends "cannot forget that I am now their king, and I cannot ignore how their behavior has changed toward me" (Paolini, *Inheritance*, p. 219), but his words earlier indicate that *he's* being neglectful. A simple change of those words would give him a good reason for being out there. Instead of having nothing to do, he could have said that he was so overwhelmed with things that he decided that he need a break … thus the Erôthknurl. It's the difference of a leader having too much to do because of the burden of kingship and a leader neglecting that burden.

Nasuada, the leader of the Varden, is always busy and rarely has any time to do anything for herself. She's always dealing with problems within her camp and ambassadors, and she's not even a king. Orik should have the same problem. Thus, by not having this problem, Orik shows that his character isn't what Paolini wanted him to be. The text says that people treat him as a good king, but his own words damn him as a bad king because of the reader's meta-textual experience of what a good leader is supposed to be. He's not cutting off people's heads and putting them on spikes, but he's still neglecting his duties. Readers know that no good leader neglects his duties. In some ways, neglect could even be considered worse than if he was sticking heads on the spikes—he *could* be doing good and is *supposed* to be doing good, but isn't.

Thus, the nature of his character, that of the good and noble king, is subverted unintentionally, and his character growth moves in an unintended direction.

There are other stock characters who often appear within stories. Some of them have a greater influence on the main character than a friendly ear and providing contrast in the way that Orik is supposed to contrast with Galbatorix. The most obvious of these is the antagonist.

Seven. No Man Is an Island

Out to Get You

Stories are built upon conflict and problems that need to be solved which makes the antagonist the most important character in any good story. Without the antagonist, there wouldn't *be* a story. The antagonist is what the protagonist fights against, sometimes literally, sometimes figuratively. Antagonists are the creators of conflict. Does an antagonist necessarily have to be a person? No.

For example, if the story was about a man who wants to make a peanut butter and jelly sandwich but he has no peanut butter, the antagonist would be the lack of peanut butter. The story would be about him getting the peanut butter. It may not be the most exciting story in the world but it has a very basic plot: man wants sandwich but has no peanut butter.

In fantasy fiction, the antagonist is hopefully not as simple as a lack of sandwich spread. As fantasy tends to deal with more extremes of good and evil, it's very tempting to make the antagonist just plain evil for no particular reason at all. Except to be evil.

Being evil for evil's sake are antagonists, for example, who want to take over the world (or destroy it) but have no particular reason for doing so beyond desiring power for power's sake. Looking back at their motives, nothing about them seems to lead to them wanting to be evil. These are the shallowest and weakest of antagonists. They're an impediment and may be a very credible problem for the protagonist but, without a reason for their evil, they're just cardboard characters. The more real the character's motivations are, the more realistic the character becomes. This isn't to say that the authors need to give detailed psychological examinations of why the antagonist does what he does, but he should have an idea in mind. Antagonists need to be built up almost as well as the protagonist because of their importance to the story. After all, their job is to thwart the protagonist, much like the protagonist's job is to thwart the antagonist. For example, instead of a villain wanting power for power's sake, he could just not want to be *powerless* because, at some point in their history, he *was* powerless and it hurt him enough to never want to be in that position again.

It's rare for a person to see himself as a villain; after all, villains *lose* in stories. Ninety-nine percent of the time, the villain will lose, and no

The Tropes of Fantasy Fiction

one wants that to happen. Usually, to go back to the idea of the antagonist taking over the world, villains want to do so because they think that they—for some reason—are better suited to rule than the current leadership. This is, of course, the same reason a protagonist will try and stop *them*. The protagonist feels like the antagonist is doing a bad job or will do a bad job and that he should be stopped.

Now, there are some antagonists who do the things they do because they are insane. Those are the wild and unpredictable ones, like the Joker. But even they have their own motives that make sense to them, if not to anyone else, even if they're something like "the toaster told me to." Sometimes, these talking toasters may actually be possessed objects themselves, and so the intelligence possessing them is actually the antagonist, whose motives must be carefully noted.

Of course, an author must be cautious when portraying their antagonists. The author has to make sure that the reader agrees that the antagonist needs to go. Unless the purpose of the story is to tell the bad guy's point of view, the writer should ensure that readers' sympathy is with the protagonist.

An antagonist's reasons for doing what he does don't have to be great and world-changing. He could be doing it just for the money. But even then there's a deeper reason for that. He wants money to live comfortably, just like everyone else does. No one wants to be poor. It's just that the antagonists go about it in such ways that are detrimental to the world around them or that are against the laws of society.

The laws of society are very important because they can turn behavior that may, to the reader, seem abhorrent into something normal and everyday for the characters. This could be anything from slavery being legal and not considered something that needs to be outlawed to outlawing magic users or allowing duels between people for any perceived insult.

Robert Jordan was particularly fond of creating situations in which things quite normal for one society was considered abhorrent in another. Within the *Wheel of Time*, the protagonists had to deal with societies where in one a woman could only braid their hair when they were considered to be an adult—that of Two Rivers—and one where only young girls braided their hair—that of the Aiel. While this isn't as drastic a societal custom as slavery, it shows that what may be wrong for one

Seven. No Man Is an Island

country may be right in another. While the readers may not care if hair is braided or not, and thus consider the customs silly, for the protagonists from the Two Rivers, it's quite an important part of becoming an adult.

So, while the antagonist may own slaves, it may not be a reason for the protagonist to rail against him, if such a thing is accepted in the protagonist's society. The protagonist herself might even own slaves. In such a situation, what would make the antagonist worthy of destruction would be *how* she treats her slaves. If she treats them poorly and there are laws against doing so, then she's clearly working against society and thus, if not evil, she is someone who needs to be brought to justice or taken out.

It is important for the antagonist to be shown working against society's morals in some way so that the readers believe that he or she needs to be gotten rid of. The antagonist ruler who protects his people and doesn't lead his cities into ruin is going to be a harder sell as a bad guy than someone who puts people's heads on spikes for fun times.

The protagonist's reactions to the antagonist are also very important. He can have the same reaction to two different kinds of antagonists, which may cause different reactions in the readers. To go back to the previous two examples: the protagonist killing the ruler who protects the people is going to provoke a different reaction from readers than killing the ruler who puts people's heads on spikes. Thus, the antagonist helps define what sort of person the protagonist is. The actions of the protagonist can be the same, but who they're applied to makes all the difference in reader response. Which, once again, proves the importance of the antagonist.

Antagonists are what shape the story and the protagonist. They are the impetus of the plot; without them, there would be nothing for the protagonist to do.

A great many of them fall into the categories of the dark selves as explained in *The Seven Basic Plots:* the Dark Father, an authority figure who stands in the way of the protagonists, a "powerful tyrannical figure, representing strong male authority in its most heartless, egotistical guise" (Booker, *Seven*, p. 241); the Dark Mother, the Dark Father's female counterpart; the Dark Rivals, who are the "younger characters, of the same sex as the hero or heroine and roughly of similar age and status, who also act as oppressors" (Booker, *Seven*, p. 242); and finally the Dark Other Half, "a character of the opposite sex who seems to hold out the possibility of union with the hero or heroine, but in fact self-seeking and treacherous, or in some other way inadequate" (Booker, *Seven*, p. 242). They are all monsters who need to be overcome.

However, the important thing to remember is that the reader's definition of treacherous and oppressive may be different than the protagonist's. Of course, the protagonist is always going to see the antagonist as being in the way of what he wants—that *is* the antagonist's job—but the readers might feel like the antagonist isn't exactly oppressive or tyrannical. While the antagonist might be trying to kill the protagonist, thus being quite oppressive and monstrous to the protagonist, the antagonist might be doing this because the protagonist is a danger to those around him and those under the antagonist's protection. The readers are likely, then, to see the protagonist as the dark figure getting in the way of the antagonist's desires.

A good author will make sure that these things are intentional. He needs to make sure that the readers' sympathies lie in the right place, that they don't end up rooting for the antagonist to "win," be it if the antagonist is good or evil. It is the antagonist's job to be the one defeated in the story. He doesn't have to be the main character of the story, but they have to lose. The readers may sympathize with the antagonist or wish that he would win, but the story should lead up properly to his defeat, because otherwise the writer has failed in telling a story about a character overcoming the obstacles of the story.

All You Need Is Love?

Just as every story requires an antagonist, it seems like almost every story requires a love interest, or at least the temptation of a love interest. This is the person to whom the protagonist is attracted and oftentimes is part of the protagonist's reward at the end of the story for saving the world—beyond riches and the world still being in existence.

Romantic love also helps tie the story together and, hopefully, make for a happy ending. A great many protagonists in fantasy are "young"—not necessarily in age so much as in their way of life. For example, they lack responsibility, thus giving them the freedom to go on the adventure. While they may have family, they aren't usually the ones with children

Seven. No Man Is an Island

but instead are the children, or their family is conveniently killed off. So, they are, essentially, single and orphans. They are children. As the story progresses, they go, with any luck, from child to adult. And part of being an adult is taking on more responsibilities, including starting a family. This is where the love interest comes in. With love comes the possibility of marriage and starting a family, one of the prominent signs of adulthood. As has been recounted in countless other books.

It's interesting to note that since marriage is considered to be the "end" of the story, there are very few married protagonists. Even characters that are of the proper age to be married, like Harry Dresden, aren't. Why? So that they can fall in love during the story. It's as if the characters can't have a proper story when starting out married, with a living spouse they still want to be with. It's as if some writers don't feel like they can create an interesting story with a married couple as the protagonists, as there isn't any good conflict.[1]

While this may seem a bit ridiculous, this is why Spider-Man and Mary Jane's marriage was retconned in the storyline "One More Day." Marvel's editor-in-chief, Joe Quesada, "made it clear he was not a fan of the marriage of Peter Parker and Mary Jane, feeling it just never felt right for Peter to be married" (Jonah Weiland, "The 'One More Day' Interviews with Joe Quesada, Part 1 of 5," ComicBookResources.com, December 28, 2007). In 2011, DC Comics rebooted its universe with the New 52 initiative. Now Lois Lane and Clark Kent are no longer married, nor does Lois know his secret identity. Aquaman and his queen were also no longer married despite her being still being his queen. Publisher Dan DiDio says this is because "[h]eroes shouldn't have happy personal lives" (Heidi MacDonald, "Marc Andreyko Taking over Batwoman and More from DC Nation at Baltimore," ComicsBeat.com, September 7, 2013). Which means, essentially, that if they have happy personal lives, if they have a happy ending, they can't go on being heroes. In his opinion. Of course, then again, the Invisible Woman and Mr. Fantastic have been married for quite a while now and still have grand and crazy adventures plus plenty of conflict ... and then there's the stuff that happens with their two children.

However, marriage means maturity, in theory, and maturity means endings. After all, the point of the quest and story is to grow and it's easier to show that growth through someone who still needs to do a lot of it. Marriage can happen during the series, and often does, but it's rare for it to happen before the series starts. Especially with the protagonists. As an aside, an interesting thing about many love interests is that they are often the first person a protagonist could be interested in, despite all the other people they could and do meet. It's almost like love at first sight, even if the characters don't realize it at the time. They don't meet, date, break up and go on to other people. There is only room for the one romance. Or they eventually end up with the person they first met even if there were others in between. The first person wins. In the *Dresden Files* series, the first eligible person of the opposite sex appears to be Karrin Murphy—though the series isn't over yet—but Dresden's first love interest was Elaine Mallory when he was sixteen (and whom he thought he'd accidentally killed for years), while the first person the readers saw him date was Susan Rodriguez. The love between Harry and Susan was strong enough to be considered true love, protecting Harry from the White Court vampires. He was planning to propose to her.[2]

We need to examine not so much the purpose of the love interest—which is to be the reward for other characters—as the *kinds* of love interests and the *necessity* of them, as well as making sure they're portrayed correctly. "Correctly" means that the two characters in love should actually *seem* like they're in love, as opposed to just the narrative and characters *claiming* they're in love because the plot says so.

The most obvious way to gain a love interest in fantasy is for the hero to save the kingdom and get the princess' hand in marriage, or for the hero to save the princess and she falls in love with him, willingly agreeing to marry him. The princess in this case is the helpless person who requires rescuing. They don't necessarily have to be princesses themselves, or even female, but they are like the helpless princesses who are always in need of rescuing, often found in the early Disney animated movies like *Sleeping Beauty* or *Snow White*. These types of stories don't often have much in the way of relationship development. The two characters could know each other for all of a few days before realizing that they're madly in love with each other, that they are the one and that they have one true love.

Male princesses aren't as common, because most of fiction is told from the male perspective where women traditionally end up being weaker and the ones in need of rescue. However, more male princesses are being written as more women become protagonists and heroes. Female protagonists have a difficult line to balance because it's very easy for them to become the ones in need of rescuing; old habits die hard in writing and readers' expectations. Guys are supposed to get the girls, not the other way around, even if the end result is the same. And so, in this spirit, the person being rescued who becomes the love interest becomes the princess.

Then there's the give-and-take relationship. Both characters are assumed, by the text, to be equal. They are both capable fighters, talkers, and intellectuals. One might be better at one thing than the other, but they complement each other. Here, the love interest is often introduced early in the story and helps the hero on their journey to defeat the villain. The love interest and the hero may start off as rivals or as antagonistic to each other but, as the journey continues and they learn more about each other, they realize that they do love each other. Sometimes, the two come from the same place and are childhood friends. Sometimes the love interest is rescued by the hero (or heroic character) and decides to join them because they, too, have a stake in defeating the Villain. Sometimes the hero has no place to put them safely so they must tag along. Or the guy or girl might have a crush on the hero, and the hero doesn't realize it until much later in the story, though it has been completely obvious to everyone else. As they travel together, they realize they make perfect companions. This would be an evolution of the princess.

These are the two major kinds of love interests. They are almost equivalent to the balanced hero/passive heroine (the princess) and balanced hero/active heroine (give and take) that Booker discusses in *The Seven Basic Plots*. Booker describes these character balances in strictly gendered terms. For the balanced hero/passive heroine, "to set her free[,] the hero has to demonstrate his own masculine power," and the heroine herself "stands for the soft, yielding, flowing, loving feminine" (Booker, *Seven*, p. 269). Meanwhile, in the case of the balanced hero/active heroine, "it is the life-giving power of the feminine which itself helps draw the hero up to his final state of wholeness" (Booker, *Seven*, p. 270). However, this idea just casts the woman as an accessory or tool for the man. It doesn't allow for female characters to be active agents on their own, which they clearly are and can be, as well as ignoring balances that involve same-sex couples. Both of these could fit into these types of roles if not for the apparently strict need to follow gender identities of feminine and masculine.

It might work out better to have the balanced protagonist (or Hero) and the passive counterpart and the balanced protagonist (or Hero) and the active counterpart. In this case, the counterparts would give the Hero the motivation needed—which could possibly be called the desire to protect and the need for help—without bothering with gender identity, which is quite fluid in real life and which is becoming more and more visible in modern-day fiction.

Which raises the question of whether a love interest is even needed.

If what the protagonist requires is a counterpart, then the love interest could be eliminated without any problems. There are fantasy books without romance, such as *The Hobbit*. Bilbo relies on the dwarfs as his balance. They are the ones that are in need of rescuing from the elf king of Mirkwood, and the ones who need him to help deal with the dragon. While the dwarfs are rescued by Gandalf from the goblins, Bilbo rescues himself from Gollum through nothing but his wits. So it's clear here that Bilbo is the "balanced hero" and the dwarves act as his counterparts. There aren't any female characters in the book.

In *The Lord of the Rings* trilogy, the only romance featuring a main character is the one between Aragorn and Arwen, which is not the trilogy's focus. The closest thing, instead, is that of Frodo and Samwise. Here, Sam becomes Frodo's partner in loyalty, refusing to leave Frodo behind. Their friendship helps Frodo carry the ring and go to Mount Doom. The two of them balance each other out, and it could be said that by the end of the book, Sam is the hero because he was the only one who was able to let the ring go. He carried it for a while and gave it back to Frodo. Some might say this is because he didn't carry it for a long time. But even then he was in the ring's presence for as long as Frodo was and it still held no real sway over him. So then the balance from heroic counterpart to hero shifts, and Frodo balances out Sam. Sam becomes the active participant, getting Frodo to Mount Doom and protecting him from various Orcs, Shelob a giant spider, Gollum and the Ring itself. And despite what some fans may think, Frodo and Sam are most definitely not in a romantic relationship. They are quite fond of each other and care about each other deeply, but they are not romantic. Sam is not Frodo's love interest in the same way that Arwen is Aragorn's love interest. They are able to part ways, and Sam goes on to have his own large family (thirteen children!) with Rosie Cotton. So it's clear that Frodo didn't need romance so much as companionship.

The Mother, the Maiden and ... the Other One

Beyond the love interest, there are two other kinds of companions for the protagonist: the mentor and the sidekick. The mentor is the older and wiser individual who teaches the protagonist, while the sidekick is usually of the same age and gender of the protagonist. Both are used for exposition purposes. The mentor usually tells the protagonist what's going on; the protagonist usually tells the sidekick what's going on. They give the author a way to explain things to the reader without having the protagonists talk out loud to themselves. Of course, if authors aren't careful, they may fall into "as you know, Bob" territory, but that's more a problem with the craft of writing than one caused by the roles the characters play.

Interestingly, if all three are together—the mentor, the sidekick and the protagonist—a trio forms rather like the Mother, Maiden and Crone from mythology. The mentor figure becomes the crone, the protagonist the mother, and the sidekick the maiden.

While this may seem like a strange concept, it works. The mentor figure is fairly obvious, as mentors are usually older and wiser. They're the ones who teach the protagonists and impart wisdom. They are also the ones closest to dying and, usually, the ones who *do* die.

Now, one would think that the protagonist would be the maiden because they are supposed to be starting on their journey and innocent in the ways of the world, but this isn't quite true. They may be innocent but they're also setting out to protect the world. They become heroes under the idea that they have to do something. They may not want to at first, but they end up protecting and saving the world. They also can end up ushering in a new age. So, they're mothering the world. They're protecting it like it was their child; saving it from evil and making sure it survives to grow up. The protagonists also have to be active elements in the world around them. They can't rely on things happening *to* them to succeed; they need to *make* things happen. It's their job to save the world or whatever else needs to be done, be it finding the McGuffin or destroying the Dark Lord or saving someone. The maiden is passive. She's waiting for the hero to come and rescue her. The mother cannot wait around for someone to save her children; she has to protect them herself.

So, by the sheer act of wanting to stop the darkness or evil, the hero takes on the protective and nurturing role of the mother. He or she is also the one who gives birth to the new age of freedom that usually follows the defeat of the dark lord. It could be said that the climactic battle could even be the birth pangs. It's exhausting, it takes everything that the hero has, and if he or she fails, everyone will die. Sometimes the hero may lose his or her life, but in the end, the new world is born.

This leaves the sidekick as the maiden. It's the sidekick who is the actual innocent in the world. A sidekick can be combined with the love interest, if the protagonist is going to fall in love with him during his journey. But the idea is that the sidekicks are the ones who don't know what's going on. They're less talented and important than the protagonist, because otherwise they would *be* the protagonist. Instead, they're someone for the protagonist to protect when they get into trouble—again acting as the mother. They're the reflection of who the protagonist used to be, because their character growth isn't usually as great as the protagonist's. They do and should go through changes, but while the protagonist is busy saving people and going through major alterations in how he sees the world, the maiden sidekick is less affected. She is here to support the protagonist and help him or her get to the point where he or she can give birth to the new world.

In stories where there are only two characters—the hero and the mentor, or the hero and the sidekick—the hero tends to pick up the missing role. The hero mentors and teaches the sidekick like the crone, while still mothering and saving the world. And in cases where there isn't any sidekick, the hero will start off as the maiden and slowly move into that of a mother figure. Or perhaps, once the mentor figure dies, the hero will pick up a sidekick.

Examples of this three-way structure range from Gandalf, Frodo and Sam in *The Lord of the Rings* to Ebenezer McCoy, Harry Dresden and Molly Carpenter in *The Dresden Files. The Dresden Files* characters

Seven. No Man Is an Island

even have the addition of the master-apprentice relationship as well as the mother, maiden, crone.

Interestingly, in Terry Pratchett's Witches sub-series of the *Discworld* novels, he has the mother, maiden and crone trio with Nanny Ogg, Magrat and Granny Weatherwax but, if using the trio in relationship to the hero, sidekick and mentor paradigm, they don't fit into the same roles. Instead, Granny, the crone, takes on the role of the hero more often than not, with Nanny taking on the role of mentor and Magrat the role of the sidekick. This dynamic happens because it's usually Granny who does the final solving of the problems in the books while Nanny supports and helps her, usually reminding her of what is what. Magrat continues to be the maiden and the sidekick because she doesn't have the same life experiences that the other two witches. While she does do some hefty changing through out the series, she still is—by the sheer force of Granny's personality—stuck in the role of maiden and sidekick. Granny is much more active than she is, while she tends to be more reactive. However, when she does start to react, she reacts boldly; bold enough to shoot an elf in the eye with an arrow through a keyhole.

A side effect of the close relationships that these characters form is the fan reaction to them. The fans will often feel like the hero and mentor or hero and sidekick have better chemistry than the hero and his love interest. Because of this, they'll start preferring these other couples (or ship them) more than the official couple. Sometimes, the pairings that fans come up with are a bit strange and don't seem to follow any sort of logical sense from the story they came from. *Harry Potter*'s Draco and Hermione is one such couple. Fan reasons for shipping the two characters can range from "the two characters are pretty" to "they just seem to like each other better." To many fans, Draco and Hermione were clearly more interested in each other than in the love interest Rowling chose for Hermione, Ron Weasley.

This can happen frequently when the love interest isn't a major character in the story. When the *Lord of the Rings* movies came out, Aragorn got shipped with Legolas much more than he got shipped with Arwen. Why? Because Aragon and Legolas shared more screen time. While Aragon had a dream of Arwen after falling off a cliff in *The Two Towers*, which helped him survive, it was his reunion with Legolas that held all the emotion.

Unfortunately, there's no real way to avoid this sort of thing. The readers will always have their own ideas of what should happen, as the innumerable amount of fan fiction proves. The best an author can do is accept this and take it with good humor. After all, he probably did (and does) the same thing.

NPCs

One final group of characters must be explored before we finish the discussion on characters that surround the protagonist and their friends: everyone else. As in, "everyone else that exists in the world the characters inhabit." The people they see on the street, the farmers that grow the food they eat in the inns. They are the crowds in crowd scenes, the people who boo or make up the armies. The nameless. The true everymen and everywomen. Why are they important? Because they show what kind of person the protagonist is when dealing with non-important people. People that aren't important to the plot. People like the readers themselves.

In various kinds of games, from table-top to video, there are NPCs (non-player characters). They are those folks wandering around and getting in the way as the players try to get across the screen. They are the shopkeepers from whom the players buy supplies. And in a lot of games, they have really very little value. The players can go into their homes with impunity and steal their things. Nothing bad ever happens to the player characters, unless it's a plot point. Guards aren't called to arrest them. The players can take the money and essentially run. Why? Because it's a convenient way for the players to quickly get supplies and it's not the real world. For table-top games, it's fairly similar; the players can often get away with killing people and then looting their bodies. Depending on the gamemaster and game, this may or may not have dire consequences; however, the players are more likely to kill or harm random people than they would in real life.

What does this have to do with protagonists and books? Well, in a story, a writer is generally trying to create a world as realistically as possible. And that means his characters should interact with the people around them as realistically as possible and not treat them like NPCs.

Seven. No Man Is an Island

An example of treating people like NPCs happens in *Brisingr*. The elf Arya runs into Eragon and he wants to know where she got the dress she's wearing because it's not her usual clothing. Her response? "I had an unfortunate encounter with a pair of ox herders soon after I left the Varden, and I stole this dress directly afterward" (Paolini, *Brisingr*, p. 146).

There is a lot of character information to unpack in this rather simple-sounding statement. Ox herding is generally not something that wealthy people engage in, so the people that Arya encountered were more than likely poor. Poor people are not usually threats to trained warriors. While farm implements can be dangerous weapons, it's unlikely that the ox herders would have been a threat to Arya. Two non-combatants, at least one of them a woman in a society that doesn't generally allow women fighters, against an elf with super-elfy skills isn't a fight or even a contest. With her super-elfy skills, it's quite possible that she could have even completely avoided the confrontation all together. So, it's quite likely that she deliberately caused the confrontation for the direct purpose of obtaining the dress so she could have an easier time passing as a human. Some people may say that it was unavoidable and she did need the dress. However, there are some important details that seem to have been forgotten here to prove that this was completely unnecessary.

First, Arya is a powerful spellcaster. She could have changed her own clothing into a dress, if need be. She even tells Eragon that she made the stolen dress she's currently wearing fit better by using magic: "One of the advantages of being a spellcaster is that you never have to wait for a tailor" (Paolini, *Brisingr*, p. 146). So it was unnecessary for her to steal the dress. If she needed to hide her elf features ... it's also known that elves can change how they look. The elf Blödhgarm has given himself catlike features and bluish fur. It should be easy for Arya, who is considered a highly skilled mage, to use magic to change her own looks. Finally, since Arya knew that she was going into human lands and was going to have to look like a human woman, she could have *taken a dress before she left the Varden*. There are plenty of human women in the Varden who wear dresses. She could have found a dress she liked, hopefully *not* stolen it, and modified it with magic to fit her. Then she wouldn't have had any unfortunate incidents with ox herders.

Her callous disregard for the ox herders, the ordinary people that the Varden are supposed to be trying to protect from Galbatorix, makes her seem inhuman and uncaring, which is counter to what Paolini wants us to think about her. However, the ox herders are merely an excuse for Arya to get a dress. Thus, they aren't real people and aren't important. They're just NPCs to get slaughtered since they were in the way.

One would hope that Eragon would feel something in the way of shock (or any sort of uncomfortable emotion, really) after learning that Arya has killed these innocent people. However, his only comment on the incident is that the dress fits nicely. Thus, the series hero is shown to be utterly callous about the people he is trying to free. These people don't have names, nor were they given any screen time, so the characters don't have to be emotionally invested in them. But by not being emotionally invested in these characters, even a little, even by a simple comment about how maybe they didn't need to be killed or couldn't their deaths have been avoided, Arya and Eragon come off as heartless, unrealistic or both.

On the other side of things is Sergeant Angua from Terry Pratchett's *Discworld*. During *The Fifth Elephant*, she travels back home to Uberwald in werewolf form and on the way takes chickens to eat. Now, out in the middle of nowhere and/or in small villages, where a great many people that she runs into live, a chicken is a very important creature which can provide livelihood for its owners. The hens will give eggs which can be eaten; the owners can raise chicks which can be sold or traded for other goods; and the chickens themselves can be eaten. With winter fast on its way at the time of the story, stealing a chicken, as Angua does, could mean the difference between life and death for the owners. So she *pays* for the chickens. She even ends up overpaying for them. While the owners never actually see her breaking into the hen houses, she *always* leaves money. Why? As Carrot says, "Because animals don't" (Pratchett, *Elephant*, p. 102).

She knows that she has to treat people with respect and pay for the goods she takes, even if she never interacts with them, because that's what *people* do, not animals. If you want something that belongs to someone else, you pay for it. You don't kill the people—which she's more than capable of doing—and then take their things, even if they're just random, nameless poor people.

Seven. No Man Is an Island

To go back to the previous example with Arya, one would assume that the ox herders would be more than willing to help her out. After all, she's an elf fighting against the supposedly evil tyrant Galbatorix. Elves are supposed to be good and she obviously has money, for she has paid for the room she and Eragon are staying in. However, since the ox herders weren't willing to part with the items she needed, that leads to the conclusion that (a) Galbatorix isn't as bad as the readers thought he was, and thus they're rooting for the wrong team, and (b) elves aren't the good, wonderful, perfect people that Paolini is trying to portray. Perhaps, then, it was a good thing that Galbatorix killed off all the dragon riders, since many of them were elves. He clearly cares for his nameless people, as they've always fought *against* the Varden instead of joining them to overthrow Galbatorix's rule. Why? Because that's what good rulers do, which is evident in the reactions of the people to the Varden.

It is likely that the only reason that the people never willingly give up their cities when the Varden arrive is because the Plot Says So. These cities never have any rebels that are fighting against Galbatorix's rule for the Varden to contact. It's always the entire city against the Varden. It wouldn't make Eragon or Roran or others look as good if they had the help of the rebels to take out these cities. It would be more realistic, but it wouldn't allow Roran and Eragon their moments of awesome glory in defeating the city of people who just want to live their lives and not have to deal with the Varden trying to invade. By forcing the NPCs to all work against the Varden for plot reasons, the story, if looked at realistically, makes the main characters look bad. And this is why it's important for authors to keep their characters' interactions with the little and normal people in mind: it's one of the best ways to define who they are. It's one thing to steal from a bandit; it's another to steal from a chicken coop.

Every character that the protagonist interacts with is important, from the love interest to the people on the street. Every action he takes with these characters inform the readers about what sort of person he is. And the authors must take care that what they want to portray is what they actually *do* portray. If they're not careful, they'll end up with kings who look lazy and heroines who steal from the poor for their own gain, so it's imperative for an author to make sure that his characters treat people as real people.

Protagonists do not exist within a vacuum. Every relationship, from it one that lasts for years to one that lasts for seconds, has an impact on both the protagonist and the reader. After all, even in books, actions speak louder than words. And how the protagonist interacts with friends, antagonists and the nobodies of the world will tell the reader more than what the writer says in the text. It's one of the most important and obvious ways they affect the world around them and make things happen.

Chapter Eight

Fairies and Dragons and Dwarfs, Oh My!

> Let sleeping dragons lie, for they find you crunchy and good with ketchup.
> —bumper sticker

The fantasy genre has what could be called stock races that writers pull out of the bag to populate their worlds. These are the things that people roll their eyes at when discussing fantasy: the unicorns, the dragons, the sparkly magical creatures that can do everything, and the long-lived elves. Superficially, every iteration of these races seems to be the same. All elves are tree-loving, long-lived, pointy-eared people of perfect goodness. All dwarfs are short, hairy and love to work in the earth, drink beer and hate elves. Dragons are fire-breathing monsters that love treasure, fly and eat people. These are things that everyone knows about fantasy creatures, and non-genre readers tend to complain about the sameness. And so do genre readers when discussing certain facets of the genre. Although they're more likely to complain about the plots of the stories than the creatures within the stories, they will still complain when a race seems to be too close to Tolkien's or another writer's depiction. The closer to how Tolkien presented his races, the more upset the readers are likely to be. Because of *The Lord of the Rings*' place within the realms of modern-day fantasy, it seems like almost every version of these fantasy races can be derived from Tolkien or seen as trying to subvert Tolkien.

The Minions

Every Dark Lord needs henchmen and minions. They're the groups of supposedly evil creatures that terrorize the regular masses of humanity and try to overwhelm the heroes in battle, giving them someone to fight against before getting to the big bosses. They make up the armies of the Dark Lord because they're evil and only evil people would follow the Evil Dark Lord unless they've been mind-controlled. Usually they're very animalistic or ugly, thus reinforcing the idea that they are evil. Evil people in fiction are generally ugly, especially the minions. Sometimes the minions are the faceless men in masks, like the Storm Troopers in Star Wars, but even then the helmets are a sort of grotesque and inhuman shape, thus creating a sense of otherness in them, which makes them more like monster races.

The minion races must be inhuman for the sake of the Hero and his companions, as well as the reader. The Hero needs to face challenges on her way to the Dark Lord, and one of the things that Dark Lords tend to do is try to take over the world. Taking over the world requires an army, so the minions are thrown at the heroes. This is where a problem arises. Heroes are often reluctant to kill innocent people, and yet the Dark Lords often send groups of minions to kill the heroes.[1] Small groups of three to six minions are quite a lot different than faceless armies. There isn't time for individual description of soldiers because it would be like trying to describe every bit of sand. With small groups, however, the writer is capable of giving each minion a bit of a description. But by doing this the writer can create an identifiable creature for both the reader and characters. The heroes may become reluctant to kill something familiar, so the minion must become something monstrous.

Monsters are okay to kill. By killing them, the Heroes are getting rid of something dangerous in the world, something that, in theory, cannot be reformed. The evil is obviously deeply ingrained into the soul of the monster, which becomes nothing more than a wild and dangerous animal that must be put down for the safety of the world. Making the minions monsters erases the idea that the Heroes are killing intelligent and sentient individuals.

In fact, monstrous minions are often described as not being as intelligent or ethical as regular people. Tolkien describes his goblins as "cruel, wicked and bad-hearted. They make no beautiful things, but they make many clever ones... Hammers, axes, swords, daggers, pickaxes, tongs, and also instruments of torture, they make very well... It is not unlikely that they invited some of the machines that have since troubled the

Eight. Fairies and Dragons and Dwarfs, Oh My!

world, especially the ingenious devices for killing large numbers of people at once" (Tolkien, *The Hobbit*, p. 59). Clearly creatures that delight in creating weapons and torture devices, of creating pain and suffering, are deserving of death.

The Wargals in John A. Flanagan's *Ranger's Apprentice* series aren't even that intelligent. Instead, they're "stocky, misshapen beings, with features that were halfway human, but with a long, brutish muzzle and fangs like a bear or a large dog" (Flanagan, *The Ruins of Gorlan*, p. 1). They "had no spoken language, relying on a primitive form of thought awareness for communication. But their minds were simple and their intellects basic" (Flanagan, *Ruins*, p. 2). Looking like a bear or dog (even if they have some sort of human shape) and possessing no intelligence makes it easier for the protagonist, Will, to kill them without making it murder. Their monstrous appearance also gives Will something to be afraid of when they charge or try to kill him.

Now the writer has something easy for the heroes to kill while still putting the Heroes in some sort of peril. In some ways, minion monsters are rather like the monsters that Odysseus or other mythological heroes had to face on their journeys.

Not every minion monster is visibly evil. Terry Goodkind went in the opposite direction when he created Darken Rhal's elite killing squads known as a "quad," a group of four nearly identical men trained to hunt and kill Confessors. They were usually good-looking, large and blond. Not the sort of people one would assume to be monsters, if they go on the idea that pretty people are good and evil people are ugly. However, quads are quite monstrous on the inside. "Although larger than most men, they could move with stealth and quickness and stalk their prey without being detected, as well as cut down their enemies in a heartbeat. Their voices were typically deep, even friendly. Pain usually did not bother them. They were relentless. They would not stop, did not know the meaning of it, and never thought of anything but their objective" ("Quads," *Sword of Truth* Wikia). This seems to be consistent with some of the ideas in Goodkind's series; monsters can be friendly and seem reasonable, but in the end they're still monsters.

And then, perhaps taking a chance to avoid continued accusations of plagiarism of Tolkien's mythos, Christopher Paolini took his Urgals and their smarter counterparts, Kull, and turned them into noble savages. He says that they aren't really evil, despite their looks and actions; they just like war a lot. Also, Galbatorix tricked them. Garzhvog explains that "'[Galbatorix] promised us good land if we killed his enemies. He tricked us, though. His flame-haired shaman, Durza, bent the minds of our war chiefs and forced our tribes to work together, as is not our way. When we learned this in the dwarves' hollow mountain, the Herndall, the dams who rule us, sent my brood mate to Galbatorix to ask why he used us so.' Garzhvog shook his ponderous head. 'She did not return. Our finest rams died for Galbatorix, then he abandoned us like a broken sword. He is *drajl* [N.B. an Urgal insult meaning "spawn of maggots"] and snake-tongued and a lack-horned betrayer. Lady Nightstalker, we are fewer now, but we will fight with you if you will let us'" (Paolini, *Eldest*, p. 608). This is after Paolini admits that they like war and killing people.

However, the Urgals say they were mind-controlled; they aren't really like this. They want to kill Galbatorix, too. It is sort of like turning the Klingons from the evil implacable villains in the original series of *Star Trek* to barely trusted allies in *Star Trek: The Next Generation* but with very little transition shown on screen. At least the Klingons made actual attempts at diplomacy and never claimed to be mind-controlled.

By doing this, Paolini tries to take the monsters that the heroes are supposed to fight and turns them into reluctant allies. He uses them to create a new civilization that he can, in theory, explore, moving them away from the stereotypical monsters they were presented as, the sort that like to kill babies and stick their bodies on pikes, which they did in one of the early chapters of *Eragon*. As Brom put it, people who could do those sorts of things "wear many faces and go by many disguises, but there is only one name for them: evil" (Paolini, *Eragon*, p. 131). This is never brought up again, even when the Urgals ask to join the Varden. Instead, it's glossed over with a "you like to kill us because we're ugly and we like to kill you because we like killing things, but we both hate Galbatorix, so let's kill him" sort of negotiations, as mentioned earlier. And mind control only excuses them so far because they were trouble and problems even before Galbatorix took control of them. The king merely organized them; they were still foes to be feared before him.

In his usual way of doing things, Terry Pratchett turned the idea of the crafty but unintelligent orc on its head. In *Unseen Academicals*, we get Nutt, a very polite gentleman from Überwald who talks like he's eaten a thesaurus and has read entire libraries of books, though he has no practical life experience. He is the quintessential bookworm ... and nothing at all like Tolkien's cruel and bad-hearted orcs. Nutt is aware that he can be dangerous but refuses to give in to the temptations presented to him for violence. Nutt plays with the idea of nurture versus nature. He is an orc, which by his nature should make him a horrible creature capable of untold cruelty, and yet he was treated horribly and cruelly by people until he was rescued by Omnian priest Mightily Oats. When Nutt's friend Glenda goes looking for information about orcs from Dr. Hix, the professor of Postmortem Communications[2] at Unseen University, she's shown three seconds of the only known orc battle though the eyes of a man who lasted all of three seconds in it. While Glenda sees the orcs fighting in those three seconds, she also sees men on horseback with whips driving the orcs into battle (Pratchett, *Unseen*, p. 293). Here, in the Discworld, the orcs are creatures *made* for battle, much like in other places ... but they're not necessarily evil. They need whips to be driven, because anyone who is heading into a hail of arrows would need some sort of incentive.

Minion Minders

Besides the mindless masses of monstrous minions, authors also have created the minion minders who aren't as mindless, if ever-loyal to their master. These creatures are the ones who drive the minions forward; they're monstrous enough that the hero doesn't feel completely horrible when he kills them. Sometimes, they are human but are so horrible that they might as well be monstrous in form as well. Other times they are actual creatures. It depends on how magical a world is and what sort of creature the Evil Lord of Darkness is. Sometimes these lieutenants are created by the Dark Lord when he offers them power and then ensnares them through their lust for that power, rather like the devil dealing with souls.

To use video-game terms, these lieutenants are mini-bosses. As the Dark Lord must be saved for the climax of the book, or, in a trilogy, the last book, the Hero needs someone to fight that has some brains and that presents a challenge beyond the merely physical. The lieutenants are acting on their master's wishes, trying to further his plans. By thwarting them, the hero and his or her companions get one step closer to defeating the Dark Lord without actually confronting him.

This, of course, brings up the question of why the Dark Lord doesn't just kill the hero and company before they can do such a thing ... or even before the hero can become a problem. And there are multiple reasons for this, but basically (and perhaps annoyingly) it comes down to "because the plot says so." There wouldn't be a story if the Dark Lord discovered that the callow youth is destined to destroy him so he went ahead and killed him before he could become a danger. Sometimes he actually does so, though oftentimes this fails, mostly because the Dark Lord kills the parents/loved ones/village/dog/what have you instead of the hero-to-be, thus sending the hero onto his path. This is an odd failing of many Dark Lords.

However, that being said, sometimes the Dark Lord just doesn't know about the hero because the hero hasn't become a problem yet. When he does become aware of the hero, he may have other things to do and thus sends his lieutenants to take care of it for him, as that's the lieutenants' job. They take care of the problems of the Dark Lord that the mindless minions can't manage. It's their job, rather like the special squads sent out by the army to take care of problems. In fact sometimes the lieutenants have their own sub-squads of mindful lieutenants. This is common in the longer series or trilogies.

Now, these may not seem like a race of minions, but in a sense they can be considered so. Especially when you get things like Ringwraiths from the *Lord of the Rings*, which are no longer quite the race of men that they started from but are instead undead creatures, or the Shades from *Eragon*. Both kinds started out as men, but through foul magic were changed into something completely and utterly unlike men, beyond sharing the shadow remains of the human form. The Ringwraiths do this by accepting a rink from Sauron and the Shades by taking in summoned spirits they couldn't control.

Terrorific Elves

There have been plenty of books that discuss where elves come from, but in a meta-textual context, it's important to see where elves are

Eight. Fairies and Dragons and Dwarfs, Oh My!

going. First, there are the terms "elf" and "fairy." For many people, they refer to completely different things. Elves are the creatures that are found in books like *Lord of the Rings* and fairies are like Tinker Bell. Elves are tall, stately creatures that are in tune with nature and better than people. Fairies are tiny, silly things with insect wings and also in tune with nature. They are of the natural world, whereas man is of the urban and technological world. Fairies and elves are mysterious and magical; men are mundane and must beware lest they stumble into their realms and never be seen again.

Up until recently, elves had faded from popular culture mythology, with only the tiny fairies being seen. Shakespeare is largely responsible. With *A Midsummer Night's Dream* and *Romeo and Juliet,* written during the mid–1590s, Shakespeare radically transformed traditional fairy lore, both by representing fairies as physically diminutive and by rooting their behavior in a new socioeconomic context. In virtually all accounts of the folkloric English fairies which predate these plays, the fairies are described as being the size of small humans. The members of the fairy retinue of *A Midsummer Night's Dream* would, of course, have appeared onstage as human-sized, yet their very names and Shakespeare's descriptions of their activities suggest that the audience views magnified versions of tiny creatures: Peaseblossom, Cobweb, Moth, Mustardseed, and their colleagues "creep into acorn-cups" (2.1.31)" (Marjorie Swann, "The Politics of Fairylore in Early Modern English Literature," *Renaissance Quarterly* 53, no. 2 [Summer 2000]).

Tolkien agreed with this and added Michael Drayton to the parties at fault. "Drayton's *Nymphidia* is one ancestor of that long line of flower-fairies and fluttering sprites with antennae that I so disliked as a child, and which my children in their turn detested" (Tolkien, *Tolkien Reader,* p. 38). He preferred the older versions of elves, the ones with grace and dignity, such as the Tuatha de Danaan from Irish mythology. In fact, since his stories claim to be from an earlier age of human history, his elves are the seeds of what later became the Tuatha de Danaan, as the latter are said "quite specifically, to have sailed out of the West to Ireland to fight the evil Fomorians, to have defeated them, and then to have themselves been defeated by a new invasion of evil creatures, the Fir Bolg. The Tuatha then sailed back into the Far West, and did not return. (Significantly, they are ... remembered ... as tall, beautiful, high beings of Light, great warriors and magicians, immortal and wise)" (J.E.A. Tyler, *The Complete Tolkien Companion*, p. 199). Tinker Bell they are not.

Much as Shakespeare turned elves into tiny creatures, Tolkien gave them height again, especially in fantasy literature. When *Dungeons and Dragons* was first created, heavily influenced by the Tolkien mythos, Gary Gygax and Dave Arenson took the elves as Tolkien described them. Those elves were probably a lot more appealing to the men who created the games than the tiny creatures with names like Buttercup and Appleseed. Ferdir (Beech-Tree) and Nínimdir (Snowdrop)[3] are much more interesting. These kinds of elves were magical and in tune with nature but they weren't capable of large feats of magic, such as creating fireballs or turning someone into a poodle, unless they took the wizard class.

Eventually, as readers got tired of the clichéd Tolkien elves, they started to change once more as writers started to take the name "fairy" back, especially in urban fantasies.[4] There, the elves couldn't live in the regular world because it was too technological for them, so they retreated back to the lands of Faerie. Faerie is outside of our world, a different dimension or space. It's accessed through things like fairy rings—circles of mushrooms found in forests—and through trees, old tombs or crossroads. Once Faerie was brought back, other creatures returned into the literature, things like redcaps and the Wild Hunt. Pixies and sprites were now the tiny creatures that fairies used to be. Other classifications arose as more of the old folklore was brought back, such as the Seelie (good or light or nicer elves) and Unseelie (bad or dark or really nasty elves) courts.

Fairies and elves become not-so-nice and perfect in an effort to expand beyond the Tolkien meta-textual idea of what an elf is. In a way, his elves have become what Shakespeare's fairies had: the only concept of what an elf is and what everything must fight against.

In some cases, they become downright ugly, like the Harry Potter series' house-elves. These elves are little creatures with "large, bat-like ears and bulging green eyes the size of tennis balls" (Rowling, *Chamber of Secrets*, p. 12). They are the happiest when they're working in the kitchens or cleaning the house for someone and really would rather *not* be set free. They like their work. They prefer their work. Even Dobby, considered strange for a house-elf, talks Dumbledore down from ten Galleons a week and weekends off to a galleon a week and one day off a month when he demands payment for his services. (Rowling, *Goblet*,

Eight. Fairies and Dragons and Dwarfs, Oh My!

p. 379). As he says, "Dobby likes freedom, miss, but he isn't wanting too much, miss, he likes work better" (Rowling, *Goblet*, p. 379). In fact, they're more like brownies than what people have come to think of as elves—that is, those who associate Orlando Bloom's Legolas with elves. For those who picture elves as tiny folk or consider brownies to be a sort of fairy, which they are, then the association of "elf" with "house-elves" perhaps isn't so disconcerting.

The Dragon Age video-game series takes a different spin on elf culture. In most stories, where elves are human-sized and look human, they're better than everyone else. They're smarter, faster, longer-lived, and prettier than you. This isn't so in the Dragon Age games. While the elves may have started out that way, they're now a scattered people at best, and, in the worst case, second-class citizens and slaves. A great many of them live in "Alienages" that are essentially ghettos, like those used in Europe to keep the Jews separate from the rest of the world. "Alienages are a hotbed of crime, disease, alcoholism and extreme poverty, with most of their people barely managing to get by on a day-to-day basis. Some elves may manage to scrape together small savings or marriage dowries by opening a store or finding work as laborers. For the majority, however, the possibility of going hungry is simply a fact of life. Disease is also widespread in the elven slums, and virulent plagues often spring up in Alienages" ("City Elves," Dragon Age wiki).

This is quite a far throw from places like the Last Homely House east of the Sea. "That house was, as Bilbo had long ago reported, 'a perfect house, whether you like food or sleep, or story-telling or singing, or just sitting and thinking best, or a pleasant mixture of them all.' Merely to be there was a cure for weariness, fear and sadness" (Tolkien, *The Fellowship of the Ring*, p. 219). This is quite different from a hotbed of crime and disease.

And then some elves became downright scary, the Unseelie elves especially. This is a good thing. There's nothing more disconcerting for a reader than to see creatures that he assumes to be good, kind and wonderful only to find them to be utterly horrific monsters. It creates a discord which, when handled well, can unsettle readers and at the same time drive them forward. Such creatures bring back the nightmares that elves and fairies originally caused. As Terry Pratchett puts marvelously in *Lords and Ladies*:

Elves are wonderful. They provoke wonder.
Elves are marvelous. They cause marvels.
Elves are fantastic. They create fantasies.
Elves are glamorous. They project glamour.
Elves are enchanting. They weave enchantment.
Elves are terrific. They beget terror.
The thing about words is that meanings can twist just like a snake, and if you want to find snakes look for them behind words that have changed their meaning.
No one ever said elves are *nice*.
Elves are *bad* [Pratchett, *Lord and Ladies,* p. 122].

Fairies like these are interesting. They're something for the hero to be afraid of. This makes the reader question the nice stories that they've heard about Tolkien's elves and their derivatives. Are they *actually* nice and perfect? Or is that just what they want us to think? After all, what sort of creatures constantly reinforce how much better they are, how much more they know and how you should think of them as eternally wise?

Perhaps the dwarves have their own opinions on the matter.

Written in Stone

Unlike elves, dwarves have the short end of the stick (no pun intended) when it comes to diversity. While people say that all elves are the same, it's easier to refute than when people say that all dwarfs are the same. They're short, they're hairy with big bushy beards, they like axes, gold and jewels, mining and making things. Their women are scarce or look like the men. They like drinking beer or ale, sound like they're from Scotland and are a sort of boisterous bruiser type. Even Disney's dwarfs from *Snow White* have many of these symptoms. Sometimes, in some stories, dwarves are also creatures from Faerie, but even then they still have the same features as those *not* from Faerie.

And that's about it.

Dwarves suffer from what science fiction writers call the "Planet of Hats" syndrome. That is when the protagonists of the show or movie go to a brand-new world and meet a brand-new race and *everyone* is exactly the same culture-wise. The planet is filled with an entire race of people who act in the same way. *Star Trek* is exceptionally good at this.

Eight. Fairies and Dragons and Dwarfs, Oh My!

Every Vulcan is logical. *Every* Ferengi worships money and is a greedy businessman. *Every* Klingon is obsessed with honor. And so on and so on. There is no cultural diversity. The Vulcans who didn't wish to be logical became their own separate race, the Romulans. And they're *all* the same. You can't have non-logical Vulcans. Or at least they are a rarity, the odd men out. Everyone is wearing the same hat.

Fairies at least get a chance at diversity. You have good elves, you have evil elves, big elves, little pixies, tricksters and wise ones. But all dwarves are the same. There are no painter dwarves. There are no cooking dwarves. There are no dwarves that like to wear pretty silk dresses and makeup. No dwarves that aren't hardy folk that don't like gold and mining and axes. Dwarf wizards are pretty much non-existent. All dwarves like beards; the non-bearded are a rarity and considered strange.

That being said, subversions do exist, but only if they're contrasted to the stereotype. They are the exceptions to the rule.

One group of subversions comes from Peter Jackson's *Hobbit* trilogy. Since film is a visual medium and there are thirteen dwarves, it's necessary to find ways to differentiate between them for the audience. Thus, he had to come up with thirteen different dwarf designs which would indicate thirteen different personalities, which he did. There are a few axe-wielding dwarves with Viking armor in the Company, such as Gloin. But then there's the cardigan-wearing Ori, who uses a sling shot. Balin wears robes. Kili is an archer and *doesn't have a beard.* He has stubble, but not a beard. Considering he's the youngest of the dwarves, and no more than a teenager, it makes sense. Bofur has the most fantastic hat that looks like it belongs on someone from Russia rather than a dwarf. These changes were so drastic that when the designs were first released, some fans cried out that they didn't look like dwarves!

Because everyone knows that dwarves have beards, use axes and wear armor. Which is very boring and very much the same; much to his credit, Peter Jackson knew this.

Considering that most of what it means to be a dwarf seems to be cultural rather than physical, Terry Pratchett does something interesting with his dwarves. In the Discworld, "dwarfish identity is not defined by mere genetics and size, but by a whole complex culture of laws, taboos, customs, moral principles and traditional knowledge. It is not precisely a religion, but it is as vital to their sense of selfhood as any religion could

The Tropes of Fantasy Fiction

be. Height, in Discworld dwarf culture, plays no part in defining a dwarf. Dwarfishness is about what you do, not how high you do it. Captain Carrot Ironfoundersson happens to have been born of human parents and to be well over six feet tall, but his upbringing has made him socially and spiritually a dwarf" (Terry Pratchett and Jacqueline Simpson, *The Folklore of Discworld,* p. 65). By making it possible for someone other than a "dwarf" to be considered to be a dwarf, Pratchett moves "dwarf" from race to society. And in a society, it's okay for everyone to be mostly the same. This is one of the things that make a society a society: a similar belief and rule structure. It's not necessarily what you look like, but instead how you act in your day-to-day life. You still can tell a dwarf by how they look, but how they act makes them a dwarf more than what they look like.

In fact, some of the dwarves from the mountains don't consider city dwarves to be dwarves at all. "They held that those who had moved to Ankh-Morpork and other lowland cities were *d'rkza,* 'not proper dwarfs,' because they had become lax, they had let the old ways slide. [In *Thud!*] if Albrect Alrechtsson had become Low King, he would have declared all these city-dwellers *d'hrarak,* 'non-dwarfs'; this would have made their marriages and business contracts invalid and would have meant that the old dwarfs would not be allowed to be buried back home" (Pratchett and Simpson, *Folklore,* p. 75). Again, a cultural thing and not a racial thing.

It's very unlikely that a dragon could be kicked out for not being dragon-like or that an elf could stop being an elf if it wanted to be, especially if it is the sort that is vulnerable to iron. This is something that is bound up into their very being. In many stories, all of the Fair Folk are vulnerable to iron; there are just different kinds of fairies. One of the ways you can tell they're a fairy is by the iron vulnerability. In the Discworld, it seems that a person could be able to tell whether someone is a dwarf by the way he looks, but then Captain Carrot being a dwarf and the idea that entire swaths of dwarves can be considered non-dwarves just because of how they act turns dwarves into something more than just a race, but instead an actual people. This is more than they get in a lot of other works.

The idea that being a dwarf is more like a culture than a race also arises in works that don't have them. In games like Elder Scrolls, there are the Dwemer, which fill the dwarf cultural niche but aren't dwarves. Instead, they're a forgotten kind of elf. "They are often referred to as 'Dwarves' in western cultures, although they were no shorter than a human and the name seems to have been derived from a supposed encounter with Giants who saw the Dwemer as short. They were a reclusive, independent race, dedicated to the principles of Science, Alchemy, Magic, and Engineering" ("Races of the Elder Scrolls#Dwemer," Wikipedia). The science, alchemy and engineering are all very dwarf-like traits, but the Dwemer *weren't* dwarves except for being short compared to giants. Again, this is if we're going by the idea that one of the things that makes a dwarf a dwarf is his size. Had the Dwemer been short, then they would have been "true" dwarves and not dwarf-like.

All in all, writers probably would do dwarves a great service by moving away from the idea that they are a race and instead describing them as a culture. After all, if what makes a dwarf a dwarf is, for many people, its cultural trappings and appearance, then if there were a race of people who, despite being short and hairy, looked like elves or some other creature, they could still be dwarves. Or at least they could fit the niche of miners and smiths who have a fondness for axes and beer and who are stoic, dependable and just like the stone they were birthed from.

Deadly Dragons

Dragons are one of the few creatures in the modern-day fantasy racial spectrum that have the luck of duality of sentience. This means that there are stories of dragons where they're at least as sentient as humans or they're as intelligent as animals. Creatures like unicorns and griffins also suffer from this problem, but not as often as dragons do. The reasons for this lie in the origins of dragons themselves, both Eastern and Western. The two types of dragons are as different as night and day. The origins of dragons is unknown, but we should take into consideration snakes, alligators or other lizardly things, a lack of photography, vivid imaginations and dinosaur bones. Whatever its origin, though, the dragon has stamped itself firmly into the minds of people everywhere. And, of course, this has made its way into fantasy fiction. After all, what could be more fantastical than a dragon?

Eastern and Western dragons are two completely different creatures in regards to their personalities if not purpose. "In mythology both Western and Oriental dragons are reputed to be powerful and the guardians of great fortunes. (In both East and West, the figure of a dragon is commonly displayed at entrances and on doors. From its treasure-guarding activities, then, the dragon has come to be used a protective symbol.) There the similarities end. Western dragons were evil misers, while one rarely encountered an Oriental dragon without coming away with a generous gift" (Daniel Cohen, *The Encyclopedia of Monsters*, p. 264). Western dragons weren't necessarily always intelligent either, while Eastern ones always were. With the world getting smaller and the intermixing of cultures, fantasy writers are able to take the features of both kinds of dragons and mix and match to get a dragon they need for the story they want to tell.

Because of this, a dragon is one of the perfect kinds of creatures for fantasy authors to use, as readers know when the protagonists are about to encounter a dragon.[5] It's easy shorthand for the writers to give their characters a challenge or use as a measure of how powerful someone is. If a person can control or kill a dragon, they must be something to worry about. A dragon tamer is just as worrisome as a dragon killer, because the tamer might be able to sic the dragon on the protagonist.

It's the same with unicorns. Readers know that unicorns are all good—pure and almost holy creatures of magical power. How a character interacts with a unicorn tells the reader a lot about them. If someone is after a unicorn's horn and kills it, the reader knows that they're bad. If a unicorn is friendly with a person, the reader usually knows of their lack of sexual adventures. However, sometimes a unicorn detects purity of spirit as opposed to body.

This is possibly why dragon riders are such a popular trope. By riding a dragon, the character can take on some of the dragon's aspects of fierceness and power, as well as its aura of indestructibility. Dragon riders are a special caste of society, sometimes reviled but always feared. They have to be, because they're the ones associating with the large people-eating beasts, even if the dragons don't necessarily eat people. Or say they don't. Vegetarian dragons are a rarity, after all.

The interesting thing about many dragon-riding stories is the matter of choosing who becomes a dragon rider. It's not like choosing a

Eight. Fairies and Dragons and Dwarfs, Oh My!

horse to ride, especially in stories with sapient dragons. No, it's the dragon that chooses the rider. The dragon chooses the rider and something almost like a pact is made between the two of them. The dragon will give the rider prestige and power, and in return, the dragon ... gets fed dinner and someone to take care of it. It begs the question: Why does the dragon only choose one person in particular to take care of it, as opposed to hoarding a bunch of people? Why, in some stories, will dragons tie their lives to the shorter ones of humans in such a way that they'll die without the human or rider being around? The dragon most likely does the choosing because it's not going to listen to some small thing on two legs that it can eat with a snap, but that doesn't answer why dragons and their riders have to become, in some cases, life-bonded.

The life bonding comes from Anne McCaffrey's *Dragonriders of Pern* series, where the dragons are actually genetically engineered from much smaller aliens, but still dragon-like, life. Their empathy was expanded to full-out telepathy and, as a side effect, their imprinting increased as well, creating an almost overly dependent bond between dragon and human. Which, in a pseudo-scientific way, makes sense.

What *doesn't* exactly make sense is when a race of dragons, which has existed as a race of dragons long before humans showed up, suddenly decide to completely change its breeding habits and biology to accommodate riders. Or to suddenly find the perfect rider before they can hatch, even if the change means that the dragon stays in the egg for a hundred years on the off-chance that they might find someone, instead of just hatching like normal animals do and going off into the wild (which is what happens to the dragons in the *Inheritance Cycle*). Saphira says that she was waiting for Eragon, having been in the egg for about a hundred years. However, that bit of logistics is another problem altogether and is addressed in a different chapter.

Another interesting logistical problem with dragon riders and intelligent dragons comes in Novik's *Temeraire* series. Considering the lack of magic in the world and the fact that the only difference between the reader's world and the book's world is the addition of the dragons, it's strange that the dragons are sapient and able to talk. It would make more sense if they were more like animals, as that would follow the rules of "our" world, which Novik's world seems to obey otherwise. However, if Novik's dragons were just animals, a great deal of the series' plot would be nonexistent. The dragons are required to have sentience for the plot of the series to exist, even if, in terms of the setting, it doesn't make any sense for the dragons to have evolved in such ways. After all, it is a distinctly non-magical setting.

Moving on from that digression, let's look at the dragon itself and what it represents. As mentioned above, dragons can be monsters of animal intelligence or human sapience. Since they are monsters, that must mean that they should be put down; especially if they're the sort that go razing villages and stealing virgins to eat. They fill a similar role for the hero as the Evil Lord's minions except that they are a single challenge in and of themselves. The heroes will often have to fight the dragon to get some part of its horde in their quest to take down the Dark Lord. After all, dragons are known as guardians of treasure, so it makes sense that the Dark Lord would have a dragon guard his (or her) precious objects.

This leaves room for subversions of the classic scenario of the dragon guarding treasure or stealing and eating virgins. In the case of a non-intelligent dragon, it could be horribly mistreated and the protagonists could set it free instead of killing it—as Harry Potter does in *Deathly Hallows*. The heroes are still able to reach their goal, but they don't look like monsters by doing so. Instead, it makes them compassionate and more empathetic. Sure, the dragon is a fierce creature, but is a dog to be blamed for a master that mistreats it? This could lead to some problems later down the line of "well, now there's a dragon loose," but the initial action is one of sympathy and not violence.

If heroes are really clever, they may be able to get the dragon to join their side, thus gaining a new companion. If the dragon is intelligent, the dragon could be under a spell that forces it to kill people and destroy villages. This gives the hero several more problems to deal with. One, do they believe the dragon? Two, if they do believe the dragon, how do they free it from the spell? Three, if they do manage to free the dragon, how do they convince others that the dragon means no harm to others? The heroes might need to consider the third point *before* they free the dragon. After all, the dragon was just trying to kill and eat everyone!

Or the sapient dragon could be *willingly* working for the Dark Lord and the heroes could try cleverness instead of violence and convince

Eight. Fairies and Dragons and Dwarfs, Oh My!

the dragon to let them through, or even switch sides. This is probably one of the hardest tasks because dragons do find people crunchy and good with ketchup.

The dragon is always meant to be a mighty challenge. While readers may get tired of dragons getting presented in the same way, they would likely be upset if the dragons were defeated easily unless the dragons were defeated by a possible antagonist. But, in that case, it would show how much of a problem that the protagonist was going to have in the future. Otherwise, a dragon is a dragon for a reason. They are a problem.

Another purpose of the dragon is its treasure. Heroes gain treasure as a reward for their service or adventures. Defeating the dragon and rescuing the "girl" gives the hero everything they need to start their new life. They have the companionship of the girl and the treasure so that they can live their lives in comfort after having saved the world. It's their just reward and the most basic of hero stories. Defeat the dragon, get the girl, save the world and live happily ever after.

With good dragons, things are a bit different. The protagonists must still tread lightly around them, because good dragons are still dragons. But the dragon also acts as an additional resource—usually of knowledge, since dragons rarely part easily with their hordes. Having lived through centuries, dragons are ancient creatures known for accumulating things. They can act as advisors and mentors to the protagonist, carrying the added weight of millennia of wisdom. A person who can count a dragon as a friend or an advisor is someone who is quite fortunate.

Plus One Feat

There is one race that rarely gets discussed in fantasy literature, and that is the human race. Oddly, most people don't consider humans as a part of fantasy even though there are humans in almost every single fantasy novel. They are also almost always the protagonists or make some significant contribution to the story. Despite not being as long-lived as elves, as tough as dwarfs, or having any other special abilities, humans are the saviors of the world. They're strong at anything, being good or evil. They can do anything. They can be anything. This is well exemplified in games like *Dungeons and Dragons*. Looking at the character races, each description gives a suggestion as to what classes the race would favor. In the fourth edition, going through each race, dragonborn favor warlords, fighters and paladins; dwarves favor paladins, clerics, and fighters; eladrin (a more magical type of fey than the woodsy elves) favor wizards, rogues and warlords; elves favor rangers, rogues and clerics; half-elves warlords, paladins and warlocks; Halflings (the *Dungeons and Dragons* version of hobbits) favor rogues, rangers and warlocks; and tieflings (a race descended from devils and humans intermixing) favor warlock, warlord and rogue classes. Humans, however, are "able to excel at any class you choose"[6] (*Player's Handbook*, 4th ed., p. 46).

Why can humans excel at anything? Why don't they have a favored class? It would make sense that, just like other races, there would be things that they favor. Or, to reverse it, so that none of the races have a favored class. But this goes back to the idea that humans can have many different kinds of cultures but the other races only one.

This ability to excel is something else that marks those of the human race. If there is going to be a Chosen One or some sort of ability that hasn't been seen in many generations, then it's likely that a human will be that Chosen One or manifest that ability. Humans can defeat powerful creatures that no one else has been able to defeat, even though the creatures have been around for hundreds of years. Humans are creative and have imagination.

Even in stories where the main characters aren't human, humans will play a role. In the case of *The Hobbit,* for example, while Bilbo is the protagonist, it is Bard—a human—who kills the dragon Smaug. Bilbo doesn't, though he outsmarts it. Thorin doesn't, even though the dragon has destroyed his home and scattered his people. No, Bard, who has barely any emotional attachment to the dragon, does. He is the descendent of the lord of Dale, but that happened generations ago. Bard himself has had no hardship from the dragon. Smaug has been asleep his entire life.

There's an easy answer for why this is, and that's because the writers and readers are human. One of the oldest adages in writing is that you should write what you know. As writers are assumed to be human, they

Eight. Fairies and Dragons and Dwarfs, Oh My!

would know how to write humans best. And since writers are humans, they would be more inclined to have humans be the winners. In worlds where there aren't any other races, this isn't so much of a problem, but in worlds where there are other races, it does become one. It seems like there should be a way to balance out the races so that they all have equal say in the world. Or, at least, the humans shouldn't always be the dominant life forms. Perhaps because humans breed so quickly, they do become the most populous life forms around, rather like roaches, and this lets them take over. What they don't have in strength or magic or special abilities, they make up in numbers.

Often, humans are the culture or the race that is coming into their own as the elves or others start to fade away. Humans are almost always the up-and-coming new thing that the hopes of the world rest upon.

But that's because readers generally want to see humanity triumph. They're supposed to take center stage with "do everything and start everything" brilliance. Elves may be beautiful and wise, but humans have the cleverness. Dwarves might be stolid and expert smiths, but humans are innovative. Humans are what hold back the darkness. Perhaps it might be interesting to see a story where humans are the cause of the darkness and it is the other races that must band together to stop humanity for destroying everything. The question is, however, would that be as satisfying to the reader?

In a way, in books like *Twilight,* it could be assumed that with Bella's transformation into a vampire, humanity loses. Instead of turning Edward human or human-like, Bella sacrifices her own humanity to become a vampire. To her, being inhuman was more important than having Edward's love; she got married so that he would turn her into a vampire. She asked him to do so, despite him wanting her to live her life. Being human was so oppressive to her that she ached to give it up. It was the monster that did the transforming and not the man.

There are, of course, many other fantasy races, but these are the main five—all made popular by Tolkien and all sewn into the fantasy genre because of him. While he may not have created the races themselves, he created the foundation and stonework that most authors use for their creations and that they must fight against with their reading audience. While the authors can draw upon the races' previous mythological backgrounds, they are still bound by the reader's preconceptions of the races and so must find new ways to treat the same old races. The best way would be to treat them not as a single culture but instead as something as varied as humanity itself. And perhaps to treat humanity more like one of the other races: singular, good at one thing, and possibly fading.

Chapter Nine

Through the Looking Glass

Coulson: Do you remember the panic when that anti-matter meteorite landed off the coast of Miami and nearly devoured half the city?
Skye: No.
Coulson: Precisely.
—"0-8-4," *Agents of S.H.I.E.L.D.*

White Wolf Publishing Company puts out a series of role-playing games called *World of Darkness*. It's made up of several subsets, each focusing on one particular aspect of horror and fantasy fiction, such as vampires, werewolves, mages and fairies. Each subset deals with the trials of being a creature of magic and existing in the modern-day world. It often involves a lot of angst as the creatures fight against their inhuman natures, trying to prevent themselves from becoming total monsters. A big aspect of the game is preventing the "real world" from finding out about their existence. Hence, the title of the first book in the series—*Vampire: The Masquerade*. The vampires and other creatures are masquerading as humans. The important thing here is that they *must* hide. They cannot walk in the world, letting ordinary people know about them.

This is something that a great many fantasy books set on Earth have in common: magic is hidden and known to only to a select few. How it's hidden varies from series to series. In many books, the magical creatures are capable of carving their own spaces in the regular world that ordinary folk can't see or reach. Such is the case with Diagon Alley in the Harry Potter series. In other cases, there's a magical force that prevents normal people from seeing what they're actually seeing, like the Mist in the Percy Jackson series, or just plain old-fashioned glamours

The Tropes of Fantasy Fiction

worn by the magical individual. And then in a lot of cases the magical folk depend on the idea that no one will believe what they saw and, if they did believe, they wouldn't tell anyone because they'd be considered crazy. After all, not many people would believe a person who said he saw a dragon set a building on fire. It'd be much more reasonable to say that an explosion caused it. Everyone knows that dragons don't exist.

They're just things found in fantasy stories.

Fantasy isn't real.

If it were, it wouldn't be called fantasy.

The question is: why do the magical folk have to hide from everyone? The common excuse is that the masses would be frightened. People won't be able to handle the unknown and the magic suddenly appearing in their midst. Their entire world view would change and everything they knew, how they saw the world, would collapse, anarchy would reign and everything would go to pot. The normal people would rise up against the magical creatures and destroy them all.

"People fear and hate what they don't understand" is an oft-repeated refrain in quite a few movies, books and other forms of media, explaining why everyone must stay hidden. If people found out that dragons/fairies/wizards/what-have-you actually existed, they would try to exterminate them. Or they would be made into scapegoats. Many of the bigoted motives at the root of racist, anti–Semitic, anti–Islamic, and/or sexist policies support this idea. The weak have always been picked on by the strong.

And yet there's an interesting problem with this:

In a great deal of these stories, magic has always existed. The societies are hidden but have been around since long ago. They're also very good at protecting themselves from non-magical creatures. For example, in the beginning of *Harry Potter and the Prisoner of Azkaban,* Harry is working on an essay about how "witch burning in the fourteenth century was completely pointless—discuss" (Rowling, *Prisoner,* p. 1). It was pointless because when a witch or wizard was actually captured, "the witch or wizard would perform a basic Flame Freezing Charm and then pretend to shriek in pain while enjoying a gentle, tickling sensation"[1] (Rowling, *Prisoner,* p. 2). Witch burning tended to capture more non-witches than witches. Wizards are also able to teleport—or to Apparate. The only thing that seems to stop them from getting into a place by

Nine. Through the Looking Glass

Apparation is if the place is designed against it. They can even make things, such as a huge place like Hogwarts Castle, unplottable so that it can never be found on any map. With the flick of a wand, they can cause people to freeze, to float, to lose their memories and hundreds of other things.

Yet, despite all this power—power that they've had before Muggles have had firearms, the readers are led to believe—witches and wizards are the ones in hiding. This isn't to say that the wizarding world's people should be ruling over the Muggles like Voldemort and Grindelwald would like to have done (and probably others might like to do in the future). But they shouldn't have any reason to fear being integrated with non-wizards despite their smaller numbers.

In the Harry Potter universe, the wizarding society goes into hiding when the witch hunting starts to get really bad in the fifteenth century, finally "culminating with the institution of the International Statute of Wizarding Secrecy in 1689 where wizardkind voluntarily went underground" (Rowling, *Beedle*, p. 13). In that same section of *The Tales of Beedle the Bard*, it says that "genuine witches and wizards were reasonably adept at escaping the stake, block, and noose" (Rowling, *Beedle*, p. 12).

But there shouldn't be a reason for them to do so. For starters, as mentioned earlier, they do have superior firepower, including things like the Killing Curse, *Avada Kedavra*, which wasn't illegal at this point (Rowling, *Beedle*, p. 86). Also, more importantly, *wizards* weren't secret at this time. This means they hadn't been secret before and had grown up among Muggles as an everyday thing. Muggles came to them for help with aliments. They were functioning members of society. Now, admittedly, it's unknown how long wizards have existed or how they were first created or born. Rowling hasn't said what triggered the creation of magic in people. But they've clearly been around for a long time and are a force to be reckoned with. They might be in the minority, but unlike a great many minorities, they had a way to protect themselves: their magic.

This doesn't even take into account the presence of magical creatures, from unicorns and dragons to centaurs and house-elves.

So why, if the wizards were more than capable of taking care of themselves, would they need to go into hiding?

Because the stories take place in a world similar to our own. In our world's history, witches were burned. If there wasn't antagonism between the Muggles and wizards, if they didn't have to go into hiding, it's fairly likely that history would be different.

This isn't to say that magic doesn't have an effect on human history. It's not uncommon in some series for magic to be behind a great many human conflicts. In the *Percy Jackson and the Olympians* series and *Heroes of Olympus* sequel series by Rick Riordan, both World War II and the Civil War were the results of conflicts between the various half-bloods. Prohibition in the United States was punishment for Dionysus chasing after a nymph that Zeus was interested in. So, while the gods, their children and sundry monsters weren't acknowledged by the rest of the world because of the Mist—the plot device that prevents most humans from seeing magical things—they were the causes of wars and other events that greatly affected the world. As Chiron says at the end of *The Lost Hero:* "The two conflicts [the Civil War]—mortal and demigod—married each other, as they usually do in Western History. Look at any civil war or revolution from the fall of Rome onward, and it marks a time when demigods also fought one another" (Riordan, *Hero,* p. 535).

And that is the very strange conceit of most urban fantasies. The readers *must* believe that these creatures of great power have to be in hiding from humanity. Now, in some cases, there may be good reasons for it: the Fair Folk often have issues with iron, and modern-day cities are full of iron. This is one of the reasons why the elves retreated from the mortal world in Mercedes Lackey and Ellen Guon's *Urban Elves* series. But the idea that they *had* to hide from mortals is a strange disconnect for one very good reason: the mystical creatures rarely, if ever, have to hide in a secondary world fantasy. Why would they have to hide in the primary world, if not in the secondary world?

But it's not the existence of magic that causes the need for hiding, as secondary worlds prove. A wizarding school—or any sort of school where magic is taught—is not a rare occurrence in secondary fantasy worlds. *The Heralds of Valdemar* series has the Collegium. In Garth Nix's Old Kingdom trilogy, Sabriel learns how to cast Charter Magic at her boarding school—a boarding school that is in a world similar to World War I-era England.

In K. E. Mills' *Rogue Agent* series, which takes place in a world similar to our 1920s, people can learn magic by correspondence courses as

Nine. Through the Looking Glass

well as at wizarding schools. In fact, they have factories that make wizard staffs, and the airship industry is in serious trouble because the creation of portals makes travel quicker and safer. Not everyone in this world is capable of using magic, and there was a time when some wizards went bad, but the governments were able to come up with a solution that worked well for everyone. Now wizards and witches are part of everyday life. The more powerful wizards are part of the elite of society. But the less powerful wizards, like the protagonist Gerald Dunwoody at the beginning of the first book, are just clerks and beaker washers for higher and more powerful magic users.

There's No History Like the One You've Made Up

This is not to say that secondary fantasy worlds don't have any history. Authors—at least good ones—need to have some history in their worlds in order for them to feel real. After all, life and people and civilizations don't exist in a vacuum. They have to come from somewhere.

In secondary worlds, the authors can make up what they wish to reach the starting point of the story. They don't even have to know the full history of their world to start the story. Back story—and thus history—can be created as the story is told. And once the story is finished, the protagonist won't know everything that has happened in the world's past. This means that the *author* doesn't need to know about every country in existence in their world, who the rulers were from the founding of the kingdom to the point when the story begins, or what wars and rebellions were fought. The writers don't have to worry about contradicting something that is already there. They need to worry about contradicting something they've already written, but they don't have to say, "This story takes place in 1943 Britain, so I have to worry about what's happening there during World War II." They have to make sure they name the right kings and right presidents.

Since writers of secondary worlds don't have to worry about wars and other major events that might have been influenced, had magic always existed and been known about, they can have magic be an everyday, unexceptional item. It might be rare, but it's less likely that people will be surprised that it existed or that others believe in it.

Of course, the histories in the secondary world must also make sense. For this to happen, continuity, as always, is important. As messy as history is, it is always about cause and effect. One event can send things cascading off into hundreds of different directions with hundreds of different repercussions. Countries and nations will have histories with each other that will color their interactions. And time scale is always important.

For example, in the *Wheel of Time* series by Robert Jordan, the Seanchan are a nation of people who live across the sea on a continent of the same name. The rulers are descendants of one of the rulers of the Westlands, where the main story takes place. The Seanchan left the Westlands a thousand years before the story begins and have been forgotten by the people there. Yet, in the second book, *The Great Hunt,* the Seanchan come back to the Westlands with the idea of retaking it. They call it "the Return" and are often surprised when no one remembers who they are or refuse to give up their lands. As one of the Seanchan tells a trader, they think that the Westlands' people should remember the oaths "to obey, to wait, and to serve" (Jordan, *The Great Hunt,* p. 423) that their ancestors knew about. But a thousand years have passed!

One thousand years ago in our history, the Holy Roman Empire still existed, Europe was in the beginnings of the Middle Ages, and Islam was in the midst of its Golden Age. Algebra didn't exist yet, nor did the printing press—though movable type was on the horizon. And a great many people still thought the sun revolved around the Earth!

While the world of the *Wheel of Time* is stuck in the usual Medieval stasis that affects a great deal of fantasy, time and culture have moved on. No one would expect people in the real world to honor oaths that their ancestors supposedly made over a thousand years ago. Or at least no one should. History should have moved on far enough that the Seanchan should have forgotten about the Westlands themselves—at least if the way history moved in *Wheel of Time* mirrored our history.

The only reason why the Seanchan remember this is so they can, in theory, have a reason to invade the Westlands, so that they have a purpose in going beyond plain conquering. Of course, there's nothing that drives forces together more than a common cause, in this case the reclamation of ancient territory.

Beyond this digression, the thing to note here is that Jordan is trying

Nine. Through the Looking Glass

to have the history of his world affect the present. He just doesn't apply it in a logical manner. Historically speaking, a great deal should have happened in Jordan's world, and in one way, it did—with the Westlands forgetting about the Seanchan but not the other way around.

For Want of a Nail

So then it could be asked: what can happen to a story that takes place on Earth but always has had magic and it's been recognized as an everyday thing, something that exists and is proven? It can create something rather like a secondary world.

At first glance, the world presented in Jacqueline Carey's alternate history series, *Kushiel's Legacy*, is not the Earth that the readers know. Terre d'Ange is a place of exceptionally beautiful people descended from men and angels. Here, in the world of Kushiel's Legacy, history took a turn at the death of Jesus. Jesus (known as Yeshua ben Yosef) died but was not resurrected, and Christianity never conquered Roman paganism. The spread of Christianity was halted, and the miraculously begotten son of Jesus and Mary Magdalene, Blessed Elua, walked the lands instead. He settled in Terre d'Ange (land of the angels), where the human inhabitants and his angelic companions interbred and passed on his legacy, encapsulated in the teaching "Love as thou wilt" (Dominique Beth Wilson, "Counterfactual Christianity: Myth and Re-Imagined Religion in Jacqueline Carey's *Kushiel's Legacy*," p. 1). Elua was born when Yeshua's blood and Magdalene's tears mixed together in the dirt and "because their union had never been sealed, Earth Herself took pity upon them and in the damp soil She quickened the divine seed of life, and of it blessed Elua was born, and he was nurtured in the womb of Earth" (Carey website).

From this one event, history spun into a completely different direction. Beyond the historical changes caused by Christianity not becoming a major force in the world, Carey presents a world where angels actually, knowingly, exist, and six have interbred with humanity. These angels' descendants settled in what, in our world, would be France as this is where Elua tarried the longest. While the story takes place in the equivalent of our Renaissance era, the world is sufficiently alien that at first a reader may not realize that they're in an alternate history Earth. Just looking at the map itself proves it. The only familiar names would be Eire—or Ireland—and possibly Alba—Scotland—but the world of *Kushiel's Dart* encompasses all of England, which was taken from those countries' historical names. The rest, such as Skaldia, Caerdicca Unitas, Aragonia and Terre d'Ange itself, look like they could be found on any fantasy-world map, despite that there are plenty of reminders that this could very well be our world.

The Yeshuites are a good example of this. Fleeing from the Skaldi, Phèdre and Joscelin encounter a family of Yeshuites. The father wears Pe'ot, which are the side curls found on some orthodox Jewish men, and the Yeshuite family speaks Hebrew. When Josceline and Phèdre first run into them, Josceline greets them with "Barukh hatah Adonai" (*Kushiel*, p. 524), which in Hebrew means "Blessed are you, O Lord." The Yeshuites never stopped believing in the One God. However, they also believe in Jesus or Yeshua which makes them more like Jews for Jesus. Still, in a world where it's fairly factual that Jesus is the son of God, it possibly makes sense that this would happen.

Other similarities to our world are found in Alba. The rulers of Dalriada, or western Alba, live in the great hall of the Dalraida, which is described as echoing "the hall of Tea Muir in Eire" (Tara) and having "seven doors, though which one enters according to rank." Da Derga's Hostel is described as having "seven doorways into the house," and Fionn mac Cumhaill also encounters a magnificent hall with seven doors in the Palace of the Quicken Trees (Wilson, "Counterfactual," p. 254). Drustan the Cruarch is a Picti, which is the equivalent of a Pict, but in this world the Picts never became Scots and were never overrun by Romans.

By altering the history of the world, Carey has created a place where, as she says in an interview, "keeping the supernatural element grounded by myth makes it feel more organic to the setting and story. And the simple fact that much of the mythology, history, culture and geography is somewhat familiar to the reader probably helps make it seem more accessible" (Wilson, "Counterfactual," quoting Jacqueline Carey's interview with Juliet Marillier for Writer Unboxed, November 9, 2007).

As Carey's series proves, it's quite possible for magic to exist with normal humanity without any serious problems. The magic users aren't

Nine. Through the Looking Glass

forced to go into hiding or burned at the stake, because magic has always been a part of these people's lives, even though these people live on Earth. Is it possible then for magic to return to the world and live out in the open with humanity? Yes.

Shimmer and Shadows

In Laurel K. Hamilton's *Anita Blake* series, vampires and werewolves have always existed and been a part of the world's everyday life. At the start of the series, vampirism has only been legal for two years. Because of a case brought to the Supreme Court, "the court case gave us a revised version of what life was, and what death wasn't. Vampirism was legal in the good ol' US of A. We were one of the few countries to acknowledge them. The immigration people were having fits trying to keep foreign vampires from immigrating in, well, flocks" (Laurell K. Hamilton, *Guilty Pleasures*, p. 3). And this is a very interesting problem that people suddenly have. While vampires have been around and acknowledged in this world, they've never had any legal rights. Now suddenly they do. "All sorts of questions were being fought out in court. Did heirs have to give back their inheritance? Were you widowed if your spouse became undead? Was it murder to slay a vampire? There was even a movement to give them the vote. Times were changing" (Hamilton, *Guilty*, p. 3). Even before vampires were given legal status as living beings, people knew of their existence. There is a vampire district in St. Louis where tourists go for the safe thrill of meeting a vampire. After all, if vampires want to keep up the pretense that they deserve the rights they've earned, they can't go around and kill people.

Another bonus that comes with vampires being legal is the promise of eternal youth and life. In this case, it is expressed in the form of the Church of Eternal Life. "The first church in history that could guarantee you eternal life, and prove it. No waiting around. No mystery. Just eternity on a silver platter. Most people don't believe in their immortal souls anymore. It isn't popular to worry about Heaven and Hell, and whether you are an absolutely good person. So the Church was gaining followers all over the place. If you didn't believe that it destroyed your soul, what did you have to lose? Daylight. Food. Not much to give up" (Hamilton,

Guilty, p. 93). Of course, Anita also points out that vampires can still die and then what happens to a person's soul afterward?

This is an interesting aspect and effect of a world where vampires are out of the shadows. They are able to increase their numbers by, basically, advertising the good points of being a vampire. In this way, people willingly come to them and no one can do anything about it, as long as they are of legal age.

Other benefits that come with having the monsters out in the open are the uses of zombies. In Anita's world, they aren't always shambling mindless creatures. If raised soon after they're dead, they can almost pass for human and speak. This allows lawyers to do things like settle contested wills and have zombies give testimony in court cases.

Though not every kind of supernatural creature is welcomed as readily in her world. Lycanthropy is considered to be a disease on par with AIDS and, like people with AIDS, they're discriminated against, even though legally they can't be. Also, full-blooded fey aren't allowed into the United States, though those with fey ancestry can immigrate.

And while the series appears to slowly devolve into plotless porn as it progresses, the world Hamilton has created is a world without a mask and explores the possibilities within it. People deal with the creatures in the night with common sense and laws. Humanity may be afraid of them, but the vampires and others want to survive and flourish as much as the humans. This gives humans the advantage. They offer the vampires status as near-equals and, in return, the vampires police themselves, lest they lose this privilege.

Another take on the unmasked world can be found in the popular role-playing game *Shadowrun*. In-game, in the year 2011, magic returned to the world. The world was already dissolving into chaos when "suddenly a percentage of children all around the world were born 'deformed.' Many people called these babies mutants; others called them elves and dwarfs, for that was exactly what they resembled" (Boyle, *Shadowrun*, p. 25). Then the great dragon Ryumyo appeared over Mount Fuji. Called the Awakening, huge storms of magic wrecked the globe, though they resurged the power of old magical sites like the standing stones in Britain. Game play starts—in the fourth edition—about sixty years later. In this world, meta-human (all player races besides humans) and human relations are as smooth as racial relations in the real world. There's a

Nine. Through the Looking Glass

positive quality called "human-looking" that allows elves, dwarfs and orks to pass for human in most cases (Boyle, p. 78) and a negative quality called "elf poser" that humans can take that lets them look like elves, because elves are Just That Cool. However, "real elves consider them an embarrassment, many humans think of them as sellouts, and even the other metatypes generally consider posers to be pathetic" (Boyle, p. 81).

And yet somehow society functions with the meta humans and other mythological creatures in its midst. The UCAS—the remains of the United States and Canada after the major computer crash in 2029—elected a dragon as its president.[2] Even though Dunkelzahn was assassinated at his inaugural ball, he was still elected. There are other problems with the society—like the fact that mega-corporations are practically their own sovereign nations, a great deal of the environment is going to the pits, and Chicago has been infested with insects that want to take over people's minds. These sorts of problems make the fact that magic exists in and of itself a bit of a minor thing.

Perhaps it's easier to do such a thing because the change happens at the modern point and is completely global. But these creatures have come out from the shadows and found some sort of acceptance and magic has been assimilated into the society. So it's fairly reasonable to believe that such a thing could happen in any other sort of urban fantasy. It's not necessary for the mask to continue. In theory, there would be upheaval, but eventually it would settle down.

Instant Disguise: Just Add Glasses

In various comic book series, such a thing has happened. The appearance of superheroes and villains are almost everyday fare in the DC and Marvel universes. They appeared—depending on the continuity—relatively recently and have earned mixed responses. In the DC universe, they've been welcomed mostly with open arms. People aren't afraid of Superman or Wonder Woman; they look up to them as celebrities. Some characters, like Booster Gold, have been paid to endorse products as a way to earn a living. Superheroes in the Marvel Universe don't always have it so easy. Characters like Spider-Man and the various and sundry X-Men are more often than not feared and hated rather than looked up to. It's hard to imagine any newspaper in the DC universe calling Superman a menace unless the accusation was in an editorial written by Lex Luthor, yet this is a common problem for Spider-Man.

On the other hand, despite the openness of the inhabitants in comic book worlds to the strange, magical and heroic, there is still a masquerade going on—literally. Almost every superhero in both universes, as well as others, wears some form of facial covering. Spider-Man wears a full facial mask, while Hal Jordan (Green Lantern) just has the domino mask. Superman wears a mask as well, though it's in his civilian identity; as Clark Kent, he wears glasses.

This masquerade is similar to the masquerade used in fantasy books where the supernatural creatures hide. If the masquerade is to hide for safety, then the superheroes must hide in plain sight for the protection and safety of those around them. When Peter Parker told the world that he was Spider-Man, for example, his Aunt May was targeted by one of Spider-Man's villains, the Kingpin, and almost fatally shot, in *Amazing Spider-Man* #538. And this led to the even more unfortunate *One More Day* storyline where Peter Parker and Mary Jane's marriage was erased from existence when Peter made a deal with Mephisto, Marvel's version of the Devil, to save Aunt May's life. Had Peter never revealed himself, then the villains wouldn't be able to hunt down his family using ordinary means and then hire people to kill them. In such a world, where superpowered individuals exist and they have no officially sanctioned superpowered police force, it makes sense that those that become superheroes keep their identities secret. It's the only way they can keep their families safe.

Those few superheroes who don't have secret identities, like Aquaman or Iron Man or the Fantastic Four, have the means to protect those they love by themselves. Aquaman is the king of Atlantis (most of the time) and, even more, he's a member of a race that lives in the depths of the oceans, which makes him a member of a superpowered—compared to humans—race. If someone wanted to hurt him, they would have to get down to Atlantis and hope that their equipment holds out, and that's only for starters. Tony Stark is insanely rich and a genius inventor. He also doesn't have much in the way of family, so he's able to build inventions that keep him safe and doesn't have to worry about people threatening his loved ones. As for the Fantastic Four, they have

Nine. Through the Looking Glass

Reed Richard's insane genius as well as the other three members' powers to protect them. They are able to create a place where Reed and Sue's two children Franklin and Valeria Richards can be safe from supervillain attacks. So, those heroes with the capabilities to protect themselves, usually because of money or station in life, are able to go without the mask while others aren't and thus must keep themselves hidden. There is no mask on the world itself, but instead the heroes use the mask in the same way that an undercover cop does: to keep their families safe.

For a writer, one of the biggest benefits of the masquerade is the additional layer of conflict it adds to the story. With the magical world hidden and forced to remain so, the characters have to worry about things like the magical authorities—the White Council in *The Dresden Files,* for example—coming down upon the protagonists' heads and causing more problems. They have to make sure they're not seen, lest the wrong people, like the government that usually knows about these things but keeps them covered up, come looking for them or hurt others. It restricts their movements to places they can and can't go, lest someone see them. With this problem always lingering in the background, the readers have an unexpected bit of tension running through their minds.

When things are hidden, it creates a better illusion for the reader. It lets them imagine things like, "Well, maybe this could be happening here." It lets the readers blur the line of reality. Since mundane people in the book world don't see anything happening, what's to say that the strange things that happen in the real world aren't because of the same reasons? That creaking and thumping happening in the walls, that funny smell that is always around this one particular building, that funny-looking guy wandering the street ... who's to say if they're just strange things or something else that mundane people can't know or see?

In a lot of primary-world cases it would make sense for the world to be unmasked, but it is easier for authors to make it masked. It saves them from having to rewrite world history in many cases and adds that extra layer of tension in all cases. The meta-textual conflict is forgiven for the sake of ease and story. It's a device that most people don't think about when reading primary-world fantasy and comparing it to secondary world fantasy. The two worlds are extremely divided and different enough that readers don't connect the idea that since magic is accepted in the secondary world, it should be accepted in the primary world. They accept the mask without question and without realizing it. It's easier for them to accept the idea of the hidden world because it reflects the world they know, thus letting them suspend disbelief in the story as well as giving them hope that maybe that secret world really does exist in ours, too.

Chapter Ten

The Fundamentals

> Is this you? Are you happily engrossed in inconsequential cartoon trivia? To the point that your socks can probably stand by themselves? Well, if you are, there's hope, there's help. There's the Please, Please, Please Get a Life Foundation!
> —Yakko Warner in the "Please, Please, Please Get a Life Foundation" episode of *Animaniacs*

Writers and teachers often discuss the most important elements in creating a story. They bring up the plot, the setting and the characters as the three fundamental and essential things needed to create a good story. The three of them spin together to create a story. They don't always need to be equal to make it enticing to an audience. One could argue that the *Star Wars* series has serious flaws when it comes to story and characters—especially in prequel episodes—but the setting itself is amazing. The world and cultures that George Lucas created in the original trilogy were fascinating and made the viewers want to be a part of the movies' world. The plot itself, especially in *Star Wars: A New Hope*, was basic: Luke Skywalker was going through the Hero's Journey.

Yet there is something even more basic and fundamental to writing that most people don't necessarily realize is there but people will notice and complain and nitpick about if it's absent from a story, and that is continuity. Without it, nothing in a story holds together or makes sense.

World building is one of a fantasy writer's hardest jobs. Many people say that writing fantasy is easy; you just have to make everything up. But that's exactly what makes writing fantasy, especially secondary-world fantasy, hard. The writers have to make *everything* up, from what sorts of creatures inhabit the world to the number of moons a world has. They can't Google or visit the locations they want to describe. They can't look up the history of a country or of racial interactions between dwarves and elves. They can't go to a restaurant or ask a friend to see what a crokal tastes like. They can't even find a picture of what a crokal *looks* like. While they can use some real-world references for cultures or religions and science, they have to be careful in how they're used. Otherwise, the writers get accused of things like, "Oh, they're just Romans with pointy ears" or "That's just Christianity but they worship a woman." When they borrow parts of a culture and its quirks, they have to make sure that they change it enough so that the audience won't recognize it for what it used to be. Unless the resemblance to the borrowed culture is done intentionally, as in Butcher's *Codex Alera* series. They are basically playing God when they create a world.

And just like in the real world, secondary worlds *must* have rules. Not only that, but these rules *must* be consistent. There must be continuity. If there isn't any, then the seams in the world are evident and the illusion of story is broken. Continuity is how stories reflect the real world. People don't change overnight in the real world, their opinions shifting from one extreme to the other. The rules of how gravity works or how cats act don't change overnight. A person's natural hair color or eyes won't change suddenly (beyond dyeing or special contact lenses). By creating an illusion of reality with these basic ideas that reflect the real world, the author is free to create the new and spectacular elements. But even the new and spectacular elements must be continuous. Otherwise, they won't match what happens in the real world. Because of this freedom, a fantasy writer has to be even more alert to contradictions in their continuity and watch out for those errors.

There are several different kinds of continuity errors, some more forgivable than others, though all of them will likely be nitpicked by fans. Errors can come from the world building and the characters. Sometimes errors are made accidentally—which can happen in large series that can fill several book shelves or many seasons—or intentionally, for plot purposes. The latter is worse than the former. However, it's unreasonable to expect a person to be completely familiar with every single *Doctor Who* episode or read of every appearance of Wolverine. And even in those cases, there are bound to be contradictions because different writers have different ideas on how to handle characters and set-

Ten. The Fundamentals

ting. And even in lengthy series written by a single author, there are bound to be continuity errors ... though a good author will have a friend or friends look over things to catch continuity problems.

Big Gaffs, Little Gaffs

While it may seem like any continuity issue could be considered a negative mark against the author, indicating that he or she doesn't care enough about the world to make it the same throughout, some problems can be forgiven. Little errors don't always impact the rest of the series, or even the rest of the story.

One forgivable error is a minor character detail that changes between, say, the first book and the rest of the series. With first books, the authors may not have the full details of the world and story they're creating settled. In Anne McCaffrey's very first book about the Dragonriders of Pern, *Dragonflight*, we're introduced to Lytol, a craftsman who later becomes the Lord Warder for Ruatha's underaged, just-born Lord Jaxom. Lytol used to ride dragons himself, with a dragon named Larth. The first time he is mentioned he is said to be "a green rider from S'lel's wing" (McCaffrey, *Dragonflight*, p. 16). Also, Larth is a male dragon when it's later shown that all green dragons are female. However, beyond that one mention, whenever Larth is brought up, he is said to be a brown dragon, not a green one. Even *Dragonflight*'s Dragondex, found at the back of the book, mentions Larth as a brown dragon (McCaffrey, *Dragonflight*, p. 299), though the dragondex was written about ten years later, after several other books in the series were written.

Now, there are several reasons as to why Larth was changed from a green dragon to a brown dragon. Green dragons, at the time of the first book, are only impressed by gay men. It could be, then, that McCaffery didn't wish for Lytol to be gay. Attitudes at the time that the books were initially written weren't favorable to homosexuals; she might not have felt comfortable having such a major character identified as such. Or it could just be that she forgot the color of the dragon and never thought it important enough to look up. After all, Larth is dead and never shown onscreen. Lytol never has any sort of romance throughout the series and so his sexuality isn't confirmed or contradicted. As Larth's color is kept consistently brown throughout the rest of the series, it becomes nothing more than a piece of trivia for really devoted fans.

Harry Potter and the Sorcerer's Stone, however, has a huge scattering of potentially damaging inconsistencies. While Rowling's world has never been great about continuity, the first book is sprinkled with things that the characters—especially the wizarding ones—should have known. Even in the first book! Two examples come up rather quickly once Harry gets to the train station. One involves Molly Weasley and the other involves her son, Ron. When Harry is trying to find platform nine and three-quarters, he overhears a woman asking, "Now, what's the platform number?" (Rowling, *Sorcerer*, p. 92), followed by Ginny giving the proper number. The problem with this is that while this is Ron's first year at Hogwarts. Molly has five older boys, all of whom have gone to or are still going to Hogwarts. The platform number doesn't change at all throughout the entire series. Even in the epilogue that jumps ahead to when Harry is an adult with children of his own, the platform number is the same. And it's more than likely that the platform number was the same when Molly was going to Hogwarts as well. So why would she need to be reminded of the platform number?

Then, once on the train itself, when Ron and Harry are talking, Ron mentions that George and Fred taught him a spell to change his pet rat Scabber's fur yellow. The spell is nothing like they learn later in the book. The one he recites is "Sunshine, daisies, butter mellow, turn this stupid fat rat yellow" (Rowling, *Sorcerer*, p. 105). Since Ron is from a pureblood wizarding family—he mentions that the only Muggle (which should be actually be called an Squib) in the family might be an accountant[1]—he must see (and does see) his family cast spells all the time. So he would know that what his brothers told him wasn't an actual spell. Wizard spells in the Potterverse often tend to be one or two words that are somewhat Latin-sounding such as *Accio,* which brings things to the caster; *Expelliarmus,* which causes something that the caster is pointing at to fly away from its owner; and *Lacarnum Inflamari* which sends a ball of fire at the target. All of which are quite different than the spell that Ron uses, which sounds like a nursery rhyme. If someone had told *Harry* it was a spell, then it would have made more sense as, in the first book, he is ignorant of the rules of how magic works. This

Ten. The Fundamentals

spell is never mentioned again. It's an odd thing—as if Rowling had written it before realizing exactly how she wanted magic spells to be cast.

And then there's the use of the word "Muggle." While talking to people after dinner at his first day of Hogwarts, Neville Longbottom mentions that his family thought he might be "all-Muggle for ages" (Rowling, *Sorcerer*, p. 125). As he is a pure-blooded wizard, there is no way that he could be all-Muggle. After all, Muggles are those with no magic and not from wizarding families. Hermione is Muggleborn, for example. No one in her family has any magic. The correct term for someone from a magical family with no magic is a "Squib." The term Squib first appeared in *Harry Potter and the Chamber of Secrets*, referring to Argus Filch, the caretaker of Hogwarts from about 1973 on. He believes that Harry has petrified Mrs. Norris, his pet cat, because he's a Squib.

> "He did it, he did it!" Filch spat, his pouch face purpling. "You know what he wrote on the wall! He found—in my office—he knows I'm a—I'm a—" Filch's face worked horribly. "He knows I'm a Squib!"
>
> "I never touched Mrs. Norris!" Harry said loudly, uncomfortably aware of everyone looking at him, including all the Lockharts on the walls. "And I don't even know what a Squib is" [Rowling, *Chamber*, p. 142].

Later on, Ron explains that "a Squib is someone who was born into a wizarding family but hasn't got any magical powers. Kind of the opposite of Muggle-born wizards, but Squibs are quite unusual" (*Chamber*, p. 145). Squibs are most definitely not Muggles, so Ron should have never called that accountant second cousin a Muggle, nor should Neville say that his family was worried that he'd turn out to be a Muggle. However, it's clear that in *Sorcerer's Stone* Rowling hasn't completely figured out how the wizarding society works.

Throughout the rest of the books, there are more continuity issues but they're generally ignored because they're small things and the way Rowling presents the Wizarding world is rather like a fairy-tale land where things don't always make sense. To enter it, after all, Harry must step through portals and go into places that Muggles can't ever find.

In stories where the world isn't as fantastical or like fairy tales, the constant changes in setting would be harder to take.

Changes

Setting-change problems that are harder to take can be found in Kevin Herne's fourth book of *The Iron Druid Chronicles: Trapped*. This book skips forward twelve years into the future. The first books take place in the modern-day world, the actual first book, *Hounded*, being published in 2011. And there's nothing in it to indicate that it isn't 2011. The last book before the time skip appears to take place around 2012. That should make it 2024, when *Trapped* begins. However, nothing within the book indicates that it *is* 2024. Nor is there anything in the previous books that indicate that they take place earlier than 2011. While there is nothing wrong with jumping twelve years forward, it brings its own special challenges, especially since it takes place in the primary world. The world would have changed a great deal, from technology to culture to politics.

Technological progress has been moving rapidly lately in the past twenty to thirty years. There are things that existed in 2011 that didn't exist in 2001 and things in 2001, like floppy disks, that were considered obsolete in 2011. In 2001, Facebook, Twitter and the iPhone didn't exist.[2] And yet in 2011 they were ubiquitous and almost-necessary parts of many people's lives. The iPhone 4 became one of people's most-used camera devices in 2011. *PC* magazine reported in 2011 that the iPhone 4 was the most-used camera on the website Flickr. "The data is based on the types of devices members use to upload photos to Flickr. The iPhone 4's five-megapixel camera recently leapfrogged the Nikon D90 to become Flickr's top camera" (Leslie Horn, "The iPhone 4 Is Officially the Most Popular Camera on Flickr," *PC*, posted June 22, 2011). Facebook had over one billion users by 2012. Tablets were things from *Star Trek* and other science fiction series in 2001.

It makes sense, then, to believe that technology would have leap-frogged even further in the twelve years between *Tricked* and *Trapped*. Google Glasses might have gotten off the ground; people would have cell-phone watches; self-driving cars would be on the market. But none of these sorts of changes are found within the world of *Trapped*. The world is still recognizable as today's. If the books didn't say that they had skipped ahead twelve years, it'd be impossible to tell.

Now while technological stasis is almost inevitable and expected

Ten. The Fundamentals

in most secondary-world fantasy books, it's not something that is realistic in primary-world books. Since they have to mimic the real world as well as add fantasy elements, they have to keep an eye on the changes and progress made in the real world. This is especially important in a series like the *Iron Druid Chronicles*, where Atticus has no issue working with technology. Harry Dresden doesn't know much about modern-day technology because his magic interferes with it. While he is up with some things in modern-day culture—like eBay—likely from friends, he can't use things like cell phones, computers or even go into hospitals for fear of ruining the more delicate equipment. The same problem applies to the Harry Potter series, where magic ruins how Muggle technology works. The worlds of the Dresdenverse and the Potterverse are much more insular than the one Atticus runs in.

While most people wouldn't notice that there was a lack of technological advancement in the twelve-year time skip—after all, they're reading a fantasy novel, not a science fiction book—it's still somewhat sloppy writing. The fact that the story has skipped twelve years into the future is jarring enough, but it's hard to believe that it really *is* the future. If there isn't going to be any indication that the story is set in the future, what's the point of setting it in the future?

In this case, it's to skip ahead to when Granuaile can get her druidic tattoos. It takes twelve years to train to become a druid. This isn't necessarily a bad reason; it's just important to remember the implications that go with skipping ahead into the future.

Doing What I Want

Characterization is one of the trickier things to worry about when dealing about continuity because characters are one of the few things that are *expected* to change and grow throughout the stories. If they *don't* change, it's considered to be a bad thing. After all, real people change and grow through their experiences, so it's natural to expect characters to do so. In some ways, that's the point of a story, to see how a character changes and grows. Everything around them facilitates their hopeful growth.

However, sometimes characters do stupid things for the necessity of the plot. The writer needs them to hold the "idiot ball" so that the

The Tropes of Fantasy Fiction

story can progress. If the characters had the smarts they're supposed to have, they likely wouldn't do what they do. This is something that happens a lot in comedies to facilitate the plot but it can, of course, happen in other kinds of stories.

This is the case with October Daye in *Rosemary and Rue* by Seanan McGuire. In the prologue of the book, October (or Toby, as she prefers to be known) had been turned into a fish for about fourteen years. The book proper starts with her working the night shift at a Safeway which she'd chosen "because it was so far away from the likely haunts of the people I'd known in my other life" (McGuire, *Rosemary*, p. 16). However, it's not far enough away from those haunts, because within paragraphs one of those people shows up at her checkout stand—someone whom she'd grown up with and had clearly run into before, as he'd previously given her his phone number.

If Toby didn't want to have any contact with her former life, then why did she stay where people from that life could reach her? Why did she stay in San Francisco? If, as she claimed, she truly didn't want the contact, to the point where she actively ignored any overtures that an old friend was making towards her, why was she close enough for that to happen? She could have left the city and gone somewhere else, from Sacramento to Los Angeles to New York. The United States is a large place; even for someone who is fourteen years behind the times, there are plenty of places to go.

Why doesn't she leave? For plot reasons. If she wasn't in San Francisco, then Countess Evening Winterrose probably wouldn't have contacted her for help. If the countess hadn't been able to contact her, hoping that she'd get there in time, Toby wouldn't have been drawn back into the world of Faerie, causing her emotional problems and angst and, well, the plot of trying to solve who killed Winterrose. This is basically the point of the first book: Toby being dragged back into the world of Faerie and solving the murder. Had she been sensible and moved anywhere else, the likelihood of it happening would have decreased dramatically. So she clutches onto that idiot ball and stays where she can be easily found.

Toby suffers a lot from writer-forced plot problems. This isn't the same as problems caused by the plot of the story. Those are what characters confront when dealing with the problem they're trying to solve.

Ten. The Fundamentals

Toby also suffers from lack of growth and change. This is another form of continuity problem, because she's expected to change over the course of the series, considering what happens to her. However, she always ends up back in the stasis of the series' beginning. The best example is in *One Salt Sea*. At the end of *Late Eclipses,* Toby was given the knowe, a space made in Fairy by one of the elves, of the late Winterrose. Suddenly, she had a great responsibility thrust upon her. After all, taking care of a knowe is no easy task. These are semi-intelligent habitations that are reluctant to take orders from anyone except their owners, and Toby must prove that she is up to the task of ruling it, as well as taking care of the people who live there.

This is a massive change and should completely turn her life around. No longer would she have to live in a small apartment, worrying about making the rent. Now she would have other problems, with people depending on her to give them a safe home. These are great responsibilities and, considering her active and often dangerous life and line of work, it would greatly impact those around her and those who depend on her.

But at the end of the book, what does she do? She fobs off the responsibility to someone else. As she says, "I never asked to join the nobility. It's not something I'm prepared for. But the sons of Saltmist ... they *have* been prepared. They've been trained. Patrick Lorden was a noble of the land before he left for the Undersea. I propose Goldengreen be granted to Dean Lorden, to bring unity to the land and sea" (McGuire, *One Salt Sea,* p. 340). While it's definitely true that she is using this as an opportunity to help unite the land and the sea realms in the San Francisco area, it's also true that she's using it as an opportunity to get rid of the responsibility of taking care of Goldengreen. She says she never asked to join the nobility, but sometimes responsibilities drop into peoples' laps and they have to learn to deal with them. How the characters deal with them shows what sort of people they are. In this case, she's running away.

While this could be considered a character trait of Toby's, it contradicts what the book says she's supposed to be like. (That is, someone who cares about people and feels responsible for them.) She told Lily at the end of *Late Eclipses* that she would take care of the changelings who depended on her and her knowe since Lily died. She didn't want the responsibility, but she would take it.

"A choice needed to be made. I could tell her 'no.' I could tell her I'd done everything I could to take care of them, I had problems of my own, I had the Queen of the Mists gunning for me and a possible death sentence hanging over my head. I could tell her that Lily didn't possibly think I could really save them."

"Yeah," I said, looking from her to Walther. He was smiling like the sun. "Has either of you been to Goldengreen?" [McGuire, *Late Eclipses*, p. 359].

So she'd made her choice to take care of them in Goldengreen, the knowe she'd been given. And yet, one book later, she gives them to someone else to take care of. What this shows is backwards character growth. Instead of going forward with taking care of Goldengreen, she goes back to her small apartment, just like she'd been at the beginning of the book. She's been reset, similar to the end of most sitcom episodes. Now, at the start of the next book, she can have the same worries about laundry and making rent that she had at the start of this book ... as opposed to an entirely new set of problems.

Now, is this a bad thing? Yes and no. By moving Toby into the role of countess, she is taken away from her role of gritty private investigator who wants no one to depend on her and needs no one to help her. Rather like Sam Spade or Philip Marlowe from the old hard-boiled detective genre. The back of *Rosemary and Rue* even has a blurb by T.A. Pratt comparing the writing to Raymond Chandler. Since hard-boiled detectives aren't supposed to have an easy life, it would be against Toby's character as a hard-boiled detective to live in a fancy castle-like thing.

On the other hand, it also could show that Toby feels like the best way to take care of the people she was given is to hand them off to someone else who knows how to rule and run things. It might have worked better if Toby had indicated that she was still going to be somewhat involved with taking care of Goldengreen, but it could just be her way of making sure everything is as taken care of as possible.

You Are Here

In many ways, settings are like characters themselves. In his introduction to the book on setting, Jack Bickham says that setting "is not merely the physical backdrop of the tale. It may also include the historical background and cultural attitudes of a given place and time, the

Ten. The Fundamentals

mood of a time, and how the story people talk" (Bickham, *Scene & Structure*, p. 1). However, instead of *may*, it's more like a setting *does*. It's required to have these things so that the reader can get a full sense of the world around the characters, especially those in non-Earth worlds. The setting is where the characters live, and characters, much like people in real life, do not live in an empty, blank space. Unless, perhaps, they're mimes. Writers, as mentioned earlier, need to keep this in mind, as it concerns what their characters have and do. It also can give the lie to what they say. In some ways, it can make the viewpoint character unreliable, but that's not usually the intention when things within a setting go awry or become contradictory.

In Lisa Tuttle's book *Writing Science Fiction and Fantasy*, she describes such an incident: "Here's an example I remember from a workshop many years ago. The story was set in an overcrowded, polluted near-future. The main character came back to her tiny apartment from work, had a meagre [sic] meal of tofu and rice, and took a bath. She lay there soaking, mourning lost comforts as she thought about food shortages, power outages, etc. Someone else in the workshop pointed out that given this background, soaking in a hot bath was an improbable luxury. It would be more likely—and make the future seem more real—for her to wash herself in a few inches of tepid water, which her husband would then use for his bath, following which the water would be carefully stored or put through a purifier for reuse" (Tuttle, p. 39).

This is also what happens in Suzanne Collins's *The Hunger Games*. In the beginning, the protagonist, Katniss Everdeen, complains constantly about how she and her family are constantly poor and hungry. But nothing in the setting seems to indicate it. She and her family appear to get enough to eat. Even then, it would be possible to get more food as her sister, Prim, has a goat and other people around have goats. Prim could breed her goat with another person's and then have two goats. And from the two goats, she could make more cheese and get more milk, which she could sell. And from there, she could get another goat and maybe some chickens. With chickens, she could get eggs, sell the eggs and the milk and the cheese and butter, and so on.

There's no reason for her not to do this except to make things desperate for Katniss and her family, to make them seem worse off and to make the reader feel sympathy. Katniss needs to be made the underdog;

the readers need to see that she has absolutely no chance in winning. They will thus be rooting for her when she gets into the games and starts being clever.

Of course, that doesn't explain why Katniss hasn't gotten a job after her father died. Her sister has a small business of selling cheese and milk; her mother has a small apothecary and she's apparently quite brilliant at healing people and bringing them out of depression. Which also begs the question: if Katiniss' mother is so good at helping people, why isn't she making more money? The readers are told that Katniss could be executed for poaching and then that she's her family's only breadwinner. So it would make more sense for her to try and get a job rather than to poach and risk her life. There's no reason given for why she can't get a job. She might be in school ... but why does she have to stay there? And why would the Capitol even *want* the children in District Twelve to be educated? It's a waste of resources if they're just going to be miners. But if she did get a job, Katniss wouldn't be super-awesome at archery. Which is what she uses to save her life in the Arena. So, while there is no foundation for her not being able to get a job, she *can't* get a job, because otherwise she wouldn't be super-awesome at archery and be able to survive in the Arena.

And then there's District Twelve. It's a mining district. The miners have to go deep into the ground since they're in the Appalachians and they've been mining coal there for hundreds of years. Mines, especially the ones as deep as District Twelve's, would require a lot of electricity to run, and yet Katniss says that "we're lucky to get two or three hours of electricity in the evenings" (Suzanne Collins, *The Hunger Games*, p. 5). And since she's discussing the electric fence that's supposed to keep her inside of the district, it seems as if she's speaking about the district as a whole that doesn't get electricity for more than two or three hours at night.

So how are the mines run? Since they're digging up coal for the entire country, it would be poor production to *not* use electricity. That doesn't even raise the concept of alternative energy sources. Are solar or wind or hydraulic power not available in other places? It would seem that in a world where people can create mutants, it would make sense that they would be using some sort of alternative energy sources.

Finally, there are the games themselves. Why do the parents allow

Ten. The Fundamentals

them to happen? Parents have done amazing and incredibly stupid things to protect their children, and yet these parents just stand there without doing anything. They should have done something years ago to prevent the games. And yet they just let their children go. Why do the participants themselves fight? What would happen if they just refused to fight and kill each other? It would make for lousy games, certainly. But it would be more realistic and more human.

The people in the series don't act like real people. The parents allow their children to be taken away without a cry of protest. Peeta's father doesn't make a sound when Peeta's name is called, even though he's supposed to be the kindly parent. Because, apparently "[f]amily devotion only goes so far for most people on reaping day" (Collins, *Hunger*, p. 26). When Katniss sees Peeta crying, she doesn't think he's doing it because he's actually frightened and doesn't want to go but instead that it must be his strategy for surviving in the games. "To appear weak and frightened, to reassure the other tributes that he is no competition at all, and then come out fighting … [b]ut this seems an odd strategy for Peeta Mellark because he's a baker's son. All those years of having enough to eat and hauling bread trays around have made him broad-shouldered and strong. It will take an awful lot of weeping to convince anyone to overlook him" (Collins, *Hunger*, p. 41). Because he could just not want to be there and not want to kill. This idea seems horribly foreign to Katniss; she seems remarkably comfortable with the idea that she has to kill other people. She just hopes she doesn't have to kill Peeta … but only because he was kind to her when she needed help.

But these are afterthoughts. It's the situation of the story, the grander setting which is unusual enough that readers want to keep on reading. When *The Hunger Games* was first published in 2008, there weren't very many books featuring dystopian futures where children were forced to kill each other for the amusement of others. It wasn't another quest for destroying an evil overlord. It didn't feature robots taking over the world. It wasn't vampires or other supernatural creatures. It was different enough to catch people's attention.

With this idea as the focus of the story, however, other things get left behind. Readers believe in the torment of Katniss, but they don't have time to dwell on how horrible her real life actually is because she's swiftly taken away from it. The setting is only hinted at. Katniss tells the readers that her life is horrible and that she's miserable, and since the story is in her point of view, readers will take her word for it, busily trying to see what happens as the story progresses. They're so caught up in the newness of the situation that they don't always see the holes in story and setting.

However, there's still a conflict between what the characters say and what actually is. The text of the world should reflect what Katniss says or Katniss' words should reflect the world around her. It's quite possible to still feel sorry for her because she is poor or because she's worried about her sister. It's still possible to wonder if she'll make it through the games without having to feel sorry for her being poor. The supposed suffering just adds an extra sort of kicker to the readers to make them feel for her.

So, while the entire story is built upon a fundamentally flawed and unrealistically built setting, the story couldn't exist without it.

In creating a setting, however, one doesn't need to approach it as Tolkien did with hard-lined, obsessive detailing. C.S. Lewis, much to Tolkien's dismay, was hardly exact. "Lewis disregarded Tolkien's exacting formula for making a 'secondary world.' Narnia was not self-enclosed and consistent. It lifted figures and motifs in whole cloth from a motley assortment of national traditions, making no effort to integrate them into any coherent mythos. Tolkien had carefully revised later editions of *The Hobbit* to remove a reference to tomatoes (if Middle-Earth is meant to be an early version of Europe, then tomatoes, a New World import, would be anachronistic), while Lewis thought nothing of giving Mrs. Beaver a sewing machine!" (Laura Miller, *The Magician's Book: A Skeptic's Adventures in Narnia*, p. 244).

While it might be highly anachronistic to give Mrs. Beaver a sewing machine in a place that doesn't even have factories or a way to make them, and thus sloppy world building on Lewis' part, sloppier writing than even the goats in *The Hunger Games*, it has one thing in its favor. It's a sewing machine that belongs to a *beaver*. Beavers can't talk, much less wear clothes, much less use sewing machines to make clothes to wear. Since the beavers *can* talk and *can* wear clothes, the sewing machine helps create the setting of the mystical, magical place that is Narnia. It is a land of fairy tales, as Miller pointed out; Lewis had no problems stealing things from everywhere to create his land. Talking

Ten. The Fundamentals

animals are familiar from fairy tales and fables. Since the *Chronicles of Narnia* are essentially fables, it makes sense within the setting of Narnia for beavers to be able to talk, wear clothes, and even use sewing machines.[3]

The previous two examples discussed initial world building issues and how some worlds have foundational problems. But sometimes culture and identity change in a series for no explicit reason beyond The Author Says So. In *Eragon,* the first book of the *Inheritance* series, elves are treated with a sort of mysterious air. Eragon knows little about them beyond the fact that they were dragon riders, they could speak the ancient language and they could use magic. Nothing indicates that they ever had anything to do with the Palancar Valley and Carvahall. For Eragon, they're like Tolkien's traditional elves: wise, all-knowing, powerful, beautiful and mysterious.

But in *Inheritance,* something completely different happens. One of the Carvahall women gives birth to a child with a catlip. It's possible for Arya to easily heal the baby; however, she does not. "If I rework the child's appearance, people will say I have stolen her and replaced her with a changeling" (Paolini, *Inheritance,* p. 69). The type of elf that this describes is completely different than the one in the previous books. This is more like the Fae and Sidhe, who are known to steal children, as opposed to Tolkien's elves. It's also more than likely that Eragon would have mentioned such a connection to the elves when he was originally trying to remember what they were like way back in *Eragon.* After all, stealing children is a rather large and important detail to remember about a people. This is a problematic change for the series, as it completely turns around how people thought of the elves earlier in the series. It's unlikely that they would be so happy to have elves protecting them as dragon riders or to have dragon riders themselves be considered such good and honorable people if elves were known for stealing children.

So, why did the villagers suddenly distrust Arya?

Because Paolini wanted Eragon to heal the baby's harelip.

In previous books, it was mentioned that Arya—and elves in general—were better healers, so it would make sense for her to be the one to heal the baby. Eragon even points that out. So Paolini needed another reason to explain why Eragon had to heal the baby. A good reason, if one were to look at the mythology of the elves, would be that they steal children. This would be a legitimate reason for the villagers to not trust Arya. It also makes sense because one of the criticisms of the elves in the *Inheritance* trilogy is that they were too much like Tolkien's elves. By doing this, Paolini was trying to distance himself from Tolkien's elves. Unfortunately, the last book of the series is a little too late to do such a thing, especially after there have been numerous interactions with the elves and humans and no such hint of such problems. Again, there's no foundation given in the entire series for humans to feel this way towards elves. The entire section appears to show how awesome Eragon is and has no other real purpose.

Obviously, this is shoddy world building. The author should be able to come up with a logical reason—one that doesn't contradict what had gone before—why Eragon had to be the one who healed the baby's lip. Perhaps Arya was out on patrol and it would take too long for her to get back and the lip needed healing immediately. With Arya out of the picture, then Eragon would have to heal the lip by himself. Then the portrayal of the elves in the beginning of the series and in this book wouldn't contradict each other.

Inheritance also suffers from another odd continuity problem. This is best exemplified in Roran's assault on Aroughs, a southern city in the Empire. This takes place over several chapters, but each chapter doesn't feel like it's been affected by the events in previous ones. Roran and his men break into the city using barges to break through the waterway gates. They are met with opposition and soldiers who, of course, fight back. This involves a few loud explosions. The chapter ends and the next one begins with Roran and his men sneaking into the city proper. Despite everything that just happened, the city is still asleep and quiet. "All of the buildings—cold and forbidding with the empty stare of their black windows—appeared to be warehouses or storage facilities, which, coupled with the early-morning hour, meant that it was unlikely anyone had noticed the Varden's clash with the guards" (Paolini, *Inheritance*, p. 182).

But this shouldn't be. There should be alarms ringing in the city—alarms sent by the guards, as they should have sent someone to alert the rest of the city. There aren't any nearby guards from the other gates. There's no indication in the previous chapter that Roran and his men managed to get all the guards in the house. Some of them should have

Ten. The Fundamentals

run to get help. There should be *some* continuity between the chapter of the attack and the chapter after the attack. But there isn't.

The silence of the city seems to indicate that Roran and the Varden managed to sneak through undetected. But they most certainly did not, especially when they came down the river in a group of barges, slamming into the gates. But if they had been detected, then Roran and the others couldn't sneak through the quiet, oddly empty streets.

The actions of one chapter don't flow into the consequences of the next chapter. The reader is left to believe that a loud explosion doesn't get the attention of anyone. That no one comes to investigate. There aren't even any guards around the warehouses, watching for thieves. What sort of merchant wouldn't hire someone to watch over their merchandise? This is a standard problem that any spy or thief has to overcome when trying to get into a warehouse. They have to sneak past the guards. And yet there aren't any here.

Again, this is done to allow a large group of characters to sneak through the city undetected. This way, they can have their grand confrontation at the palace itself instead of having to fight through to it. But there's less at stake now. The readers don't have to worry as much about Roran making it to the end.[4] It's unrealistic and shows that Paolini either doesn't have an understanding on how a city works, or that he doesn't care about inconsistency as long as it helps his plot to get to where he wants it to go. Cities are almost like living things and one the size of Aroughs should have people moving around it all the time, especially in the middle of a siege.

While plot *is* important, it's also important to not put the plot above the setting. They have to work in harmony. If the author has created a setting, then he needs to stick to its rules. Cities have identities and rules; erasing those rules for the sake of plot causes a conflict for the reader. The story becomes unrealistic. And while there is definitely unrealism in fantasy, that makes it more important for the normal things that readers would identify with to *stay* normal, unless there's a reason for them to do otherwise. But the readers aren't given a reason for the emptiness of Aroughs during the attack. Unneeded conflict is created and the illusion is broken.

Had Roran wondered about the emptiness of the city it wouldn't create conflict, as he would be on the same page as the reader. But since he takes this as an everyday thing and it's not something that the reader would believe to be true, it does create that metafictional vs. fictional conflict.

Wibbly-Wobbly Magicy-Wagicy

Of course, one can't talk about fantasy fiction and its structure without discussing the existence of magic. Magic is one of the foundations of fantasy, and how it's applied can often make or break a story. Much like any other law of reality establishing how things happen in the world, magic should have a set of rules and regulations. There isn't a set rule on how magic should work beyond what the author says should happen. The vaguer the author is, the easier time they have letting things happen. Instead, as Brandon Sanderson says, "An author's ability to solve conflict with magic is directly proportional to how well the reader understands said magic" ("Sanderson's First Law," Sanderson website). This means that the vaguer the magic, the easier it is for the author to use it to solve random problems.

In Robin McKinley's *Chalice*, there is most definitely magic. Mirasol, the Chalice, is part of the Circle that holds the Willowlands demesne together. The Chalice helps keep the land lines calm and the demesne itself whole, hale and happy with the help of the Master and other members of the Circle such as the Grand Seneschal, Oakstaff and Clearseer. But the readers are never given any reasons to *why* the world requires such people to hold the land together. It doesn't explain how the land is held within the cities mentioned or what a Clearseer exactly is and does. It doesn't even really explain how a Chalice does what she does beyond using water, honey—in Mirasol's case—and various cups to bind and heal things. By leaving out exactly how powerful Mirasol is and what exactly the Chalice can do in protecting her lands, the story leaves room for her to save the demesne from an outblooded master.

Magic is merely background to this world and setting. It's more about Mirasol struggling to become a proper Chalice for the Willowlands rather than what exactly a Chalice is. There are rules in place, of course. The Chalice must use a cup of some sort with her liquid of choice. Water from local wells near the problems she needs to fix tends to work better. Outblooded Masters can potentially ruin a demesne for generations to come. And so these are rules that are reinforced by the characters and the story itself. She never once does her duties without a chalice of some sort and always uses honey. The outblooded heir is repulsed by the land, even though the Overlord is forcing him upon the Willowlands. The land would rather have its Master be a priest of fire who can barely remember what it's like to be human than a human who wasn't part of the land. Had it been otherwise, then the readers would more than likely be upset.

On the other side of things is Sanderson himself, who employs well-written and well-defined systems of magic. Magic does what magic does and this is why and how. The backs of his books are filled with all sorts of information on how magic works in his various worlds, from what "lashings" are in the Stormlight Archives to what sort of metals can do what in the *Mistborn* series. With these hard-and-fast rules bound and discussed within the texts themselves, Sanderson can use the magic as tools. But at the same time he must stick with his rules. Rules are rules, after all. They are how magic, how the world, works in his stories. If he were to randomly change something or have a character do something others cannot, the other characters must question why. They cannot just accept what the character has done as normal.

In a way, creating an inflexible rule system for magic can make it harder for writers, as they can't just say, "because of magic" to solve problems. They have to show exactly how the magic can help solve the problems and they can't just "because magic" away something if the rules say they can't. At the same time, it gives them structure and a more solid foundation of the world because the magic has definable rules. Readers can count upon them like they count upon gravity and the sun rising. It is, in a way, making the world more realistic, turning the magic into a sort of science than vague hand-waving. And this helps with the immersion in the story.

As long as the writer doesn't just break the rules without commenting on it.

Joking Around

Writers are, despite what some people may think, human, too. They have their own likes and dislikes, favorite shows and favorite stories.

And, like anyone else, they like sharing what they enjoy with others. One way they do it is by dropping references into their works. They're the winks and nods to audiences of, "Hey, I'm a fan of this and it's really cool." Or, in some cases with larger fandoms, the writers will put things in to say, "Hey, we recognize the fans and what they think." For example, on the television show *Castle*, they often drop references to *Firefly*, the show that Nathan Fillion previously worked on including having Castle dress up as Mal Reynolds for Halloween one episode. Even this book itself is no stranger to such things. There are dropped references of everything from Monty Python to Terry Pratchett within the text.

However, references to other works can't just be dropped into a work willy-nilly. They have to fit in to the world around them. As funny as references to *Monty Python and the Holy Grail's* man-eating rabbit might be, if the character mentioning it isn't the sort that thinks about those sorts of rabbits, it would be rather odd. Instead, it would sound like the author was trying to be overly clever. That quality can also come from the author trying to shoehorn in a joke that makes it blatantly obvious that this is what he's doing. In some cases, depending on the tone of the work, this is okay. In other cases, it's not.

The Inheritance Cycle has several of these references. In *Brisingr*, for instance, Eragon and Arya are sitting out one night on their way back to the Varden. Arya writes a poem referencing a "lonely god" that "wanders from shore to distant shore, upholding the stars above" and that is "adrift in a sea of time" (Paolini, *Brisingr*, p. 204). According to Paolini in his acknowledgments of the book, this is a reference to the Doctor from *Doctor Who*. As he says, "my only excuse is that the Doctor can travel everywhere, even alternate realities" (Paolini, *Brisingr*, p. 763). The Tenth Doctor is referenced as the lonely god in several episodes, the first time in the episode *New Earth*.

Now, why is this a problematic reference? First of all, Arya is an elf. The elves have been shown to be atheists. They feel that religion is silly and the fact that the dwarfs worship gods makes them superstitious and backwards. There is no proof of gods, so why should you believe in them? In *Eldest*, while holding a conversation with a dwarf, Arya even "implied that the dwarf gods did not exist, question[ing] the mental capacity of every dwarf who entered a temple" (Paolini, *Eldest*, p. 120).

So why would Arya write a phrase referencing a god? Especially in

Ten. The Fundamentals

a manner that would indicate some sort of belief in them? The lonely god is doing something important. He is not being mocked or made fun of. What makes it even worse is that Arya has no idea why she wrote the lines. Eragon asks her what they mean and she says she doesn't know. So she's unconsciously writing a *tribute* to gods, something she doesn't believe in.

Why?

Because Paolini wanted her to. He wanted to put in a reference to the Doctor in them. This isn't a bad thing. The problem was who he used to make the reference. Had it been one of the dwarves, say Orik, mentioning a lonely god while discussing his religion, which he does do later on in the book, it would have been less noticeable and less out of character. Even if Orik couldn't explain much about the lonely god, the reference would still mean more coming from him than from Arya, whose only explanation for writing the words was, "I don't know." Her out-of-character behavior bumps the conscious reader out of the story.

Another shoehorned-in joke happens in *Eldest*. Roran is leading the survivors of his village to meet with the Varden. They need a way down the river for the group of them, and so Roran and a few others go looking for transportation. They find a man who is willing to take them on his barges and make arrangements. Later that night, when Roran tells the villagers, this is what happens: "Marching to the forefront of the group, Loring raised his arms for attention. 'Barges?' said the cobbler. 'Barges? We don't want no *stinking* barges!'" (Paolini, *Eldest*, p. 413).

This is, of course, a reference to the line from Mel Brooks's *Blazing Saddles*, which is a mangled reference to the line from *The Treasure of Sierra Madre* by B. Traven. It is shoehorned-in because there is no reason for Roran to have to use barges. Boats would have been just fine. It would still cause the same problems that he encounters—that of not having enough money to pay the man they're hiring and wondering if they're going to rob him at the end. The fact that Loring protests even turns into a non-issue because his problems aren't brought up again after Roran says that they can take the barges or they can walk. When the villagers load up onto the barges, no one argues with Roran that it's a bad idea. There's no point for the entire thing beyond giving Paolini a chance to have a character say, "Barges? We don't want no *stinking* barges!"

What makes this phrase stand out even more is that none of the other characters ever speak in such a way.

The Fairy Godmother by Mercedes Lackey has two homages to Terry Pratchett's Discworld series within its pages. The first one is found when Ella is at the mop fair hoping to find a job that would take her away from her stepmother and stepsisters. As it approaches midnight, she sees that the only people left are herself, a sausage seller and a boy and his father. He was "a gangly boy with no tokens of experience, all elbows and knees, wearing clothing that was three sizes too big for him apparently made of tent-canvas" (Lackey, *Godmother,* p. 51). This corresponds to a scene in Pratchett's *Mort* when the titular character is waiting at the hiring fair with his father. There, Mort is wearing "a loose fitting brown garment of imprecise function, which had been understandably unclaimed by a previous owner and had plenty of room for him to grow, on the assumption that he would grow into a nineteen-legged elephant" (Pratchett, *Mort,* p. 6). When Elle is picked up after the sun sets, the boy is heard to say that he wasn't leaving "'Tain't tomorrow, yet. I'm stayin' till midnight" and "[Ella] looked back at them, until the cart turned a corner and they were lost behind buildings, wondering what would happen to the poor lad" (Lackey, *Godmother,* p. 53). What happens is right before the stroke of midnight, Death comes and takes Mort away as an apprentice, though Ella doesn't know this, because she left hours earlier.

The second homage happens when Ella is visiting the nearby village to drop off some supplies. She runs into three women. One is a "cheery, round-faced woman who had three happily grubby little children trailing behind her," the other is "thin and careworn, with a grimace," and the third is "a sweet-faced girl" (Lackey, *Godmother,* p. 157). While the girl, named Rosalie, turns out to be somewhat important to the plot of the book, when presented with the other two women she becomes reminiscent of Magrat, one of the three original witches in the Witches subseries in the *Discworld* novels, the other two being Nanny Ogg, who is round-faced and has lots of young grandchildren, and Granny Weatherwax, who is thin and never much for smiling.

Neither of these two sets of cameos influences the plot in any way; however, they make sense for the world and for how Lackey places them within the story. Mort is looking for a job at the apprentice fair, which

Ten. The Fundamentals

is similar to the mop fair in everything but the name. His being there helps impress how lonely and worthless Ella seems to the others. It's just her and this boy with no tokens of experience whatsoever, waiting determinedly for someone, *anyone,* to take them. And then it allows Ella to feel just that much better as she's not the last one. Plus, it shows her compassion that she wonders what happens to the boy who stood resolutely there in the square, determined to stay until midnight.

Meanwhile, the appearance of the three witches as women in the village also makes sense within the context of their cameo. They are presented as merely people who live within the village, much like their Discworld counterparts, and had someone been unfamiliar with the Discworld series, their appearance wouldn't seem out of place. Round-faced women with grubby children and careworn women who don't smile a lot are the sorts that would be found in such places.

So, while it doesn't make sense for Arya to speak of a "lonely god," as she doesn't believe in gods, the presence of Mort and the three witches does make sense because they blend into the setting without jarring the reader.

In the end, it's important to remember that things should happen in a logical manner. For every action, there's a reaction. There has to be a foundation for anything to happen, even if the characters themselves don't know it. Like a Rube Goldberg device, the plot, setting and characters intertwine with each other to create the story. But it has to be able to stand by itself without the creators to nudge it along in places where the ball might have gotten stuck. Despite all the differences, the pieces of a good story will work together and create a fantastic invention that does something very simple: give the audience a thing to enjoy and a way to escape and think about something different for a while.

Chapter Notes

Introduction

1. I use the term "fantasy story" to include all forms of media, for I am not focusing on the manner of presentation but the story itself.
2. "Throughout the series, my goal has been to steer the covers away from traditional fantasy covers because I'm not writing fantasy. I'm accidentally published by a fantasy publisher so I get thrown in with that genre, but my books are no more fantasy than a detective novel is a 'gun book.'" —Terry Goodkind, "An Interview With Terry Goodkind," by David Craddock, December 10, 2007.
3. That is, when the author pulls something that's not quite a *deus ex machina*—it's not exactly coming out of nowhere, but it still reverses what has happened before in a situation. In this case, the readers believe the two characters are related, but to allow them to be together without breaking society's taboos, the author must change their relationship by saying, "What I said before was wrong. Sorry. Here's how it actually is." It is likely coined from the idea in tabletop role-playing games where characters must roll dice to prevent or save themselves from having something bad happening to their characters.
4. However, with the popularity of *Harry Potter*, this concept has probably changed a little.

Chapter One

1. Unless all the other animators had been sacked.
2. Obviously, this couldn't be done if Thursday had been in the real world, but she is able to have conversations in the footnotes as well as astonish characters from the BookWorld that she can tell them apart even if they don't have "said" indicators during long sequences of dialogue with no character tags.
3. In *Hogfather*, Death asks Nobby, "And have you been a good bo ... a good dwa ... a good gno ... a good individual?" (*Hogfather*, p. 151).
4. As seen in *Men at Arms,* though, the two adventurers in question had good dark vision already.
5. As the squad in *Monstrous Regiment* discovered when locked up in a kitchen.

Chapter Two

1. In most cases. Sometimes, it is quite possible to be utterly off meaning. People would be hard-pressed to say that William Carlos Williams's poem "The Red Wheelbarrow" was about how important it was to keep the Red menace of the Soviet Union away from the United States.
2. All of these are actual titles.

Chapter Three

1. SCIENCE! is different than Science! Science follows the laws of nature,

as are found in the real world. SCIENCE! perverts all of that in the name of science! It is like magic but with machines.

Chapter Four

1. Or dwarfs, trolls, orcs, werewolves, vampires, zombies, personifications of ideas made real.
2. The city council reminds us that angels do not exist and we should not be thinking about them, acknowledging their existence, or speaking to them. To do so will require treatment. Also, the ones behind Ralphs are liars.

Chapter Five

1. This list includes such advice as: "56. My legions of terror will be trained in basic marksmanship. Anyone who cannot learn to hit a mans-sized target at 10 meters will be used for target practice," and "12. One of my advisors will be an average five-year-old child. Any flaws in my plan that he is able to spot will be corrected before implementation (http://www.eviloverlord.com/lists/overlord.html).

Chapter Six

1. Such as in *The Mask of Zorro*, *Star Wars: A New Hope*, Indiana Jones in *Raiders of the Lost Ark* and *Indiana Jones and the Last Crusade*, *Spaceballs*, various James Bond movies, Terry Pratchett's *Monstrous Regiment*, and many others.

Chapter Seven

1. The obvious joke here is that those writers have never been married.
2. Admittedly Susan ends up losing because she gets killed, twelve books in, in *Changes*, but Murphy is still the first eligible person whom Harry interacts with in *Storm Front*.

Chapter Eight

1. Thus giving the heroes, especially the heroes that are swept up from their ordinary lives, the chance to learn how to use their weapons and magic and gain useful experience which will allow them to defeat the Dark Lord later.
2. But not necromancy. Necromancy isn't allowed.
3. Names generated from an online elf-name generator.
4. But that still doesn't stop them from looking like *Lord of the Rings* elves. In Kevin Hearne's *Hounded*, the protagonist describes some fairies come after him as looking like Orlando Bloom's Legolas (*Hounded*, p. 5).
5. As any *Dungeons and Dragons* player can tell you.
6. Interestingly, in the main text of the human race's description, it does say that "their self-reliance and bravery inclines humans towards martial classes such as fighter, warlord and rogue. They often prefer to find hidden reserves of strength in themselves rather than trust to the magic of wizards or clerics" (*Player's Handbook*, 4th ed., p. 47).

Chapter Nine

1. Of course, this begs the question: how did the witches or wizards make it look as if they had been turned into charred corpses while they were being burned alive ... or after? They might fake screaming in pain but, in the end, they still needed to look like they'd been burned to a crisp.
2. Then again, who would vote against a dragon?

Chapter Ten

1. Which then begs the question: why *wouldn't* wizards have accountants? They have money and banks, obviously. Unless only goblins do accounting, but even

then that doesn't quite make sense. However, it does *sound* good. After all, only boring Muggles—like the Dursleys—would be interested in becoming an accountant instead of doing magic.

2. Released/created in 2004, 2006 and 2007, respectively.

3. Never mind the fact that there is a lamppost in the middle of nowhere which stayed lit for who knows how long and does so without any visible means of power. However, the strangeness of this is commented on by the Pevensie children, when they find it again as adults.

4. Never mind the fact that Roran seems to have some sort of strange "plot armor" that lets him get into situations that would kill normal people but allows him to survive—despite being an ordinary human.

Bibliography

"Alienage." *Dragon Age Wikia*. Dragonage.wikia.com/wiki/alienage. Accessed September 19, 2013.

"Almost Got 'Im." *Batman the Animated Series*. Writer: Paul Dini. Director: Eric Randomski. The WB, November 10, 1992.

Anspach, Peter, ed. "Peter's Overlord List." www.eviloverlord.com/lists/overlord.html. 1997. Accessed February 3, 2014.

Baker, Keith. "Dragonmarks 4/4: Good and Evil." *Keith Baker*. April 4, 2012. http://keith-baker.com/dragonmarks-44-good-and-evil/. Accessed September 25, 2013.

Baker, Keith, and Bill Savicsek. *Eberron Campaign Setting*. Renton, WA: Wizards of the Coast, 2004.

Bickham, Jack M. *Setting: How to Create and Sustain a Sharp Sense of Time and Place in Your Fiction*. Cincinnati: Writer's Digest Books, 1993.

Booker, Christopher. *The Seven Basic Plots*. London: Continuum, 2004.

Bowers, Maggie Ann. *Magic(al) Realism*. New York: Routledge, 2004.

Boyle, Rob, and Robyn King-Nitschke. *Shadowrun*. Chicago: FanPro, 2005.

Butcher, Jim. *Furies of Calderon* (Book One of the Codex Alera). New York: Ace Fantasy, 2004.

_____. *Grave Peril* (Book Three of the Dresden Files). New York: Roc, 2001.

_____. *Proven Guilty* (Book Eight of the Dresden Files). New York: Roc, 2006.

_____. *Storm Front* (Book One of the Dresden Files). New York: Roc, 2000.

Carey, Jacqueline. *Kushiel's Dart* (Book One of Kushiel's Legacy). New York: Tor Books, 2002.

Centers for Disease Control and Prevention. "Zombie Preparedness." http://www.cdc.gov/phpr/zombies.htm. Accessed July 8, 2013.

Clasen, Tricia. "Taking a Bite Out of Love: The Myth of Romantic Love in the Twilight Series." In *Bitten By Twilight: Youth Culture, Media and the Vampire Franchise*, edited by Melissa A. Click and Jenifer Stevens Aubrey. New York: Peter Lang, 2010.

Cohen, Daniel. *Encyclopedia of Monsters*. Essex: Fraser Steward Book Wholesale, 1991.

Collins, Suzanne. *The Hunger Games* (Book One of The Hunger Games). New York: Scholastic Press, 2009.

Craddock, David. "An Interview with Terry Goodkind." *Fantasy Book Critic Blogspot*, December 10, 2007. http://fantasybookcritic.blogspot.com/2007/12/interview-with-terry-goodkind.html. Accessed December 24, 2012.

Ella Enchanted. Director: Tommy O'Haver. Miramax Films, 2004.

Fforde, Jasper. *The Eyre Affair*. New York: Penguin, 2001.

_____. *Lost in a Good Book*. New York: Penguin, 2002.

_____. *Something Rotten*. New York: Penguin, 2004.

_____. *The Well of Lost Plots*. New York: Penguin, 2003.

Flanagan, John. *The Ruins of Gorlan*. New York: Philomel Books, 2005.

Bibliography

Foglio, Phil, and Kaja Foglio. *Girl Genius Vol. 6*. Studio Foglio, April 10, 2006. http://www.girlgeniusonline.com/comic.php?date=20060410. Accessed February 11, 2014.

Goodfriend, Wind. "Relationship Violence in Twilight." *Psychology Today*, November 9, 2011. http://www.psychologytoday.com/blog/psychologist-the-movies/201111/relationship-violence-in-twilight. Accessed November 21, 2013.

Grant, Mira [Seanan McGuire]. *Feed*. New York: Orbit Books, 2010.

Hamilton, Laurell K. *Guilty Pleasures*. 1993. New York: Jove Books, 2002.

_____. *The Laughing Corpse*. 1994. New York: Jove Books, 2002.

Hart, Stephen M., and Wen-Chin Ouyang, eds. *A Companion to Magical Realism*. Woodbridge: Tamesis Books, 2005.

Hearne, Kevin. *Hounded*. New York: Del Rey Books, 2011.

Heinsoo, Rob, Andy Collings, and James Wyatt, eds. *Dungeons and Dragons Player's Handbook*, 4th ed. Renton, WA: Wizards of the Coast, 2008.

Horn, Leslie. "The iPhone 4 is Officially the Most Popular Camera on Flickr." *PC Mag*, June 22, 2011. www.PCmag.com/article2/0,2917,2387452,00.asp. Accessed January 31, 2014.

"Imperial Order." Sot.wikia.com, Sword of Truth Wikia. http://sot.wikia.com/wiki/Imperial_Order. Accessed February 25, 2013.

Inchoatus Group. "Review—A Storm of Swords." *Inchoatus Group*, August 21, 2004. http://web.archive.org/web/20080325003052/http://www.inchoatus.com/Reviews/ Review_____. A%20Storm%20of%20Swords,%20George%20Martin.htm. Accessed February 11, 2014.

"Innocence." *Buffy the Vampire Slayer*. Writer: Joss Whedon. Director: Joss Whedon. The WB, January 20, 1998.

James, Edward, and Farah Mendlesohn, eds. *The Cambridge Companion to Fantasy Literature*. Cambridge: Cambridge University Press, 2012.

Jones, Diana Wynne. *The Tough Guide to Fantasyland*. New York: Firebird, 2006.

Jordan, Robert. *A Crown of Swords* (Book Seven of the Wheel of Time). New York: Tom Doherty Associates LLC, 1996.

_____. *The Dragon Reborn* (Book Three of the Wheel of Time). New York: Tom Doherty Associates LLC, 1994.

_____. *The Eye of the World* (Book One of the Wheel of Time). New York: Tom Doherty Associates LLC, 1990.

_____. *The Great Hunt* (Book Two of the Wheel of Time). New York: Tom Doherty Associates LLC, 1991.

Kirschling, Gregory. "Stephenie Meyer's 'Twilight Zone.'" *Entertainment Weekly*, July 5, 2008. www.ew.com/ew/article/0,,20049578,00.html. Accessed July 15, 2013.

Lackey, Mercedes. *Arrows of the Queen*. New York: DAW Books, 1987.

_____. *The Fairy Godmother: A Tale of the Five Hundred Kingdoms*. New York: Luna Books, 2004.

_____. *The Last Herald-Mage* (Valdemar: The Last Herald-Mage #1–3). New York: Guild America Books, 1990.

_____. *One Good Knight: A Tale of the Five Hundred Kingdoms*. New York: Luna Books, 2006.

MacDonald, Heidi. "Marc Andreyko Taking Over Batwoman and More from DC Nation at Baltimore." *Comics Beat*, September 7, 2013. http://comicsbeat.com/mark-andreyko-taking-over-batwoman/. Accessed October 21, 2013.

McCaffrey, Anne. *Dragonflight* (Volume One of the Dragonriders of Pern). 1968. New York: Del Ray Books, 1987.

_____. *Dragonquest* (Volume Two of the Dragonriders of Pern). 1971. New York: Del Ray Books, 1989.

McGuire, Seanan. *Late Eclipses* (An October Daye Novel). New York: Daw Books, 2011.

Bibliography

_____. *One Salt Sea* (An October Daye Novel). New York: Daw Books, 2011.

_____. *Rosemary and Rue* (An October Daye Novel). New York: Daw Books, 2009.

"Magical Realism." *Wikipedia*. http://en.wikipedia.org/wiki/Magical_Realism. Accessed February 11, 2014.

Marillier, Juliet. "Interview: Jacqueline Carey Pt. 2." *Writer Unboxed*, September 11, 2009. http://writerunboxed.com/2007/11/09/interview-Jacqueline-Carey-part-2/. Accessed December 25, 2013.

Martin, George R. R. *A Game of Thrones*. 1996. New York: Bantam Spectra, 2011.

Martin, Julia, and John Rateliff, eds. *Dungeons and Dragons: Player's Handbook*. 3.5 ed. Renton, WA: Wizards of the Coast, 2003.

Meyer, Stephenie. *Breaking Dawn*. 2008. New York: Little, Brown, 2012.

_____. *Twilight*. 2005. New York: Little, Brown, 2006.

Miller, Laura. *The Magician's Book: A Skeptic's Adventures in Narnia*. New York: Little, Brown, 2008.

Mohan, Kim, David Noonan, and Jennifer Clarke Wilkes, eds. *Dungeons and Dragons: Arms and Equipment Guide*. Renton, WA: Wizards of the Coast, 2003.

Monty Python and the Holy Grail Directors: Terry Gillam and Terry Jones. Python (Monty) Pictures, 1975.

Morrison, Grant. *Scorched Earth* JLA #25. Art: Howard Porter. Inks: John Dell. Colors: Pat Garrahy. Letters: Ken Lopez. New York: DC Comics, January 1999.

Newcomb, Robert. *The Fifth Sorceress*. New York: Del Rey Books, 2002.

Nix, Garth. "FAQ." *Garth Nix Website*. www.Garthnix.com/faq.html. Accessed June 26, 2013.

_____. *Lirael: Daughter of the Clayr*. New York: Harper Eos, 2001.

_____. *Sabriel*. 1995. New York: Harper Eos, 1996.

Paolini, Christopher. *Brisingr, or, The Seven Promises of Eragon Shadeslayer and Saphira Bjartskular*. 2008. New York: Alfred A. Knopf, 2010.

_____. *Eldest*. 2005. New York: Alfred A. Knopf, 2007.

_____. *Eragon*. 2003. New York: Alfred A. Knopf, 2005.

_____. *Inheritance, or, The Vault of Souls*. 2011. New York: Alfred A. Knopf, 2012.

Pearson, Helen. "Big Bird had Swift Legs." *Nature: International Weekly Journal of Science*. www.nature.com/news/2006/061025/full/news061023-9.html. Accessed July 4, 2013.

Pratchet, Terry. *Guards! Guards!* 1989. New York: Harper Torch, 2001.

_____. *Interesting Time*. 1994. New York: Harper Torch, 2000.

_____. *Jingo*. 1997. New York: Harper Torch, 2000.

_____. *The Last Hero: A Discworld Fable*. New York: HarperCollins, 2001.

_____. *Lords and Ladies*. 1992. New York: Harper Torch, 2000.

_____. *Men at Arms*. 1993. New York: Harper Torch, 2000.

_____. *Mort*. 1987. New York: Harper Torch, 2001.

_____. *Moving Pictures*. 1990. New York: Harper Torch, 2002.

_____. *The Thief of Time*. 2001. New York: Harper Torch, 2002.

_____. *The Truth*. 2000. New York: Harper Torch, 2001.

_____. *Witches Abroad*. 1991. New York: Harper Torch, 2002.

Pratchett, Terry, and Jacqueline Simpson. *The Folklore of Discworld*. 2008 London: Transworld Publishers, 2009.

Pratchett, Terry, Ian Stewart, and Jack Cohen. *The Science of Discworld II: The Globe*. 2002. London: Ebury Press, 2008.

Roberts, Thomas. *An Aesthetics of Junk Fiction*. Athens: University of Georgia, 1990.

Rowling, J. K. *Harry Potter and the Cham-*

Bibliography

ber of Secrets. New York: Scholastic Press, 1999.
_____. *Harry Potter and the Deathly Hallows*. New York: Scholastic Press, 2007.
_____. *Harry Potter and the Goblet of Fire*. New York: Scholastic Press, 2000.
_____. *Harry Potter and the Sorcerer's Stone*. New York: Scholastic Press, 1997.
Sanderson, Brandon. *The Alloy of Law (A Mistborn Novel)*. 2011. New York: Tor Fantasy, 2012.
_____. "The Final Empire Introduction," *Brandon Sanderson Website*. http://brandonsanderson.com/books/mistborn/the-final-empire/. Accessed February 11, 2014.
_____. *The Hero of Ages (A Mistborn Novel)*. 2008. New York: Tor Fantasy, 2009.
_____. *The Rithmatist*. New York: Tor Fantasy, 2013.
_____. "Sanderson's First Law," *Brandon Sanderson Website*. http://brandonsanderson.com/sandersons-first-law/. Accessed February 11, 2014.
Shakespeare, William. *A Midsummer Night's Dream*. Edited by Barbara A. Mowat and Paul Werstine. New York: Washington Square Pocket, 1993.
Skyfall. Director: Sam Mendes. Metro-Goldwyn-Mayer, Columbia Pictures, 2012.
Swann, Marjorie. "The Politics of Fairy Lore in Early Modern English Literature." *Renaissance Quarterly* 53.2 (Summer 2000): 449. Accessed September 16, 2013.
Tiffin, Jessica. *Marvelous Geometry: Narrative and Metafiction in Modern Fairy Tale*. Detroit: Wayne State University Press, 2009.
Tolkien, J. R. R. *The Hobbit, or There and Back Again*. 1937. New York: Marine Books, 2012.
_____. *The Lord of the Rings*. 1954–1955. New York: Houghton Mifflin, 1994.
_____. *The Tolkien Reader*. New York: Ballantine, 1966.
Tuttle, Lissa. *Writing Fantasy and Science Fiction*, 2d ed. London: A & C Black, 2005.
Twilight: Breaking Dawn Part 2. Director: Bill Condon. Summit Entertainment, 2012.
Tyler, J. E. A. *The Complete Tolkien Companion*. New York: Thomas Dune Books, 2004.
Valentine, Amanda, ed. *The Dresden Files Roleplaying Game: Volume One; Your Story*. Evil Hat Productions, 2010.
Weiland, Jonah. "The 'One More Day' Interviews with Joe Quesada, Pt. 1 of 5." *Comic Book Resources*, December 29, 2007. http://www.comicbookresources.com/?page=article&old=1&id=12664. Accessed October 21, 2013.
Wendell, Sara. "Twilight by Stephenie Meyer." *Smart Bitches, Trashy Books*, August 27, 2008. http://smartbitchestrashybooks.com/blog/twilight-by-stephenie-meyer. Accessed November 21, 2013.
Wilkes, Jennifer Clarke, and Jon Pickens, eds. *Dungeon and Dragons Monster Manual*, 3.5 ed. Renton, WA: Wizards of the Coast, 2003.
Wilson, Dominique Beth. "Counterfactual Christianity: Myth and Re-Imagined Religion in Jacqueline Carey's *Kushiel's Legacy*." *Literature and Aesthetics* 19.2 (2011).
Zamora, Lois Parkinson, and Wendy B. Faris, eds. *Magical Realism: Theory, History, Community*. Durham: Duke University Press, 1995.

Index

Abhorsen 92
An Aesthetics of Junk fiction 8–9
Agents of S.H.I.E.L.D. 157
The Alloy of Law 80, 83
alternate history 65, 71, 163–167; *see also Kushiel's Legacy*; *The Rhithmatist*; *Thursday Next*; *Tremiare* series
Angel (TV series) 90
Animaniacs 18, 171
Anita Blake (series) 50, 165–166; *Guilty Pleasures* 165
Antagonist 96–118, 120–124, 127, 136, 153
Anuga (character) 134
Aquaman (character) 125, 168
Aragorn (character) 67, 128–129, 131
archetype characters 7, 11, 32, 123, 126–132, 153; *see also* Chosen One; damsel in distress; hero
Arenson, Dave 75, 144; *see also* Dungeons and Dragons
Arms and Equipment Guide (Dungeons & Dragons) 78
Arrows of the Queen 88
Arwen (character) 128–129, 131
Arya (character) 133–135, 185–186, 190–191, 193
audience 18
authorial imperative 31–33, 45, 99, 104, 110, 119–122, 132, 135, 139, 149, 161, 177, 185–188

Baker, Keith 77; *see also* Eberron
Batman 97, 98, 111
Batman: The Animated Series: "Almost Got him" 97
The Bedford Glossary of Critical and Literary Terms 42, 95
Bella Swan (character) 38–46, 50, 58–59, 155
Beowulf 7, 55, 73
"Beowulf to Batman: the epic Hero and Pop Culture" 97
Bickman, Jack 180–181
Bitten by Twilight: Youth Culture, Media & the Vampire Franchise 40, 43, 46
Booker, Christopher 95 123–124, 127

Booster Gold (character) 167
Bowers, Maggie Ann 70
Boyle, Rob 166–167
Breaking Dawn: book 48; movie 47–49
Brisingr 104–105, 133–135, 190
Buffy the Vampire Slayer (series) 47–49, 55; "Innocence" 90–91
Bugs Bunny 18
Butcher, Jim Codex: Alera 15, 84–86, 172; *Cursor's Fury*; *First Lord's Fury* 85; Dresden Files 11, 15, 55–57, 88–89, 125–126, 130, 169, 177; *Furies of Calderon* 86; *Proven Guilty* 56; *Storm Front* 56; *see also* Harry Dresden (character)

The Cambridge Companion to Fantasy Literature 6, 7
Campbell, Joseph 116
Captain Carrot Ironfoundersson (character) 25, 27, 29, 32, 97, 98, 100–102, 134, 148
Carey, Jacqueline 163–165; *Kushiel's Legacy* 163; *Kushiel's Dart* 164
Centers for Disease Control (CDC) 53–54
Chalice 188–187
character 1–2, 6, 10–11, 13–15, 17–24, 27–28, 30–36, 42, 44–47, 49–50, 52–58, 60, 171, 177, 119
Christie, Agatha 66
The Chronicles of Narnia 184–185; *the Lion the Witch and the Wardrobe* 20
Cinderella 8–9, 62
Click, Melissa A. 40, 46
Codex Alera (series) 15, 84–86, 172; *Cursor's Fury* 85; *First Lord's Fury* 85; *Furies of Calderon* 86
Cohen, Daniel 150
Cohen, Jack 17
Collins, Suzanne *The Hunger Games* 181–184
The Complete Tolkien Companion 144
Condon, Bill 47
continuity 171–175, 185–187
"Counterfactual Christianity: Myth and Re-Imagined Religion in Jacqueline Carey's Kushiel's Legacy" 163–164

Index

Craddock, David 195
A Crown of Swords 112
Cursor's Fury 85

The Dark Griffin 116–117
dark lords 7, 75, 79–80, 116, 137–142, 152, 196
DC Comics 72, 98, 111, 125, 167–169
designated hero 99, 104, 107–109, 115; villain 99, 106–107; love interest 7, 110
The Desolation of Smaug 11
Detective Conan 52
Didio, Dan 125
Discworld 17, 24–25, 27, 29, 32, 37, 100–102, 147–148, 193, 195; *see also* Anuga (character); Captain Carrot Ironfoundersson (character); *The Fifth Elephant*; *The Folklore of Discworld*; Granny Weatherwax (character); *Guards! Guards!*; *The Hogfather*; *Interesting Times*; *Jingo*; *The Last Hero*; *Lords and Ladies*; *Men at Arms*; *Monstrous Regiment*; *Mort*; *Moving Pictures*; *Nightwatch*; *The Science of the Discworld II: The Globe*; Sir Sam Vimes (character); *The Thief of Time*; *Thud!*; *The Truth*; *Unseen Academicals*; *Witches Abroad*
Doctor Who 1, 172, 190–191, 193
Draco Malfoy (character) 131
Dracula 12
Dragon Age 145
The Dragon Reborn 113
dragon riders 150–152
Dragonflight 173
Dragonriders of Pern 151, 173–174
dragons 3, 6, 25, 26, 28, 32, 65–66, 71, 76–78, 84, 119, 128, 148, 149–153, 154, 158, 159, 166–167, 173–174, 196
Dresden Files (series) 11, 15, 55–57, 98–99, 125, 126, 130, 169, 177; *Proven Guilty* 56; role playing game 56–57; *Storm Front* 56
Dungeons and Dragons 55, 75–78, 144, 154, 196; *see also* Eberron
dwarves 62, 73, 84, 100–101, 106, 119–120, 128, 137, 140, 146–149, 153–155, 166–167, 172, 190–191

Eberron 35, 76–79, 90
Eberron Campaign Setting 77–79
Edward Cullen (character) 39–46, 58–59, 118, 155
Elder Scrolls 148–149
Eldest 140, 190–191
Elementary 52–53
Ella Enchanted: book 8–9, 48–49; movie 48–49
elves 3, 7, 27, 73, 77–79, 84, 106, 133, 135, 142–147, 149, 153–155, 160, 166–167, 172, 185–186, 190, 196, 237

The Encyclopedia of Monsters 150
Eragon (book) 2, 106, 140, 142, 185
Eragon (character) 104–107, 119, 133–135, 151, 185–186, 190–190
everybody knows 25–28, 147
evil 7, 69, 75, 77, 79–80, 108, 116, 137–141
Evil Overlord's List 35, 75, 196
The Eyre Affair 19

fairy 7, 55, 67, 69, 143–145, 147 148, 160, 179; *see also* elves
The Fairy Godmother 8–9, 30–31, 192–193
Faith of the Fallen 68
The Fallen Moon Trilogy 116–117
fan fiction 34, 35, 109–112, 131
The Fantastic Four (characters) 168–169
Feed 54–55
The Fellowship of the Ring 36, 145
Fforde, Jasper 6, 14, 19, 20–23, 69, 71; *The Eyre Affair* 19; *First Among Sequels* 23; *The Great Samuel Pepys Fiasco* 23; *Lost in a Good Book* 69; *Nursery Rhyme Series* 23; *Something Rotten* 20–23; *Well of Lost Plots* 19–23
fiction vs. metafiction 50, 188; *see also* meta-text; text vs. meta-text
fictional world 18, 20–23, 171–172
The Fifth Elephant 134
The Fifth Sorceress 107–109
Firefly 55
First Among Sequels 23
First Lord's Fury 85
Flanagan, John A. 139
The Folklore of Discworld 148
Fortune's Fool 33
fourth wall 17–18, 24
Frodo Baggins (character) 128–129, 130
Funk, Cornelia 19–20
Furies of Calderon 86

Galbatorix (character) 104–107, 120, 134–135, 140
A Game of Thrones 86–88
Gargoyles (TV show) 98, 102
Gary Stu 36, 109–115
genre savvy 53–61
Girl Genius 52, 60–61
The Goblet of Fire 91
Goldman, William 66–68, 112
Goodfriend, Wind 41
Goodkind, Terry 6, 15, 64, 68–69, 73, 106, 139, 195
Granny Weatherwax (character) 34, 131, 192
Grant, Mira *see* McGuire, Seanan
Grave Peril 55–56
The Great Hunt 162
The Great Mouse Detective 52

Index

The Great Samuel Pepys Fiasco see *First Among Sequels*
Guards! Guards! 25–26, 100
Guilty Pleasures 165
Guon, Ellen 160
Gygax, Gary 75, 144

Hamilton, L.K. 50, 165–166
Harry Dresden (character) 11, 55–57, 98, 125–126, 130, 177, 196
Harry Potter (character) 34, 62, 91, 102, 152, 158, 174–175
Harry Potter (series) 1, 5, 34, 55, 61–62, 91, 102–103, 116–117, 131, 144, 152, 157–160, 177, 195
Harry Potter and the Chamber of Secrets 144, 175
Harry Potter and the Deathly Hallows 62, 152
Harry Potter and the Goblet of Fire 91, 102, 144–145
Harry Potter and the Half-Blood Prince 103
Harry Potter and the Prisoner of Azkaban 158
Harry Potter and the Sorcerer's Stone 103, 174–175
The Heralds of Valdemar (series) 82, 88, 160; *Arrows of the Queen* 88; *The Last Herald Mage* 82; *Mage Winds* 82
Hermione Granger (character) 34, 62, 131, 174–175
Herne, Kevin 15, 176–177
hero 7, 11, 13, 46, 60, 77, 80–81, 86–83, 95–110, 115–117, 123, 138, 141–142, 152–153; anti-hero 7; balanced 128; Chosen One 34, 88, 107, 112, 154; designated 7, 99, 104–109, 115; as monster 95, 97; as protagonist 96; role of 80–81
The Hero of Ages 82
heroic character 95–100, 103–106, 109, 127–128
Heroes of Olympus (series) *see* Percy Jackson series
hidden world 157–161, 170; *see also* secondary world
The Hobbit 25–26, 75, 116, 128–129, 154; book 11, 25–26, 128–129, 138–139, 184; movie 11, 147
The Hogfather 26, 195
Hounded 176, 196
humans (race) 153–156
The Hunger Games 181–184

in-jokes 189–193
Inchoatus Group 89–90
Inheritance 105, 119–120, 185–188
Inheritance Cycle 142, 151, 185; *Brisingr* 104–105, 133–135, 190; *Eldest* 140, 190–191; *Eragon* 2, 106, 140, 142, 185; *Inheritance* 105, 119–120, 185–188; *see also* Arya (character); Eragon (character); Galbatorix (character)
Inkheart 19, 20
Inkspell 20
Interesting Times 29
"An Interview with Terry Goodkind" 195
The Invisible Woman (character) 125, 168–169
The Iron Druid Chronicles 15, 176–177
Ironman (character) 168

Jackson, Peter 11, 67, 75, 147
Jacob Black (character) 43
James Bond (character) 108
Jingo 27–28
JLA (comic book) 72
Jones, Diane Wynne 75, 95
Jordan, Robert 2, 80, 112–113, 122–123, 162–163; *A Crown of Swords* 112; *The Dragon Reborn* 113; *The Great Hunt* 162; *Lords of Chaos* 112

Kafka, Franz 96
Katniss Everdeen (character) 181–184
Kirschling, Gregory 59
Kushiel's Dart 164
Kushiel's Legacy 163–165
Kustritz, Anne 110

Lackey, Mercedes 8–9, 30, 82, 160, 32–35; *Arrows of the Queen* 88; *The Fairy Godmother* 8–9, 30–31, 192–193; *Fortune's Fool* 33; *The Last Herald Mage* 82, 112, 114–115; *The Mage Winds* 82; *Phoenix and Ashes* 8–9; *Urban Elves* (series) 160
The Last Herald Mage 82, 112, 114–115
The Last Hero 28–29
Late Eclipses 179–180
Legolas (character) 131, 145, 196
Levine, Gail Carson 8–9, 48–49
Lewis, C. (Clive) S. (Staples) 20, 184–185; *The Chronicles of Narnia* 184–185; *The Lion the Witch and the Wardrobe* 20
The Lion the Witch and the Wardrobe 20
Lirael 92
Lord of Chaos 112
Lords and Ladies 145
The Lost Hero 160
Lost in a Good Book 69
The Lord of the Rings: books 11, 78, 128–129, 130, 131, 142; *The Fellowship of the Ring* 36, 145; movies 11; *The Two Towers* (movie) 131; *see also* Aragon (character); Arwen (character); Legolas (character)
love interest 32, 34, 39, 41–46, 49–50, 58,

Index

110, 114–115, 118, 124–129, 130–131, 135, 155; designated 7, 110; kinds of 126–129; marriage 125–126

MacDonald, Heidi 125
magic 6, 61–62, 64, 65, 110–112, 133, 158, 184; belief in 25, 31; everyday 85, 160–161, 163–168; hidden world 157–160, 169–170; lack of in a fantasy story 65–68; races 77–79, 137, 141–155, 158; special objects 7, 11, 34; systems 12–13, 56, 75–76, 174–175, 188–189; and technology 82–83, 90–93, 177
magic book of genre fiction 1
Magic(al) Realism 70
Magical Realism 69–73
The Magician's Book: A Skeptic's Adventures in Narnia 184
"Marc Andreyko Taking Over Batwoman and More from DC Nation at Baltimore" 125
Marion, Isaac 50–51
Martin, George R.R. 7; *A Game of Thrones* 86–90; *A Song of Ice and Fire* 7, 13, 89–90; *A Storm of Swords* 89
Marvel Comics 125, 167–169
Marvelous Geometry 27, 29–30
Mary Sue 36, 109–115
McCaffery, Anne 151, 173–174
McGuffin 130
McGuire, Seanan 54, 178–180
McKinley, Robin 188
medieval stasis 82, 162, 176–177
Men at Arms 24, 101, 195
mentor, protagonist, sidekick dynamic 129–132
metafiction 44, 49
Metamorphosis 96
meta-text 18, 27, 29, 34–35, 45, 57, 142, 144, 16; meta knowledge 77
Meyer, Stephenie 39–40, 42–43, 45–48, 51, 58–60; *Breaking Dawn* 48, 47–49; *New Moon* 40; *The Short Second Life of Bree Tanner* 59; *Twilight* 7, 39–46, 118, 155; *The Twilight Saga* 12, 14, 39, 46–47, 49–51, 58–60
A Midsummer's Night Dream 7, 143
Miller, Laura 184
Mills, K.E. 160–161
minions 137–142, 152
Mistborn 80–83, 189
Mr. Fantastic (character) 125, 168–169
Monster Manual (3.5) 76, 78; see also Dungeons and Dragons
Monstrous Regiment 195
Monty Python 18–19, 38, 190
Monty Python and the Holy Grail 18–19, 90
Morgenstern, S. 66

Mort 192
mother, maiden, crone dynamic 129–132
Moving Pictures 27

Narrativium 27–28
New Critics 68
New Moon 40
Newcomb, Robert 107–109
Newsflesh Trilogy 54–55
Night Watch 100
Nix, Garth 80, 91–93, 160; *Abhorsen* 92; *Lirael* 92; *Sabriel* 92
non player characters (NPC) 132–136; see also minions; ordinary people
Nosferatu 12
Novik, Naomi 6, 15, 65, 71, 151
Nursery Rhyme Series 23

objectivism 68
Official Fan-Fiction University of Middle Earth (OFUM) 36
The Old Kingdom series 80, 91–93, 160; *Abhorsen* 92; *Lirael* 92; *Sabriel* 92
"On Fairy-stories" 67
"The One More Day Interviews with Joe Quesada" 125
One Salt Sea 179
Orcs 11, 67, 77–78, 128, 141, 196
ordinary people 158–160

Paolini, Christopher 104–107, 139, 185–188, 190–191; *Brisingr* 104–105, 190; *Eldest* 140, 190–191; *Eragon* 140, 185; *Inheritance* 105, 119–120, 185–188
Pearson, Helen 86
Percy Jackson Series 157, 160; *The Lost Hero* 160
the perilous realm 67, 69
Phoenix and Ashes 8–9
The Player's Handbook (3.5 ed.) 76; see also Dungeons and Dragons
Player's Handbook (4th ed.) 154, 196; see also Dungeons and Dragons
plot 1, 2, 18–23, 36, 42, 48, 96, 100, 110, 121–123, 126, 132, 135, 137, 142, 151–152, 171–172, 177–178, 187, 192, 193
plot device 19, 160; forbidden love 41; idiot ball 177; love at first sight 42; plot armor 197; prophecy 35; quest 35; true love 42, 46, 114
"The Politics of Fairylore in Early Modern English Literature" 143
popular culture 53, 57–58
Pratchett, Terry 17, 25–30, 32, 34, 68, 100–101, 131, 134, 140, 145, 147–148, 190, 192; *The Fifth Elephant* 134; *The Folklore of Discworld* 148; *Guards! Guards!* 25–26, 100; *The*

Index

Hogfather 26, 195; *Interesting Times* 29; *Jingo* 27–28; *The Last Hero* 28–29; *Lords and Ladies* 145–146; *Men at Arms* 24, 101, 195; *Monstrous Regiment* 195; *Mort* 192; *Moving Pictures* 27; *Nightwatch* 100; *The Science of the Discworld II: The Globe* 17, 25; *The Thief of Time* 24; *Thud!* 101; *The Truth* 24; *Unseen Academicals* 140–141; *Witches Abroad* 34; *see also* The Discworld primary world fiction 158–161; *see also* ordinary world fiction; secondary world fiction
The Princess Bride 66–67, 112
protagonist 9, 13, 35, 85, 87–90, 95–117, 121–124, 139, 146, 150, 152–154, 161; as hero 98–102; relationships 124–131; as villain 97, 115–117; in the world 118, 132–135
Protectors of the Plot Continuum (PPC) 36
Proven Guilty 56

Quesada, Joe 125

races *see individual entries*
Rand, Ayn 68
Rand al'Thor (character) 112–113
Ray, Supryia M. 42
reader's expectations 58–60, 87–90, 93–94, 96, 99, 109, 119–120, 124, 127, 131–132, 136, 138, 145, 158, 169, 187, 189
the real world 18, 23, 70–73, 157
"Relationship Violence in Twilight" 41
relationships 114, 126, 130–131, 136; balanced 128–129; Bella and Edward 39–44, 69; give-and-take 127–128; hero and villain 96
Riordan, Rick 157, 160
The Rithmatist 71
Roberts, Thomas J. 8–9
Rogue Agent (series) 160–161
Roh, Franz 70
role-playing games 35, 55–57, 75–79, 132, 144, 154, 157, 166–167; *see also* Dungeons and Dragons; Eberron; Shadowrun; Vampire: The Masquerade
Rollin, Roger B. 97
Romeo and Juliet 143
Ronald Weasley (character) 131, 174–175
Rosemary and Rue 178, 180
Rowling, J.K 1, 5, 34, 55, 61–62, 91, 102–103, 116–117, 131, 144, 152, 157–160, 177, 195; *Harry Potter and the Chamber of Secrets* 144, 175; *Harry Potter and the Deathly Hallows* 62, 152; *Harry Potter and the Goblet of Fire* 91, 102, 144–145; *Harry Potter and the Half-Blood Prince* 103; *Harry Potter and the Prisoner of Azkaban* 158; *Harry Potter and the Sorcerer's Stone* 103, 174–175; *The Tales of Beedle the Bard* 159
The Ruins of Gorlan 139

Sabriel 92
Samuel Vimes (character) 32, 97–98, 100–102
Samwise Gamgee (character) 128–129, 130
San Diego ComicCon 55, 84
Sanderson, Brandon 71, 80–83, 188–189; *the Alloy of Law* 80, 83; *The Hero of Ages* 82; *Mistborn* (series) 80–83, 189; *The Rithmatist* 71; *The Storm Light Archives* 189; *The Well of Ascension* 81
Sandman, Camilla 36
Scene & Structure 180–181
Science of the Discworld II: The Globe 17, 25
secondary worlds 160–163, 172, 177, 181; *see also* The Chronicles of Narnia; The Codex Alera; The Discworld; The Fallen Moon Trilogy; The Fifth Sorceress; The Heralds of Valdemar; Inheritance Cycle; Lord of the Rings; The Mistborn series; The Old Kingdom; A Song of Ice and Fire; The Stormlight Archive; Tales of the Five Hundred Kingdoms; The Wheel of Time
The Secret of Chimneys 66
setting 171, 181–185
The Seven Basic Plots 96, 117, 123–124, 127
Shadowrun 166–167
Shakespeare, William 7, 143–144
Shaun of the Dead 54
Sherlock (TV series) 52–53
Sherlock Holmes 52–53
The Short Second Life of Bree Tanner 59–60
Skyfall (movie) 108
"Slashing the Romance Narrative" 110
The Sleeping Beauty 32
Smart Bitches, Trashy Books 46
Smith, Paula 109
Something Rotten 20–22
A Song of Ice and Fire 7, 15, 86–90; *A Game of Thrones* 86–90; *A Storm of Swords* 89
sparklepires *see* vampires
Sparks, Nicholas 68
Spider-Man (character) 125, 167–168
Star Trek 55, 140, 146, 176
Star Trek: The Next Generation 52, 140
Star Wars 55, 98, 171
"Stephenie Meyer's Twilight Zone" 59
Stewart, Ian 17
stories effecting reality 54–57, 60
Storm Front 56
A Storm of Swords 89
The Stormlight Archives 189
subversions 76, 93–94, 147, 152; accidental 120; the Chosen One 88–89; evil overlords 80–81; hero 87–88; races 77–79, 139, 140–141; technologic progression 82
superhero 167–169
Superman (character) 125, 167–168

207

Index

Swann, Marjorie 143
Sword of Truth (series) 6, 35, 64, 68, 106, 117, 139

The Tales of Beedle the Bard 62
Tales of the Five Hundred Kingdoms (series) 30–35, 37; *The Fairy Godmother* 8–9, 30–31, 192–193; *Fortune's Fool* 33
Taylor, K. (Katie) J. (Jill) 116–117
technology *see* magic, and technology
Temeraire (series) 6, 15, 65, 151–152
terror bird 86
text vs. meta-text 10–14, 82, 99, 120, 188
The Thief of Time 24
30 days of Night 54
Thursday Next (series) 6, 19–24, 34, 36, 69, 195; *The Eyre Affair* 19; *First Among Sequels* 23; *The Great Samuel Pepys Fiasco* 23; *Lost in a Good Book* 69; *Something Rotten* 20–23; *Well of Lost Plots* 19–23; *see also* Thursday Next (character)
Thursday Next (character) 19–23, 69, 195
Tiffin, Jessica 27, 29–30
time travel 1
Toby Daye (character) 178–180
Toby Daye (series) 178–180; *Late Eclipses* 179–180; *One Salt Sea* 179; *Rosemary and Rue* 178, 180; *see also* Toby Daye (character)
Tolkien, J. (John) R. (Ronald) R. (Reuel) 27, 30, 67, 69, 73, 76, 79, 138–139, 141, 143–144, 146, 155, 184–186; *The Hobbit* 128–129, 138–139, 154; *The Lord of the Rings* 78, 128–129, 137, 145; *The Tolkien Reader* 67, 143; *see also* Aragon (character); Arwen (character); Frodo Baggins (character); Legolas (character); Samwise Gamgee (character)
The Tolkien Reader 67, 143
The Tough Guide to Fantasyland 75, 95
The Tradition 32–35
Trapped 176
A Trekkie's Tale 109
Tricked 176
true love 42, 46, 114
The Truth 24
Turtledove, Harry 65
Tuttle, Lisa 181
24 (TV series) 66
Twilight 7, 12, 39–46, 50, 51, 58, 118
Twilight Saga 12, 14, 39, 46–47, 49–51, 58–60; *Breaking Dawn* 48, 47–49; *New Moon* 40; *The Short Second Life of Bree Tanner* 59; *Twilight* 7, 39–46, 118, 155; *see also* Bella Swan; Edward Cullen; Jacob Black
The Two Towers (movie) 67
Tyler, J.E.A. 144

Unseen Academicals 140–141
Urban Elves (series) 160
Urban Fantasies 90, 144; *see also* Angel; Buffy the Vampire Slayer; The Dresden Files; Percy Jackson series; The Tobye Day series; The Twilight Saga

Vampire: The Masquerade 157
vampires 12, 14, 39–50, 53–60, 73, 76, 118, 126, 155, 157, 165–166; 183
Vance, Jack 76
The Very Old Man With Enormous Wings 71–72
villain 13, 69, 79, 97, 99–100, 108, 121–122, 127, 140, 167–169; archetype 96; designate villain 99, 104–109; as protagonist 115, 116–117; subversion 77; villain character 102–103, 107
villainous character 98, 102–104
Voldemort (character) 69, 102–104, 116, 159

Warm Bodies 50–51
Weeks, Brent 64
Weildand, Jonah 125
Welcome to Night Vale 72–73
The Well of Ascension 81
The Well of Lost Plots 19–23, 69
Wendell, Sb 46
werewolves 42, 55, 166
The West Wing 66
Whedon, Joss 47; *see also* Angel; Buffy the Vampire Slayer
The Wheel of Time (series) 2, 80, 112–113, 122–123, 162–163; *A Crown of Swords* 112; *The Dragon Reborn* 113; *The Great Hunt* 162; *Lords of Chaos* 112
White Wolf Publishing 157
witches 31, 34, 62–64, 160–161; Discworld 131; Harry Potter 61–62, 91, 102–103, 158–161, 196
Witches Abroad 34
wizard 3, 11–13, 32, 55, 144, 147, 154; Dresden Files 11–12, 55–56; Harry Potter 61–62, 91, 102–103, 158–161, 196
Wizards of the Coast 76
women character types 7, 32, 88, 123, 126–127, 153
Wonder Woman (character) 167
world building 111, 161, 171
World of Darkness 157
writing 8, 19, 36, 45, 51, 59, 61–62, 64, 68, 70, 100, 127, 129, 154–155, 171, 177, 180–181, 184
Writing Science Fiction and Fantasy 181

zombie 50–51, 53–55, 166

www.ingramcontent.com/pod-product-compliance
Ingram Content Group UK Ltd.
Pitfield, Milton Keynes, MK11 3LW, UK
UKHW042000140426
5217IPUK00015B/898